A Theology of Restorative Justice

DR. MAXWELL SHIMBA

Shimba Publishing LLC

Printed in the United States of America

First Printing Edition, 2023

Table of Contents

Preface

A Theology of Restorative Justice

In the realm of justice and reconciliation, where the human spirit yearns for redemption and healing, we find the profound and transformative concept of restorative justice. This book embarks on a journey into the heart of a theology of restorative justice, a journey that transcends legal frameworks and delves deep into the moral and ethical underpinnings of this approach to healing our fractured world.

Restorative justice is not merely a secular endeavor; it resonates with the spiritual and theological essence of humanity. It beckons us to explore the intersections between our faith traditions and the principles of empathy, accountability, and healing. In these pages, we embark on a quest to understand how our various theological beliefs, rooted in diverse religious and philosophical traditions, converge with the ideals of restorative justice.

Through the chapters that follow, we will traverse a rich landscape of theological perspectives, ethical considerations, and practical applications. We will journey through the theological imperative for compassion, forgiveness, and the recognition of the inherent worth of every individual. We will explore how these values find resonance in restorative justice and how, in turn, restorative justice can be a powerful vehicle for living out our faith.

As we delve deeper into this theology of restorative justice, we will encounter real-life stories of transformation and redemption. We will witness the profound impact of restorative practices on individuals, communities, and societies, all guided by the theological imperative to seek justice with mercy.

This book is an invitation—a call to engage with the profound moral and theological dimensions of restorative justice. It is an opportunity to reflect on the universal themes that bind us across faith traditions and cultural divides. It is a celebration of the transformative power of restorative justice to heal wounds, mend relationships, and fulfill the divine imperative for justice, mercy, and reconciliation.

Join us in this exploration of the theological imperative for restorative justice, as together, we seek to embody the highest ideals of our faith traditions while forging a path toward a more just, compassionate, and reconciled world.

CHAPTER 1
The Quest for Justice

God's Devine Justice:

The Bible unveils God as both righteous and just. His righteousness is a fundamental aspect of His nature, as affirmed in passages such as Deuteronomy 32:4, Psalm 119:137 and 142, Isaiah 45:21, and John 17:25. Furthermore, God is consistently described as just in all His ways, as seen in Psalm 145:17 and Revelation 15:3.

Divine righteousness can be defined as God's intrinsic and unchanging moral perfection, from which He issues commands for all things in both heaven and earth. He deems as just that which aligns with His righteousness and as sinful that which deviates from it. Throughout the Bible, one can discern a close relationship between righteousness and justice. Righteousness pertains to God's moral character, while justice relates to the actions that flow from His character. Whatever God's righteousness demands, His justice carries out—whether it is to approve or disapprove, to bestow blessings or pronounce condemnation.

What is the Quest for Justice?

The quest for justice is the fundamental and enduring human pursuit of fairness, equity, and the righting of wrongs in the world. It represents the collective and individual desire to rectify injustices, address harm, and ensure that individuals and communities are treated fairly and with dignity. The quest for justice encompasses a range of human concerns, including:

Seeking Fairness: Humans have an innate sense of fairness and a desire for equitable treatment in their interactions with others and within society.

Resolving Disputes: Justice involves the resolution of conflicts and disputes in a manner that is perceived as fair and just by all parties involved.

Accountability: It entails holding individuals and institutions accountable for their actions, particularly when those actions cause harm or infringe upon the rights of others.

Restoration: Justice often includes efforts to restore what has been broken or harmed, whether that involves repairing relationships, compensating victims, or rehabilitating offenders.

Social and Legal Frameworks: Justice is embedded in legal and social systems, which are designed to provide a framework for addressing wrongdoing and upholding the principles of fairness and equity.

Moral and Ethical Values: The quest for justice is often deeply rooted in moral and ethical values that guide individuals and societies in their pursuit of what is right and just.

Global and Local Concerns: It extends from individual, and interpersonal issues to broader societal concerns and even global questions of justice, such as addressing poverty, inequality, and human rights violations on a global scale.

In essence, the quest for justice is a foundational aspect of human civilization, reflecting our shared commitment to creating a more just and equitable world. It drives the development of legal systems, ethical frameworks, and social norms aimed at addressing and rectifying injustices and ensuring that all individuals are treated with dignity and fairness.

1.1 The Human Yearning for Justice

The human yearning for justice is deeply rooted in our nature and is driven by several interconnected factors:

Innate Sense of Fairness: Humans possess an innate sense of fairness from a very early age. Research in developmental psychology has shown that even infants and toddlers display a basic understanding of fairness, suggesting that this inclination is part of our biological and cognitive makeup.

Social Cooperation: The desire for justice is closely tied to the need for social cooperation and harmonious living. Fairness ensures that individuals can trust one another in social interactions, promoting cooperation, and strengthening social bonds.

Moral and Ethical Values: Many cultures and belief systems place a strong emphasis on moral and ethical values, including concepts of right and wrong. These values drive individuals to seek justice as a means of upholding their moral principles.

Empathy and Compassion: Humans have the capacity for empathy and compassion, enabling them to understand and share the feelings of others. When witnessing or experiencing injustice, empathy for those harmed fuels the desire for justice as a way to alleviate suffering.

Sense of Identity and Belonging: Justice is often tied to one's sense of identity and belonging to a community or society. When injustice occurs, it disrupts this sense of belonging and can lead individuals and communities to seek redress.

Psychological Well-Being: Injustice can have profound emotional and psychological effects on individuals. Feelings of anger, sadness, and disillusionment can drive people to seek justice as a means of restoring their psychological well-being.

Maintaining Order and Stability: Justice systems, both formal and informal, are essential for maintaining order and stability in societies. People yearn for justice as a means of resolving disputes, preventing chaos, and ensuring a sense of security.

Evolutionary Advantage: Some theories suggest that fairness and reciprocity may have evolved as adaptive strategies in human evolution. Cooperation and equitable resource distribution could have provided an advantage for our species' survival.

Cultural and Social Norms: Cultural and societal norms often shape individuals' concepts of justice. These norms are transmitted through generations and play a significant role in defining what is considered just and fair.

Accordingly, the human yearning for justice is a complex interplay of innate cognitive tendencies, moral values, emotional responses to injustice, and the need for social harmony. This innate desire drives individuals and communities to seek fairness and equity and to establish systems and mechanisms for addressing wrongdoing and harm.

1.2 Defining Justice

"Justice" is a multifaceted and evolving concept that has been explored and defined by various philosophers and thinkers throughout history. It encompasses principles of fairness, equity, and moral rightness, and it plays a central role in human societies and legal systems. Here's a general understanding of justice and how it's defined:

Fairness and Equity: At its core, justice is often associated with fairness and equity. It involves the idea that individuals should be treated impartially, without bias or discrimination, and that outcomes should be distributed fairly.

Moral Rightness: Justice is often linked to moral principles and ethical standards. It is about doing what is morally right and just, even when it may conflict with self-interest.

Legal and Social Systems: In a legal context, justice refers to the fair and equitable application of laws and the impartial resolution of disputes.

Legal justice involves ensuring that individuals receive their due rights and that wrongs are addressed through the legal system.

Retributive and Restorative Justice: There are different philosophical approaches to justice. Retributive justice focuses on punishment as a response to wrongdoing, with the aim of restoring the balance disrupted by the offense. Restorative justice, on the other hand, emphasizes repairing harm, healing relationships, and reintegrating offenders into society.

Social Justice: Social justice extends the concept of justice to address broader societal issues related to inequality, discrimination, and the distribution of resources. It seeks to rectify systemic injustices and promote fairness in access to opportunities and resources.

Cultural and Contextual Variations: Notions of justice can vary across cultures and societies, reflecting different cultural values, norms, and historical contexts. What is considered just in one culture may differ from another.

Historical Development: Justice has evolved over time, with ancient philosophers like Plato and Aristotle offering early philosophical foundations. Modern thinkers like John Rawls and Amartya Sen have expanded and refined our understanding of justice, introducing concepts like "justice as fairness" and "capabilities approach."

Balance of Rights and Responsibilities: Justice often involves a balance between individual rights and social responsibilities. It requires individuals to respect the rights of others while society ensures that individuals' rights are protected.

In the context of restorative justice, it represents a unique approach to achieving justice that focuses on healing, reconciliation, and repairing the harm caused by wrongdoing. It moves beyond punitive measures and emphasizes restoring relationships and addressing the needs of victims, offenders, and the community.

In essence, justice is a complex and multifaceted concept that can take on different meanings depending on the context, culture, and philosophical perspective. It is a fundamental principle that guides human interactions, societal norms, and legal systems in the pursuit of fairness and moral rightness.

1.3 The Brokenness of the World

"The brokenness of the world" refers to the recognition that our world is far from perfect and that it is characterized by various forms of harm, conflict, and wrongdoing. This concept acknowledges the existence of problems, challenges, and injustices that impact individuals, communities, and societies. Here's a deeper understanding of the brokenness of the world:

1. Prevalence of Harm and Conflict: The brokenness of the world acknowledges that harm is pervasive. It encompasses everything from minor interpersonal conflicts to more significant issues such as violence, abuse, discrimination, and systemic injustices. Harm and conflict are part of the human experience and can be found in various aspects of life.

2. Wrongdoing and Injustice: In addition to harm and conflict, the brokenness of the world recognizes the presence of wrongdoing and injustice. This includes criminal behavior, ethical transgressions, violations of human rights, and actions that go against societal norms and values.

3. Human Suffering: The brokenness of the world underscores the fact that these forms of harm and wrongdoing lead to human suffering. People experience physical, emotional, and psychological pain as a result of these issues. Victims of harm and injustice often bear the brunt of this suffering.

4. Limitations of Punitive Justice Systems: One key aspect of discussing the brokenness of the world is the acknowledgment of the limitations and shortcomings of punitive justice systems. Traditional justice systems, which primarily focus on punishment, often face challenges such as high rates of recidivism, overcrowded prisons, and an emphasis on retribution over restoration.

5. Social and Systemic Injustices: Beyond individual actions, the brokenness of the world encompasses broader issues of social and systemic injustices. This includes inequalities related to race, gender, socioeconomic status, and access to resources and opportunities. These injustices perpetuate harm and conflict on a larger scale.

6. Impact on Communities: The brokenness of the world has a ripple effect, impacting not only individuals but also entire communities and societies. Communities can be fractured, trust can erode, and social cohesion can weaken as a result of harm, wrongdoing, and injustice.

Recognizing the brokenness of the world is a crucial step in addressing these issues and seeking ways to promote healing, justice, and reconciliation. It acknowledges that there is work to be done in repairing the harm, restoring relationships, and creating a more just and equitable world. This recognition also provides the foundation for exploring alternative approaches to justice, such as restorative justice, which aim to address the brokenness of the world in a more holistic and transformative way.

1.4 The Search for a Better Way

The search for a better way in the context of justice and conflict resolution arises from the recognition of the limitations and shortcomings of traditional punitive approaches. Here's why the search for a better way is essential:

Addressing Injustice and Harm: Traditional punitive justice systems often focus on punishment and deterrence but may not adequately address the needs of victims or promote healing and restoration. The search for a better way is driven by the desire to find approaches that effectively address harm and injustice while also considering the well-being of individuals and communities.

Reducing Recidivism: Many punitive justice systems struggle with high rates of recidivism, where individuals who have served sentences reoffend. The search for alternatives stems from the need to break the cycle of crime and provide opportunities for rehabilitation and reintegration into society.

Healing and Reconciliation: The search for a better way is motivated by the recognition that healing and reconciliation are essential components of justice. Restorative approaches prioritize repairing relationships, fostering empathy, and promoting the psychological well-being of both victims and offenders.

Community Engagement: Restorative justice often involves the active participation of the affected community. This engagement builds a sense of ownership and responsibility within the community, reinforcing the idea that justice is a collective effort.

Respecting Human Dignity: Pursuing a better way is aligned with the principle of respecting the inherent dignity of every individual. It seeks to avoid dehumanizing punishment and instead treats individuals with respect and empathy.

Cultural Sensitivity: Restorative justice allows for cultural sensitivity and customization of approaches to fit the specific needs and values of different communities and cultural contexts.

Historical Roots and Global Examples: Tracing the historical development of restorative justice and exploring early examples of restorative approaches in different cultures provides evidence that alternatives to punitive justice have existed for centuries. This history inspires the search for better ways by demonstrating that such approaches have deep cultural and historical roots.

Continual Improvement: The search for a better way is an ongoing process of refining and adapting justice systems. It recognizes that justice is not a static concept but one that should evolve and improve as societies change and as our understanding of human behavior and conflict resolution deepens.

In summary, the search for a better way of justice and conflict resolution is driven by the need to address the limitations of punitive systems, promote healing and reconciliation, respect human dignity, and continually strive for more effective and humane approaches to addressing harm and conflict in society. It is a quest for justice that seeks to build a more equitable, compassionate, and restorative world.

1.5 A Theological Perspective

Theological perspective refers to the framework through which the book will examine the concept of restorative justice. It involves viewing restorative justice through the lens of religious and theological principles, values, and beliefs. Here's a deeper understanding of the theological perspective:

Religious and Moral Foundations: The theological perspective acknowledges the role of religious traditions and moral principles in shaping ideas about justice, forgiveness, and reconciliation. It explores how these traditions provide a moral compass for evaluating restorative justice practices.

Ethical Frameworks: It considers the ethical frameworks within religious traditions that guide human behavior and interactions. This perspective assesses how restorative justice aligns with these ethical guidelines and whether it resonates with the moral teachings of various religions.

Questions of Sin and Redemption: Theological perspective delves into questions of sin, repentance, and redemption found in religious teachings. It examines how restorative justice can offer opportunities for individuals to make amends for wrongdoing and seek redemption.

The Role of Forgiveness: Forgiveness is a central theme in many religious traditions. This perspective explores how restorative justice processes can facilitate forgiveness, both for victims and offenders, in alignment with religious teachings.

Community and Reconciliation: Many religious traditions emphasize the importance of community and reconciliation. Theological perspective assesses how restorative justice fosters community engagement and reconciliation efforts in the aftermath of harm or conflict.

Interfaith Dialogue: It encourages interfaith dialogue and collaboration in the pursuit of restorative justice. This perspective recognizes that different religious traditions may offer unique insights and approaches to addressing wrongdoing and promoting healing.

Diverse Belief Systems: Theological perspective acknowledges the diversity of belief systems and religious traditions worldwide. It explores how restorative justice can be adapted to accommodate various religious perspectives and values.

Moral Imagination: It encourages a moral imagination informed by religious and theological insights. This perspective invites readers to consider restorative justice as a means of embodying religious values and principles in the pursuit of justice.

Overall, the theological perspective in the book examines restorative justice as a concept deeply intertwined with religious and moral dimensions. It considers how restorative justice aligns with, challenges, or complements the teachings and traditions of various religions. This exploration sheds light on the potential intersections between faith-based values and restorative justice practices, offering a comprehensive view of how theology can inform the pursuit of justice and reconciliation.

1.6 Preview of the Journey

A preview of the journey is essential for several reasons:

Structural Guidance: It offers readers a roadmap of what to expect in the book. By providing an overview of the book's structure and the topics that will be covered in subsequent chapters, readers can better navigate the content and understand the logical progression of ideas.

Contextualization: It helps set the context for the upcoming chapters. By previewing the journey, readers can grasp the big picture and understand how each chapter contributes to the overarching exploration of restorative justice from a theological perspective.

Engagement and Interest: A preview sparks readers' interest and engages them in the upcoming content. It gives readers a sense of what they will learn, encouraging them to continue reading and explore the subject matter more deeply.

Alignment with Expectations: It aligns readers' expectations with the book's content. By providing a glimpse of the topics to come, the preview ensures that readers have a clear idea of what they can anticipate from the book, reducing the risk of confusion or mismatched expectations.

Relevance: The preview highlights the relevance and significance of the upcoming chapters. It demonstrates why the topics covered in the book are important and why readers should invest their time and attention in exploring them.

Preparation: It prepares readers for the upcoming discussions and themes. This can help readers mentally and emotionally engage with the subject matter and approach it with the appropriate mindset.

In summary, a preview of the journey serves as a helpful guide, ensuring that readers are informed, engaged, and prepared for the content that will follow in subsequent chapters. It enhances the overall reading experience and encourages readers to delve deeper into the book's exploration of restorative justice from a theological perspective.

CHAPTER 2

Theological Foundations of Restorative Justice

Interpreting the Bible through the lens of restorative justice rather than retributive theology presents a profoundly different portrayal of God and justice. Throughout the Bible, we discover a fundamental "logic of salvation" that opposes the notion of salvation solely based on satisfying an impersonal principle of retributive justice. This biblical teaching reshapes our understanding of justice, consequently redefining the very essence of God.

The Bible establishes an inseparable connection between God's love and God's justice. This vital linkage safeguards against the dehumanizing treatment of individuals in the name of "justice," where some are reduced to mere objects in a power struggle that creates winners and losers, perpetuating an unending battle.

Furthermore, holding love and justice in unity prevents the reduction of justice to a mere abstraction divorced from its role as a force that builds relationships and sustains life. Biblical justice is primarily concerned with people, prioritizing right relationships over rigid rules.

In this light, biblical justice is fundamentally corrective and restorative. It seeks reconciliation and reparation, opposing injustice but always holding open the possibility of reconciliation. Consequently, acts that result in death, such as capital punishment, are incompatible with corrective justice's principles.

This understanding of biblical justice emphasizes the importance of restoring relationships and social harmony in the face of brokenness and alienation, such as in cases of crime. It is aptly termed "restorative justice."

We can contrast retributive justice and restorative; biblical justice as follows:

Retributive Justice

(1) Rule-focused (violating the law)

(2) Emphasis on causing suffering

(3) Rewards based on what is deserved

(4) Separated from mercy

(5) Maintains the existing order

(6) Central actors: state vs. individual

(7) State (or God) seen as the victim

(8) Objective is for the offender to repay society (or God); victim is often overlooked

Restorative, Biblical Justice

(1) People-focused (causing harm)

(2) Emphasis on making amends

(3) Rewards based on need

(4) Rooted in mercy and love

(5) Transforms the current state of affairs

(6) Central actors: the entire community

(7) People (seeking peace and wholeness) are the victims

(8) Goal is to restore relationships and facilitate healing for all parties involved

Restorative justice is characterized by its personal, relational, social, and dynamic nature. It stands in stark contrast to the Western retributive justice that characterizes our criminal justice systems. While some may argue that the gap between the two is so vast that restorative justice appears irrelevant to the contemporary world, we propose that restorative justice holds tremendous potential for healing even within the brokenness and alienation of today's criminal justice systems. Countless programs worldwide demonstrate that restorative justice is not only relevant but essential, as healing is unquestionably needed.

Religious Values and Justice:

Religious values and justice are intertwined concepts that often form the foundation for ethical and moral behavior within various religious traditions. These values provide the framework through which restorative justice approaches are informed and guided. Here's a closer look at how religious values and justice intersect:

Core Values of Justice in Religions:

Christianity: In Christianity, justice is rooted in the teachings of Jesus Christ. Concepts like love, forgiveness, and reconciliation is central to Christian ethics. The idea of "doing unto others as you would have them do unto you" reflects a strong commitment to fairness and treating others justly.

Jesus occupies a central role in the biblical narrative of God's healing plan. He perceived himself as fulfilling the message of the Torah, a belief also confessed by early Christians. His teachings emphasized the importance of loving neighbors, bringing healing to broken situations, and offering forgiveness and restoration in the face of wrongdoing.

The Gospels recount Jesus' testimony to God's love, which primarily revolved around addressing issues of violence, brokenness, conflict, and alienation. As Jesus articulated, his mission was not directed toward those who were already well but toward those in need of healing (Mark 2:17). In doing so, he saw himself as continuing the legacy of Moses, the prophets, and the healing message of the Torah.

The Gospels expand on the Old Testament narrative, emphasizing fulfillment and continuity rather than discontinuity. Jesus announced the presence of God's kingdom in a profound and innovative way. He provided direct forgiveness independent of Temple sacrifices, healed individuals suffering from diseases that had alienated them from the faith community (such as leprosy, bleeding, and blindness), and liberated people from the influence of evil through exorcisms. In these ways, Jesus reaffirmed the message of God's healing work from the very beginning.

Yet, akin to previous agents of healing in Israel's history, Jesus faced vehement opposition. Religious and political leaders joined forces to arrest and execute him, unjustly accusing him of blasphemy against Israel's God. In response, God decisively raised Jesus from the dead, conclusively demonstrating that the God of justice is focused on healing rather than condemnation, inclusion rather than exclusion, and forgiveness instead of punishment.

In summary, Jesus' message can be distilled as follows: God created the world in love, but human rejection and subsequent alienation are possible. God bears witness to the need for humanity to turn away from this alienation and return to God's mercy. This witness is embodied by those who do turn to God and, in the midst of brokenness and alienation, testify to God's love. God's justice is exemplified in this costly testimony as God's people work to bring healing amid brokenness.

Jesus, as God's son, clarifies his healing mission in the face of temptations to combat injustice with coercion and violence. By resisting these temptations, Jesus underscores that authentic justice does not involve punishing wrongdoers or a form of holiness that cannot coexist with sin and evil. True justice directly engages with the world of sin and evil, seeking to bring healing and transformation, restoring wholeness to relationships.

Jesus' acts of justice extend beyond healing the afflicted; they also involve confronting those responsible for the harm. The powers-that-be retaliate, asserting their own form of justice aligned with self-interest and their laws and policies designed to preserve their authority. Jesus challenges this brand of "justice," leading to retaliation by those in power.

Through Jesus' resurrection, God fundamentally challenges the claims of the powers-that-be to act in the name of God's justice through punitive practices. These practices do not serve genuine justice but instead promote an unjust "peace and order." Jesus unequivocally conveys the message that the leaders of these rebellious human structures do not truly serve God's justice as they claim. This point in the Gospels echoes the message of the Old Testament, where both empires (such as Egypt, Assyria, and Babylon) and the Israelite nation-state served unjust powers rather than the just power of God, as they professed.

The final aspect of God's healing plan, as depicted in the story of Jesus, underscores the enduring significance of the community of God. Jesus' followers grasp God's justice, share it widely, and thereby bless all the families of the earth. Jesus assembled a community and equipped his followers with the mission to "go ... and make disciples of all nations, baptizing them in the name of the Father and of the Son and of the Holy Spirit, and teaching them to obey everything that [he] commanded [them]" (Matthew 28:19-20).

Judaism: Judaism places a high value on justice, with the Hebrew Bible (Old Testament) emphasizing concepts like "Tikkun Olam" (repairing the world) and the pursuit of righteousness (tzedek). The concept of "Shalom" (peace and wholeness) underlies the pursuit of justice and reconciliation.

Islam: In Islam, justice (adl) is one of the core principles and a fundamental value. The Quran frequently calls for justice and the equitable treatment of others. Islamic jurisprudence (fiqh) includes detailed guidelines for achieving justice and resolving disputes.

Buddhism: While Buddhism doesn't emphasize justice in the same legal sense as some other religions, it does highlight moral and ethical values such as compassion, non-harming (ahimsa), and right action. These values underpin efforts to address harm and suffering.

Foundations for Restorative Justice:

Forgiveness: Many religious traditions emphasize forgiveness as a fundamental value. Restorative justice aligns with this by providing a framework for offenders to take responsibility for their actions, seek forgiveness, and make amends.

Reconciliation: Concepts of reconciliation and healing are central to religious teachings. Restorative justice prioritizes the restoration of relationships and communal harmony, which aligns with these values.

Accountability: Holding individuals accountable for their actions is a common thread in religious values. Restorative justice incorporates accountability through processes like restitution and making things right with those harmed.

Compassion: Compassion for others, especially those who have experienced harm, is emphasized in many religions. Restorative justice processes encourage empathy and understanding, fostering a compassionate response to wrongdoing.

Interfaith Dialogue: In a globalized world, interfaith dialogue and collaboration are increasingly important. Restorative justice provides a space where individuals from diverse religious backgrounds can come together to address harm and conflict, drawing on shared values of justice, compassion, and reconciliation.

Accordingly, religious values and justice are deeply interconnected, and they play a significant role in informing restorative justice approaches. These values underscore the importance of fairness, compassion, reconciliation, and accountability in addressing harm and conflict, making restorative justice a natural extension of religious teachings related to justice and ethics

Moral Imperatives and Ethics:

Moral imperatives and ethics play a pivotal role in the context of restorative justice, and their importance cannot be overstated. Here's why moral imperatives and ethics are crucial in discussions surrounding restorative justice:

Guiding Principles: Moral imperatives and ethics provide guiding principles for individuals and societies. They offer a moral compass for distinguishing right from wrong and serve as the foundation for ethical decision-making.

Alignment with Restorative Justice: Restorative justice principles, such as forgiveness, reconciliation, and accountability, align closely with ethical and moral imperatives found in religious teachings. These principles resonate with core values such as compassion, fairness, and the pursuit of justice.

Forgiveness: Forgiveness is a central moral imperative in many religious traditions. It is viewed as a virtuous act that promotes healing and reconciliation. Restorative justice recognizes the importance of forgiveness as a means of letting go of anger and resentment, which can hinder the healing process.

Reconciliation: Ethical teachings often emphasize the importance of reconciliation and restoring relationships. Restorative justice practices prioritize the restoration of damaged relationships, recognizing the moral imperative of fostering understanding and harmony among individuals and communities.

Accountability: Ethical frameworks commonly stress the importance of accountability for one's actions. Restorative justice promotes accountability by encouraging offenders to take responsibility for their wrongdoing, make amends, and face the consequences of their actions in a constructive manner.

Compassion and Empathy: Compassion and empathy are ethical imperatives found in various religious traditions. Restorative justice encourages individuals to approach conflicts and harm with empathy, acknowledging the pain and suffering of others and responding with compassion.

Healing and Redemption: Moral and ethical teachings often emphasize the possibility of redemption and transformation. Restorative justice supports these teachings by offering opportunities for offenders to make amends, seek redemption, and reintegrate into society in a positive way.

Community and Social Cohesion: Many moral imperatives stress the importance of community and social cohesion. Restorative justice aligns with these values by involving the affected community in the justice process and promoting collective healing and accountability.

Conflict Resolution: Ethical frameworks provide guidance on resolving conflicts peacefully and justly. Restorative justice processes offer a non-violent and constructive approach to addressing harm and conflict, in line with these ethical imperatives.

Interfaith Dialogue: Moral imperatives and ethical values are points of commonality among different religious traditions. Restorative justice provides a platform for interfaith dialogue and collaboration, where individuals from diverse backgrounds can work together to achieve shared moral and ethical objectives related to justice and reconciliation.

In summary, moral imperatives and ethics are essential because they provide the ethical foundation and moral framework that underpin restorative justice principles. They emphasize the importance of forgiveness, reconciliation, accountability, and compassion, all of which are integral to the restorative justice approach and contribute to the pursuit of justice in a morally sound and ethically grounded manner.

What are Biblical Roots?

Biblical roots refer to the foundational concepts and principles related to restorative justice that can be found in the Bible, both in the Old and New Testaments. These roots provide a scriptural basis for understanding and practicing restorative justice. Here are some key biblical roots and passages:

Repentance and Forgiveness:

Luke 15:11-32 (The Parable of the Prodigal Son): This parable illustrates the concept of repentance and forgiveness. The prodigal son's return to his father and the father's forgiveness exemplifies the idea of restoration and reconciliation.

Restitution and Compensation:

Exodus 22:1 (Restitution for Theft): This verse outlines the principle of restitution, stating that if a thief is caught, they must repay what they have stolen, often at multiple times the value.

Leviticus 6:1-7 (Restitution for Sins): This passage discusses restitution for various sins and offenses, emphasizing the importance of making amends for wrongdoing.

Reconciliation:

Matthew 5:23-24 (Reconciliation Before Offering): In this passage, Jesus teaches that if you have conflicts or disputes with others, you should seek reconciliation before making offerings to God. This underscores the importance of reconciling relationships.

Justice and Righteousness:

Micah 6:8 (Act Justly, Love Mercy, Walk Humbly): This well-known verse emphasizes the importance of acting justly, showing mercy, and walking humbly with God, which align with restorative justice principles.

Isaiah 1:17 (Seek Justice, Correct Oppression): This verse calls for seeking justice, correcting oppression, and defending the rights of the fatherless and widows, highlighting the biblical imperative for addressing injustice.

Compassion and Care for the Vulnerable:

James 1:27 (Religion that God Accepts): This verse speaks to pure and faultless religion as caring for widows and orphans in their distress, reflecting a compassionate response to those in need.

Isaiah 58:6-7 (The Fast God Chooses): These verses describe a true fast as one that involves breaking the chains of injustice, feeding the hungry, and sheltering the homeless, emphasizing care for the vulnerable.

Reconciliation and Peacemaking:

Matthew 5:9 (Blessed Are the Peacemakers): Jesus' teaching in this verse highlights the blessedness of peacemakers, who are called children of God, emphasizing the importance of reconciliation and peace.

Community and Restoration:

Galatians 6:1-2 (Restore One Another): This passage encourages the community to restore a person caught in wrongdoing gently, emphasizing the role of the community in restoration.

These biblical roots illustrate the presence of restorative justice principles in the Bible, including concepts of repentance, restitution, reconciliation, justice, compassion, and care for the vulnerable. They provide a scriptural foundation for understanding and applying restorative justice principles within a faith-based context.

Interfaith Perspectives:

Interfaith perspectives are indeed important when discussing restorative justice, and here's why:

Cultural and Religious Diversity: Our world is culturally and religiously diverse, with various faith traditions coexisting in communities and nations. Understanding how different religious traditions approach restorative justice helps create a more inclusive and comprehensive understanding of this concept.

Promoting Dialogue: Interfaith perspectives encourage dialogue and collaboration among individuals from different faith backgrounds. Restorative justice is a subject where individuals of various religions can find common ground and work together to promote shared values of justice, compassion, and reconciliation.

Shared Values: Many religious traditions share common values related to justice, forgiveness, reconciliation, and accountability. Recognizing these shared values can foster a sense of unity and cooperation in addressing harm and conflict.

Learning from Others: Examining how different faith traditions approach restorative justice can provide valuable insights and fresh perspectives. It allows practitioners and scholars to learn from the rich traditions and experiences of others and adapt their own practices accordingly.

Respect for Pluralism: Interfaith perspectives promote respect for religious pluralism, acknowledging that there are multiple valid ways of approaching and interpreting concepts like justice and reconciliation. This respect contributes to a more tolerant and harmonious society.

Global Relevance: Restorative justice is a global concept, and its application is not limited to any one religion or culture. Interfaith perspectives help bridge cultural and religious divides, making restorative justice more accessible and relevant to diverse communities worldwide.

Conflict Resolution: In a world where religious and cultural conflicts can arise, interfaith perspectives on restorative justice can play a role in conflict resolution and peacebuilding. It offers a shared framework for addressing conflicts while respecting religious and cultural differences.

Legal and Ethical Considerations: In societies with diverse populations, legal and ethical considerations must account for various religious beliefs and practices. Understanding interfaith perspectives can inform legal and ethical frameworks for restorative justice implementation.

In summary, interfaith perspectives are important because they promote inclusivity, foster dialogue, and encourage cooperation among individuals from diverse religious traditions. They highlight the universal values shared by different faiths and demonstrate how these values can be harnessed to address harm, promote healing, and pursue justice in a pluralistic world.

Theological Debates:

Theological debates surrounding restorative justice are valuable for several reasons:

Theological Exploration: These debates allow theologians, scholars, and practitioners to explore and deepen their understanding of how restorative justice aligns with or challenges theological concepts within their respective faith traditions.

Doctrinal Clarity: Debates help clarify the theological doctrines related to justice, atonement, redemption, and divine mercy. They allow religious communities to examine how restorative justice fits within their doctrinal framework.

Interpretation of Scripture: Theological debates often involve the interpretation of religious texts. These debates can shed light on how specific passages or teachings within sacred texts relate to restorative justice principles.

Moral and Ethical Considerations: Restorative justice raises important moral and ethical questions that intersect with theology.

Debates provide a platform for discussing these ethical considerations within a religious context.

Practical Application: Debates not only focus on theoretical aspects but also on practical application. They help religious communities and practitioners navigate how restorative justice can be applied within their faith-based contexts.

Reconciliation with Theological Teachings: Restorative justice seeks reconciliation, which is often a central theme in religious traditions. Debates explore how restorative justice aligns with and reinforces the theological imperative for reconciliation.

Challenges and Critiques: Debates also involve addressing challenges and critiques of restorative justice from a theological perspective. This critical engagement can lead to refinements in restorative justice practices.

Interfaith Dialogue: Theological debates on restorative justice can foster interfaith dialogue. They offer an opportunity for individuals from different faith backgrounds to come together and share their perspectives, fostering mutual understanding and collaboration.

Community Engagement: Within religious communities, theological debates can engage the community in discussions about justice and how their faith informs their approach to addressing harm and conflict.

Development of Theological Resources: Debates contribute to the development of theological resources and literature related to restorative justice, providing valuable references and insights for theologians, scholars, and practitioners.

In essence, theological debates enrich the discourse around restorative justice by providing a deeper exploration of the theological dimensions and implications of this approach. They contribute to a more nuanced understanding of how restorative justice aligns with or challenges theological concepts and doctrines, ultimately helping to integrate restorative justice into faith-based contexts more effectively.

Theological Interpretations:

Theological interpretations are highly important when discussing restorative justice for several reasons:

Faith Integration: Theological interpretations allow for the integration of restorative justice principles with the theological teachings and beliefs of a particular religious tradition. This integration is crucial for aligning restorative justice with the values and ethics of that faith.

Relevance and Applicability: Different religious traditions have their own unique theological perspectives and doctrines. Theological interpretations ensure that restorative justice remains relevant and applicable within the context of each faith, addressing specific theological considerations.

Ethical and Moral Framework: Theological interpretations provide an ethical and moral framework for understanding restorative justice. They help theologians and scholars explore how restorative justice aligns with or challenges the core ethical and moral teachings of their faith.

Guidance for Practitioners: Theological interpretations offer guidance for practitioners and communities on how to implement restorative justice within a faith-based context. They provide insights into how to navigate complex theological and ethical dilemmas.

Interfaith Dialogue: Understanding theological interpretations from various religious traditions promotes interfaith dialogue and collaboration. It allows individuals from different faith backgrounds to share their perspectives on restorative justice, fostering mutual understanding and cooperation.

Contextualization: Theological interpretations allow for the contextualization of restorative justice practices. They help adapt restorative justice to the cultural and theological nuances of different communities, making it more effective and culturally sensitive.

Doctrinal Clarity: In some cases, theological interpretations clarify how restorative justice relates to specific doctrinal elements within a faith tradition. This clarity is essential for avoiding misinterpretation or misconceptions.

Social Transformation: Restorative justice seeks to bring about social transformation and reconciliation. Theological interpretations can highlight the role of restorative justice in fulfilling the broader mission of a faith tradition, such as promoting justice and peace.

Scholarly Discourse: Theological interpretations contribute to scholarly discourse and academic research. They provide valuable insights and perspectives that enrich the academic understanding of restorative justice.

Practice Improvement: Through theological interpretations, theologians and scholars can offer suggestions for improving restorative justice practices within faith-based contexts, ensuring they align with theological values and goals.

In summary, theological interpretations are crucial for ensuring that restorative justice can be effectively integrated into the diverse religious landscapes of our world. They offer a bridge between restorative justice principles and the theological teachings of various faith traditions, facilitating a more harmonious and ethical implementation of restorative justice within these contexts.

CHAPTER 3

The Biblical Roots of Restoration

Exploration of Biblical Stories:

My foundational perspective begins with the belief that we should approach the Christian Bible as a comprehensive narrative, examining it as a story that unfolds from start to finish. By grasping the essence of this narrative—the underlying plot, the points of tension, and the eventual resolution—we can gain a deeper understanding of how it addresses the concept of justice. In doing so, we can appreciate how biblical justice might serve as a potent antidote to our culture's embrace of the myth of redemptive violence, a myth that obscures the fact that the violence within our criminal justice system offers no true redemption.

The Bible introduces us to the theme of alienation early on, as we encounter instances of violence in passages like Genesis 4 (Cain's murder of Abel), 7–9 (the escalation of violence leading to the Flood), and 11 (the Tower of Babel). Right from the beginning, violence is central to the narrative, resulting in profound conflicts, even within the first family (Cain and Abel). Initially, God responds with extensive retribution, exemplified by Noah and the great flood—a response stemming from God's deep sorrow. However, a transformation occurs when "God remembers" Noah, the waters recede, and God calls humanity back together, vowing never to destroy in such a manner again. This shift prompts us to consider how God will address this prevailing alienation.

Genesis 12:1-3 offers us a model: God summons a community to experience God's healing love and to serve as a conduit for this love, bestowing blessings upon all the families of the earth. I refer to this model as "God's healing strategy" (as elaborated in my book of the same title). It embodies God's intention to respond to human alienation and injustice through a peaceful community that shares the peace it learns to embody with the entire world.

I believe that the remainder of the Bible unfolds the narrative of God's healing strategy—a story filled with numerous twists and turns. Nevertheless, I believe that we can trace this thread from Genesis through to Revelation. It is of immense significance in our biblical interpretation to recognize that in the final vision, the New Jerusalem established by God on earth features at its core a river with trees along its banks, offering leaves "for the healing of the nations."

The exploration of biblical stories related to restoration involves examining specific narratives from the Bible that illustrate instances of individuals, communities, or nations experiencing restoration. These stories often feature themes of forgiveness, reconciliation, and renewal. Here are some examples of such biblical stories:

The Prodigal Son (Luke 15:11-32): This parable told by Jesus illustrates the concept of restoration and reconciliation. It tells the story of a wayward son who squanders his inheritance but is welcomed back with open arms by his father upon his return, highlighting the themes of forgiveness and renewal.

Joseph and His Brothers (Genesis 37-50): The story of Joseph in the Book of Genesis showcases the process of reconciliation and restoration within a family. Joseph's forgiveness and reconciliation with his brothers after their betrayal is a powerful example of restoring broken relationships.

The Healing of the Paralytic (Mark 2:1-12): This story depicts Jesus healing a paralyzed man and forgiving his sins, emphasizing both physical and spiritual restoration. It demonstrates the interplay between physical and spiritual renewal.

The Woman Caught in Adultery (John 8:1-11): Jesus' response to the woman caught in adultery highlight's themes of forgiveness and restoration. He forgives her sins and encourages her to go and sin no more, offering her a chance at a renewed life.

The Return of the Israelites from Exile (Ezra and Nehemiah): The Books of Ezra and Nehemiah recount the return of the Israelites from Babylonian exile and the rebuilding of Jerusalem. This story underscores the restoration of a community and the renewal of their relationship with God.

The Story of Zacchaeus (Luke 19:1-10): This story features a tax collector named Zacchaeus who encounters Jesus and pledges to make amends by repaying those he has wronged. It exemplifies the concept of restitution and restoration.

The Healing of the Man Born Blind (John 9): This narrative involves the healing of a man born blind by Jesus. The story delves into themes of physical healing and the transformation of the blind man's spiritual understanding, illustrating restoration on multiple levels.

The Rebuilding of the Jerusalem Walls (Nehemiah 1-6): Nehemiah's leadership in rebuilding the walls of Jerusalem following their destruction is a story of restoration at the community and city level. It demonstrates the importance of unity and collective restoration efforts.

These biblical stories serve as powerful examples of restoration, forgiveness, reconciliation, and renewal. They offer insights into how these themes have been addressed within a faith context and continue to inspire contemporary efforts to promote restorative justice and healing within faith communities and beyond.

Repentance and Transformation:

Repentance and transformation are central concepts within the biblical context and are integral to the process of restoration. Here's an explanation of these concepts:

Repentance:

Repentance, in the biblical context, refers to a profound change of heart and mind accompanied by genuine remorse for one's actions. It involves:

Recognition of Wrongdoing: Acknowledging that one's actions have been morally wrong or have caused harm to oneself or others.

Sorrow and Regret: Feeling a deep sense of sorrow and regret for the wrongdoing, often accompanied by a desire to make amends.

Turning Away from Sin: A commitment to turn away from the sinful or harmful behavior and to seek a new path characterized by righteousness and obedience to God's commandments.

Seeking Forgiveness: Repentance often involves seeking forgiveness, both from God and from those who have been harmed.

In the context of restoration, repentance is crucial because it signifies a sincere willingness to change and make amends. It is the first step toward healing and reconciliation, as it demonstrates a genuine desire for restoration.

Transformation:

Transformation, in a biblical sense, refers to a profound and lasting change in a person's character, values, and behavior. It involves:

Spiritual Renewal: A transformation of the heart and spirit, often attributed to divine intervention or grace. It signifies a departure from a sinful or unrighteous way of life toward a life aligned with God's will.

New Life: A metaphorical rebirth or new beginning, where an individual is spiritually regenerated and adopts a life marked by righteousness, love, and obedience to God's commandments.

Fruit of the Spirit: Transformation often results in the manifestation of positive attributes known as the "Fruit of the Spirit," including love, joy, peace, patience, kindness, goodness, faithfulness, gentleness, and self-control (Galatians 5:22-23).

Impact on Others: A transformed life has a positive impact on others, inspiring and influencing them toward moral and spiritual growth.

In the context of restoration, transformation is essential because it signifies a genuine and lasting change in the individual who has caused harm or wrongdoing. It demonstrates a commitment to living a life that aligns with the principles of justice, love, and reconciliation.

Repentance and transformation are interconnected, with repentance often being the initial step that leads to a transformative process. Together, they play a central role in the biblical understanding of restoration, as they pave the way for reconciliation, forgiveness, and the renewal of relationships and communities.

Restitution and Making Amends:

Restitution and making amends, as found in the biblical context, are principles that emphasize the act of repairing or compensating for harm or wrongdoing. Here's an explanation of these concepts:

Restitution:

Restitution, in a biblical sense, refers to the act of making right or compensating for a wrongful action or harm caused to another person or their property. Key aspects of restitution include:

Returning What Was Taken: It often involves returning stolen property or the equivalent value to the rightful owner. The idea is to restore the victim to the position they were in before the harm occurred.

Compensating for Damages: In cases where physical harm or damage to property has occurred, restitution may involve compensating the victim for the losses incurred.

Seeking Forgiveness: Restitution is often accompanied by a sincere desire for forgiveness from the person who was wronged and, in some cases, from God.

Repentance and Responsibility: Restitution is linked to repentance and taking responsibility for one's actions. It reflects a commitment to rectify the consequences of one's wrongdoing.

Restoring Relationships: By making amends through restitution, individuals aim to restore damaged relationships and seek reconciliation with those they have harmed.

Restitution aligns with the biblical principle of justice and fairness, ensuring that those who have suffered harm receive compensation and that wrongdoers take steps to rectify their actions.

Making Amends:

Making amends involves actions taken to repair the harm caused to others, whether through words, deeds, or restitution. It includes:

Apology and Acknowledgment: Acknowledging the harm done and offering a sincere apology to the person who was wronged. This may involve expressing regret and taking responsibility for one's actions.

Restorative Actions: Taking practical steps to address the consequences of one's actions, such as repairing damaged property, compensating for financial losses, or providing support to those affected.

Change in Behavior: Demonstrating a commitment to change by refraining from the harmful behavior and adopting a more responsible and considerate approach to interactions with others.

Rebuilding Trust: Making amends often focuses on rebuilding trust with the person who was harmed. It involves consistent and trustworthy actions that demonstrate a genuine desire for reconciliation.

Making amends is a process of healing and restoration that goes beyond mere words. It involves tangible efforts to repair relationships and restore a sense of justice and fairness.

In the biblical context, both restitution and making amends are seen as important steps in addressing wrongdoing and restoring relationships. These principles emphasize accountability, responsibility, and the ethical imperative to rectify harm caused to others. They align with the broader themes of justice and reconciliation found in the Bible.

Reconciliation and Healing:

Reconciliation and healing, as highlighted in the biblical context, are essential aspects of restoration and play a crucial role in addressing harm and conflict. Here's an explanation of these concepts and why they are needed:

Reconciliation:

Reconciliation, in the biblical context, refers to the process of restoring harmony and unity within broken or strained relationships. Key aspects of reconciliation include:

Forgiveness: A central element of reconciliation is the act of forgiving those who have caused harm. Forgiveness involves letting go of resentment, anger, and the desire for revenge.

Restoration of Relationships: Reconciliation aims to rebuild trust and restore relationships to a state of harmony. It involves repairing the breach that occurred due to harm or conflict.

Conflict Resolution: Addressing the issues that led to the conflict or harm is an important part of reconciliation. It often requires open and honest communication, empathy, and understanding.

Mutual Understanding: Reconciliation involves seeking mutual understanding, where both parties acknowledge their roles in the conflict or harm and work together toward resolution.

Peace and Unity: The ultimate goal of reconciliation is to bring about peace, unity, and a sense of wholeness within individuals, families, communities, and nations.

The biblical emphasis on reconciliation is rooted in the teachings of forgiveness, love, and peacemaking found in various passages, such as the command to love one's neighbor as oneself.

Healing:

Healing, within a biblical context, refers to the process of restoring physical, emotional, and spiritual well-being that may have been affected by harm or conflict. Key aspects of healing include:

Physical Restoration: Healing can involve the recovery of physical health or the alleviation of physical suffering, as seen in biblical stories of Jesus' miraculous healings.

Emotional and Psychological Restoration: Healing addresses the emotional and psychological wounds that result from harm or trauma. It involves finding emotional stability, peace, and resilience.

Spiritual Renewal: Healing often has a spiritual dimension, involving a reconnection with one's faith, a sense of inner peace, and the restoration of spiritual well-being.

Community Healing: In cases of communal harm or conflict, healing extends to the entire community. It involves collective efforts to mend the fabric of the community and restore trust.

Transformation and Growth: Healing can lead to personal transformation and growth, allowing individuals to emerge from adversity with greater strength, wisdom, and compassion.

The biblical narrative includes numerous accounts of physical, emotional, and spiritual healing, often associated with faith, prayer, and divine intervention.

Why Reconciliation and Healing Are Needed:

Restoration of Relationships: Reconciliation and healing are needed to restore broken relationships and promote unity within families, communities, and societies.

Emotional Well-being: These processes contribute to emotional and psychological well-being by addressing trauma, grief, and emotional pain.

Spiritual Renewal: Reconciliation and healing align with spiritual values and enable individuals to experience spiritual renewal and a sense of inner peace.

Conflict Resolution: They provide a constructive approach to conflict resolution, helping to prevent ongoing harm and resentment.

Collective Healing: In cases of communal harm or conflict, reconciliation and healing are essential for the collective well-being of the community.

Personal Growth: These processes facilitate personal growth, resilience, and a deeper understanding of oneself and others.

Promotion of Peace: Reconciliation and healing contribute to the promotion of peace, both on an individual and societal level, fostering a sense of justice and reconciliation.

In summary, reconciliation and healing are vital for addressing harm and conflict, repairing broken relationships, and promoting emotional, spiritual, and communal well-being. They align with biblical principles of forgiveness, love, and restoration and play a central role in the pursuit of justice and peace.

Prophetic Messages:

Prophetic messages in the Bible are divine revelations or declarations communicated through prophets, individuals chosen by God to convey His messages to the people. These messages often emphasize themes of restoration, justice, and the renewal of societies. Here's an explanation of prophetic messages and their significance:

Divine Imperative for Restoration:

Prophetic messages frequently carry a divine imperative for restoration, which means that they emphasize the importance of repairing what has been lost, broken, or damaged. This restoration can be spiritual, social, or moral in nature.

Call for Repentance:

Prophets often call on individuals and communities to repent of their sinful or unjust actions. Repentance is seen as a crucial step toward restoration and reconciliation with God.

Justice and Righteousness:

Prophets deliver messages that emphasize the importance of justice, righteousness, and ethical living. They condemn oppression, corruption, and injustice within society and call for a return to moral and just behavior.

Reconciliation and Healing:

Prophetic messages often contain promises of reconciliation and healing. They assure the people that God is willing to forgive and restore those who turn back to Him.

Hope and Renewal:

Prophetic messages frequently offer hope and the promise of renewal. They speak of a future where brokenness and suffering will be replaced with wholeness and blessings, often in the context of God's divine plan.

Social Justice and Care for the Vulnerable:

Prophets advocate for social justice and care for the vulnerable members of society. They challenge oppressive systems and call for the fair treatment of widows, orphans, and the marginalized.

Rebuilding and Redemption:

Some prophetic messages involve instructions for rebuilding what has been destroyed, as seen in the restoration of Jerusalem after the Babylonian exile. These messages emphasize God's redemptive work in restoring what has been lost.

Covenant Renewal:

Prophets often speak about the renewal of the covenant between God and His people. This renewal is seen as a path to restoration, as it involves a recommitment to God's commands and principles.

Warning of Consequences:

Prophetic messages may also include warnings about the consequences of continued disobedience and injustice. They caution that if people do not turn back to God and seek restoration, there will be negative repercussions.

Guidance for a Righteous Society:

Prophetic messages offer guidance on how to establish and maintain a righteous and just society, often by emphasizing love, compassion, and faithfulness to God.

Prophetic messages are significant because they provide divine guidance and direction for individuals and societies. They inspire hope, call for repentance, and remind people of God's desire for restoration and justice. These messages continue to resonate with believers today, offering timeless wisdom and a call to pursue justice, reconciliation, and renewal within the context of faith.

Theological Insights:

Theological insights derived from the biblical roots of restoration offer valuable perspectives on the alignment between biblical themes and contemporary restorative justice principles. Here's an explanation of theological insights and their significance:

Alignment with Divine Justice:

Theological insights highlight that the biblical roots of restoration are rooted in divine justice. They emphasize that restoration and reconciliation are not merely human constructs but reflect God's desire for justice and the restoration of broken relationships.

Emphasis on Forgiveness:

Biblical roots underscore the importance of forgiveness as a fundamental aspect of restoration. Theological insights emphasize that forgiveness is central to both biblical teachings and restorative justice principles, promoting healing and reconciliation.

Moral Imperatives:

Theological insights highlight the moral imperatives found in the Bible, such as loving one's neighbor, seeking justice, and caring for the vulnerable. These imperatives align with contemporary restorative justice principles, emphasizing ethical behavior and social responsibility.

Transformation of Hearts:

Theological insights emphasize that the biblical narrative often focuses on the transformation of hearts and minds. This aligns with the restorative justice principle that seeks to transform both the offender and the harmed party, fostering personal growth and moral development.

Community and Collective Responsibility:

Biblical roots and theological insights underscore the collective responsibility of communities in addressing harm and conflict. They emphasize that restoration is not solely an individual endeavor but involves the entire community in supporting reconciliation and healing.

Redemptive Justice:

Theological insights introduce the concept of redemptive justice, which aligns with the idea that justice should not be solely punitive but should also aim at the redemption and restoration of individuals. This resonates with the core principles of restorative justice.

Divine Mercy and Compassion:

Theological insights emphasize divine mercy and compassion as driving forces behind restoration in the biblical narrative. These qualities align with the compassionate and empathetic aspects of restorative justice, which seek to address harm while upholding the dignity of all involved.

Reconciliation as a Virtue:

Theological insights underscore reconciliation as a virtue that reflects God's desire for harmony and unity among His creation. This aligns with restorative justice's emphasis on rebuilding relationships and achieving reconciliation.

Hope and Renewal:

Theological insights highlight the themes of hope and renewal found in the biblical narrative. They underscore the transformative power of restoration and how it can bring about renewed lives and communities.

Interfaith Dialogue:

Theological insights encourage interfaith dialogue by demonstrating how common themes of justice, forgiveness, and reconciliation are shared among different religious traditions. This dialogue promotes mutual understanding and collaboration in promoting restorative justice.

These theological insights provide a strong foundation for integrating restorative justice principles into faith-based contexts. They demonstrate the alignment between biblical teachings and contemporary approaches to justice, fostering a deeper understanding of how faith can inform and enrich restorative justice practices.

Is Interfaith Connections important?

Interfaith connections are indeed important, as they facilitate understanding, dialogue, and collaboration among people of different religious traditions. Here's an explanation of interfaith connections and why they are significant, especially in the context of examining biblical roots of restoration:

Interfaith Connections:

Interfaith connections refer to interactions, dialogues, and collaborations that take place between individuals and communities from various religious traditions. These connections involve:

Shared Values and Themes: Identifying common values, themes, and ethical principles that transcend religious boundaries. This includes exploring how themes like justice, forgiveness, and reconciliation are shared among different faiths.

Dialogue and Exchange: Engaging in conversations and exchanges that promote mutual understanding, respect, and appreciation of diverse religious perspectives.

Collaboration: Working together on common goals and initiatives that address social, ethical, and humanitarian challenges. This may include joint efforts to promote peace, justice, and social welfare.

Interfaith Study and Education: Learning about the beliefs, practices, and teachings of different religions to foster empathy and cross-cultural understanding.

Significance of Interfaith Connections:

Interfaith connections are important for several reasons:

Promoting Peace and Harmony: They contribute to peaceful coexistence by fostering respect and tolerance among individuals and communities of different faiths.

Mutual Understanding: Interfaith connections help people gain a deeper understanding of the beliefs and values held by others, dispelling stereotypes and misconceptions.

Shared Values: They highlight the common values and ethical principles that unite diverse religious traditions, including those related to restoration, justice, and reconciliation.

Collaborative Solutions: Interfaith collaborations enable diverse groups to work together on complex societal issues, pooling resources and expertise for the greater good.

Conflict Resolution: In regions with religious diversity, interfaith connections can play a crucial role in resolving or mitigating religiously motivated conflicts.

Spiritual Growth: Interfaith dialogue can lead to personal and spiritual growth by exposing individuals to different perspectives and deepening their own faith.

Promoting Restorative Justice: In the context of examining biblical roots of restoration, interfaith connections allow for a broader exploration of common themes related to justice and reconciliation, enriching the discourse and facilitating the integration of restorative justice principles across faith traditions.

In the specific context of examining biblical roots of restoration, interfaith connections allow for a broader exploration of how themes found in the Bible resonate with similar themes in other religious traditions. This fosters a more inclusive and comprehensive understanding of restoration principles and their relevance across diverse faith contexts. Ultimately, interfaith connections contribute to a more harmonious and compassionate world by promoting dialogue, understanding, and cooperation among people of different beliefs.

CHAPTER 4

The Divine Image and Human Dignity

Image of God:

The concept of the "Image of God" is a theological idea found in various religious traditions, including Christianity, Judaism, and Islam. It emphasizes that humans are created in a way that reflects certain attributes or qualities of the divine.

Theologically, the justice of God can be understood through several categories:

1. Rectoral Justice: This aspect recognizes God as the ultimate moral legislator who judges all of humanity for their thoughts and actions. Abraham acknowledged God as "the Judge of all the earth" (Genesis 18:25), and David affirmed that "the heavens declare His righteousness, for God Himself is judge" (Psalm 50:6). God righteously judges those who have been exposed to His revelation, either through written scripture (Romans 2:12) or through the moral code written on their hearts (Romans 2:14-15; cf. Romans 1:18-20).

2. Retributive Justice: This facet entails God administering just punishment to the wicked for their deeds. In Deuteronomy, the Lord declared, "Vengeance is Mine, and retribution; in due time their foot will slip; for the day of their calamity is near, and the impending things are hastening upon them" (Deuteronomy 32:35). The Apostle Paul, in addressing the Thessalonian church, affirmed that "it is only just for God

to repay with affliction those who afflict you and to give relief to you who are afflicted" (2 Thessalonians 1:6-7a).

3. Remunerative Justice: This dimension involves the distribution of rewards, often based on righteous behavior. For instance, David wrote, "The LORD will repay each man for his righteousness and his faithfulness" (1 Samuel 26:23a). He also acknowledged, "The LORD has rewarded me according to my righteousness; according to the cleanness of my hands He has recompensed me" (Psalm 18:20). Additionally, it can encompass compensation, such as the payment made by the Egyptians to the Israelites for their four hundred years of slavery (Exodus 3:22).

4. Redemptive Justice: This aspect concerns God's forgiveness and justification of helpless sinners because Christ has redeemed them by paying the price for their sins. The price for redemption is the shed blood of Christ, as Peter wrote, "knowing that you were not redeemed with perishable things like silver or gold from your futile way of life inherited from your forefathers, but with precious blood, as of a lamb unblemished and spotless, the blood of Christ" (1 Peter 1:18-19). Believers are justified as a gift by God's grace through the redemption found in Christ Jesus (Romans 3:24-25a). This redemptive justice delivers us from the penalty of sin, ensuring that "there is now no condemnation for those who are in Christ Jesus" (Romans 8:1). At the cross, God both judged our sin in accordance with His righteousness and saved the sinner, in line with His love.

5. Restorative Justice: This dimension pertains to the familial forgiveness God extends to His children who humble themselves and confess their sins. When we sin, we break fellowship with God, and upon confession, He forgives and restores us. David acknowledged this when he wrote, "I acknowledged my sin to You, and my iniquity I did not hide; I said, 'I will confess my transgressions to the LORD,' and You forgave the guilt of my sin" (Psalm 32:5). In the Old Testament, forgiveness was contingent on confessing sins (Leviticus 5:5; 16:21; Psalm 32:5; 38:18) and offering animal sacrifices (Leviticus 4:20; 5:6; 6:6-7). In the New Testament, God requires confession alone (1 John 1:9), rooted in the

once-for-all atoning sacrifice of Christ on the cross (Hebrews 10:10-14). John emphasized the importance of confession, stating, "If we confess our sins, He is faithful and righteous to forgive us our sins and to cleanse us from all unrighteousness" (1 John 1:9).

Inherent Worth and Value:

At its core, the belief in the Image of God underscores the inherent worth and value of every human being. It suggests that each person possesses a sacred and unique quality that sets them apart in the created order. This inherent worth is not based on external factors such as achievements, status, or abilities but is an inherent aspect of human nature.

Reflection of Divine Attributes:

The Image of God implies that humans reflect certain divine attributes or qualities in their nature. While the specific attributes vary among religious traditions, they often include qualities like intelligence, creativity, moral consciousness, and the capacity for spiritual relationship.

Moral and Ethical Implications:

This belief has profound moral and ethical implications. It suggests that recognizing the divine image in others requires treating them with respect, dignity, and compassion. It calls for the protection of human rights, justice, and the prevention of harm or dehumanization.

Interconnectedness and Equality:

The Image of God emphasizes the interconnectedness of all humanity and implies the equality of all individuals in the eyes of the divine. This concept challenges discrimination, prejudice, and social hierarchies that devalue certain groups of people.

Religious Significance:

The belief in the Image of God is significant within religious traditions because it shapes views on the sanctity of human life, the moral responsibility to care for others, and the divine mandate to seek justice and reconciliation.

Interfaith Perspectives:

While the concept is most commonly associated with Abrahamic religions (Judaism, Christianity, and Islam), similar ideas of the divine spark within humanity exist in other faiths as well. For example, Hinduism emphasizes the divine essence (Atman) within each individual.

Diversity of Interpretation:

Different religious traditions interpret the Image of God concept in various ways. For example, in Christianity, it is often associated with the idea of humans sharing in God's rationality and moral attributes. In Judaism, it signifies humans as God's representatives on Earth, entrusted with the stewardship of creation. In Islam, it reflects the idea that humans are created with a divine breath and purpose.

Impact on Views of Human Dignity:

The belief in the Image of God significantly shapes views on human dignity, underscoring that every person, regardless of their circumstances or background, possesses a sacred and inviolable dignity. This belief is foundational to discussions on human rights, social justice, and the treatment of individuals within various religious and ethical frameworks.

In summary, the concept of the Image of God emphasizes the inherent worth, value, and unique qualities of every individual as reflective of the divine. It carries profound ethical and moral implications and is foundational to discussions on human dignity, justice, and the treatment of others in religious and ethical contexts.

Human Dignity and Justice:

Human Dignity:

Human dignity is the inherent and inviolable worth and value possessed by every human being simply because they are human. It emphasizes the sacredness of human life and the intrinsic worth of each individual, regardless of their background, circumstances, or attributes. The belief in human dignity underlines that every person deserves respect, compassion, and protection of their fundamental rights and well-being.

Justice:

Justice is the moral and social principle of fairness, equity, and righteousness in the treatment of individuals and the allocation of resources and opportunities within society. It involves ensuring that each person receives their due, that wrongs are righted, and that individuals are treated in accordance with moral and legal standards. Justice encompasses various aspects, including social justice, distributive justice, and criminal justice, among others.

Implications of Human Dignity for Justice:

The belief in human dignity has significant implications for justice:

Equal Treatment: Human dignity requires that all individuals be treated with equal respect and fairness under the law. Discrimination, prejudice, and bias that undermine human dignity are considered unjust.

Protection of Rights: Justice involves safeguarding the rights and freedoms of individuals. Upholding human dignity means ensuring that these rights are protected and respected.

Restorative Justice: The concept of human dignity aligns closely with restorative justice principles. In restorative justice, the dignity of both victims and offenders is recognized and respected. Offenders are seen as individuals capable of transformation, and victims are offered the opportunity to have their voices heard and their harm acknowledged.

Reconciliation: Restorative justice places a strong emphasis on reconciliation, which involves the restoration of relationships and the healing of harm. Recognizing the dignity of all parties involved is essential for achieving genuine reconciliation.

Empathy and Compassion: A just society encourages empathy and compassion, recognizing that these qualities are essential for understanding the experiences and suffering of others. These qualities are closely tied to acknowledging human dignity.

Responsibility and Accountability: Justice requires holding individuals accountable for their actions. However, this accountability should be carried out in a way that respects the inherent worth of the person and seeks their rehabilitation rather than retribution.

Prevention of Harm: A just society seeks to prevent harm to individuals and communities, understanding that harm undermines human dignity. This includes efforts to address systemic injustices and inequalities.

Promotion of Social Welfare: Justice extends to ensuring the well-being of all members of society, particularly the vulnerable and marginalized. This includes access to basic necessities and opportunities for growth and development.

Accordingly, the belief in human dignity informs views on justice by emphasizing the importance of treating every individual with respect, fairness, and compassion. It calls for the protection of rights, the prevention of harm, and the promotion of social welfare. In the context of restorative justice, recognizing and upholding human dignity is central to the principles of reconciliation, accountability, and the restoration of relationships.

Challenges to Human Dignity:

Human dignity is a foundational principle that emphasizes the inherent worth and value of every individual. However, various forms of harm, injustice, and dehumanization can challenge and undermine human dignity. Here are some of the key challenges to human dignity:

Physical Harm and Violence: Physical harm, including acts of violence, assault, and abuse, directly violate an individual's bodily integrity and dignity. Victims of such harm often experience physical and psychological trauma.

Discrimination and Prejudice: Discrimination based on factors such as race, gender, religion, or nationality is a grave challenge to human dignity. It denies individuals equal treatment and opportunities and perpetuates social inequalities.

Inequality and Economic Injustice: Widespread economic inequality, lack of access to basic necessities, and poverty can erode human dignity by depriving individuals of their basic needs and opportunities for advancement.

Dehumanizing Language and Stereotypes: The use of dehumanizing language, stereotypes, and derogatory labels can demean and devalue individuals, stripping them of their dignity and reducing them to mere objects of ridicule or hatred.

Institutional Oppression: Systems and institutions that perpetuate oppression and marginalization, such as oppressive governments, corrupt legal systems, and discriminatory policies, can systematically undermine human dignity.

Social Isolation and Stigmatization: Individuals who are socially isolated or stigmatized due to factors like mental illness, addiction, or criminal history often face the erosion of their dignity as they are treated as outcasts.

Trauma and Victimization: Victims of various forms of harm, including crime, natural disasters, and conflict, may experience profound trauma that challenges their sense of dignity. The aftermath of victimization can leave individuals feeling vulnerable and powerless.

Deprivation of Basic Rights: The denial of basic human rights, such as freedom of speech, expression, and religion, restricts individuals' autonomy and dignity.

Restorative Justice and Upholding Human Dignity:

Restorative justice practices play a vital role in addressing these challenges to human dignity. Here's how:

Recognition of Harm: Restorative justice acknowledges the harm done to victims and recognizes their dignity by allowing them to express their feelings, concerns, and needs.

Empowerment: Restorative processes empower victims by giving them a voice in the resolution of the harm. This empowers them to reclaim their dignity and agency.

Accountability: Restorative justice holds offenders accountable for their actions while emphasizing their potential for rehabilitation. This approach recognizes the dignity of both victims and offenders.

Restitution and Repair: Restorative justice promotes restitution and efforts to repair the harm caused. This includes making amends, offering apologies, and taking responsibility for one's actions, which can help restore the dignity of both parties.

Community Support: Restorative justice often involves the community in the healing process, offering support and understanding to those affected by harm. This sense of community can help rebuild a sense of belonging and dignity.

Preventing Recidivism: By focusing on addressing the underlying causes of harm and promoting rehabilitation, restorative justice aims to prevent future harm and reoffending, which contributes to the long-term restoration of human dignity.

In summary, restorative justice practices help address the challenges to human dignity by recognizing the harm caused, empowering victims, holding offenders accountable, and involving the community in the healing process. By prioritizing reconciliation, restitution, and rehabilitation, restorative justice contributes to the restoration and upholding of the dignity of those affected by harm and injustice.

Restorative Justice and Human Dignity:

Restorative justice is an approach to justice that focuses on repairing the harm caused by wrongdoing, holding offenders accountable, and promoting the restoration of relationships. It aligns closely with the belief in human dignity by recognizing the intrinsic worth and value of all individuals involved in the justice process. Here's an analysis of how restorative justice approaches align with the belief in human dignity:

Recognition of Intrinsic Worth:

Restorative justice starts with the fundamental recognition that every individual, including victims and offenders, possesses intrinsic worth and dignity.

It rejects the dehumanization of offenders and recognizes their potential for change and growth.

Victim-Centered Approach:

Restorative justice prioritizes the needs and voices of victims, acknowledging their right to be treated with dignity and respect.

Victims are given the opportunity to express their feelings, seek answers, and have a say in the resolution process.

Offender Accountability with Dignity:

Restorative justice holds offenders accountable for their actions but does so in a way that respects their dignity.

Offenders are encouraged to take responsibility for their actions and make amends, recognizing the harm they have caused.

Empathy and Understanding:

Restorative justice processes, such as victim-offender dialogues, foster empathy and understanding between victims and offenders. These processes contribute to the restoration of human dignity by allowing individuals to see each other as human beings with shared experiences and vulnerabilities.

Community Involvement:

Restorative justice often involves the community in the resolution process. This community support reinforces the idea that individuals, even those who have caused harm, belong to a broader social fabric.

Community members contribute to the healing and restoration of those affected by harm.

Preventing Further Harm:

By addressing the underlying causes of harm and focusing on rehabilitation, restorative justice aims to prevent further harm and victimization.

This preventive aspect aligns with the principle of preserving human dignity by safeguarding individuals from harm.

Examples and Case Studies:

Victim-Offender Mediation: In cases of minor offenses, victim-offender mediation brings victims and offenders together to discuss the harm caused. Case studies have shown that victims often find this process empowering, as it allows them to confront offenders and regain a sense of control and dignity.

Restitution and Amends: Restorative justice often involves offenders making restitution or amends to victims. These actions, when undertaken sincerely, can help restore the dignity of both parties. For example, an offender repairing the damage they caused to a victim's property can symbolize the restoration of the victim's sense of security and dignity.

Juvenile Diversion Programs: Restorative justice is frequently applied in juvenile justice systems to divert young offenders away from punitive measures. By focusing on rehabilitation and reintegration, these programs aim to prevent juveniles from being stigmatized and dehumanized by the criminal justice system, preserving their dignity.

Truth and Reconciliation Commissions: In post-conflict settings, truth and reconciliation commissions use restorative justice principles to address past atrocities. These processes provide victims with a platform to share their experiences and seek acknowledgment of their suffering, contributing to the restoration of their dignity.

Hence, restorative justice approaches align with the belief in human dignity by recognizing the worth of all individuals, providing opportunities for victims and offenders to heal and reconcile, and involving the community in the restoration process. Numerous examples and case studies demonstrate how restorative justice practices prioritize the restoration of human dignity for all parties involved, promoting healing, reconciliation, and accountability.

Theological Perspectives on Dignity:

Theological perspectives on dignity vary among different religious traditions, but they often share common themes regarding the sacredness of human life and the moral imperative to protect human dignity. Here, we explore these perspectives from several major religious traditions:

Christianity:

Imago Dei: In Christianity, the belief in the Imago Dei, or the image of God, underscores the idea that every human being is created in the likeness of God. This belief emphasizes the inherent worth and dignity of all individuals.

Love and Compassion: Christian teachings, such as the commandment to love one's neighbor, emphasize the moral imperative to treat others with love, compassion, and dignity.

Forgiveness and Redemption: Christian theology places a strong emphasis on forgiveness and redemption, highlighting the potential for individuals to transform and be restored to their God-given dignity.

Judaism:

B'tzelem Elohim: In Judaism, the concept of "B'tzelem Elohim" (created in the image of God) parallels the Christian notion of the Imago Dei. It signifies the divine spark within each person and underscores their intrinsic worth.

Tikkun Olam: The Jewish concept of "Tikkun Olam" (repairing the world) underscores the moral duty to engage in acts of justice and compassion to uphold human dignity and mend the brokenness of the world.

Justice and Mercy: Jewish tradition places a strong emphasis on justice, mercy, and the protection of the vulnerable, reflecting a commitment to human dignity.

Islam:

Fitrah: Islamic theology holds that all humans are born with an inherent disposition toward goodness, known as "Fitrah." This concept aligns with the idea of human dignity.

Compassion and Justice: Islamic teachings emphasize compassion, justice, and the obligation to care for the less fortunate. Upholding human dignity is central to these principles.

Repentance and Forgiveness: Islam teaches that sincere repentance and divine forgiveness are accessible to all, promoting the restoration of human dignity.

Buddhism:

Respect for All Life: Buddhism promotes respect for all sentient beings, recognizing the intrinsic value and dignity of every individual, not just humans.

Compassion and Non-Harming: Buddhist ethics emphasize compassion, non-harming, and the alleviation of suffering, aligning with the preservation of human dignity.

Self-Transformation: Buddhism teaches that individuals have the potential for self-transformation and liberation, reflecting the belief in human dignity and personal growth.

Hinduism:

Atman: Hinduism teaches the concept of "Atman," the eternal self or soul present in every being. This belief underscores the sacredness and dignity of all life forms.

Dharma: Hindu ethics emphasize one's duty (dharma) and the pursuit of righteousness, which includes treating others with dignity and respect.

Karma and Rebirth: Hinduism's belief in karma and rebirth underscores the idea that individuals have the potential to evolve spiritually and regain their dignity in subsequent lifetimes.

Influence on the Criminal Justice System:

These theological perspectives influence attitudes and practices within the criminal justice system in various ways:

Emphasis on Rehabilitation: Theological teachings often encourage a focus on rehabilitation and personal transformation within the criminal justice system, promoting the restoration of human dignity for offenders.

Restorative Justice Practices: Some religious traditions advocate for restorative justice practices that prioritize healing, reconciliation, and the restoration of relationships, aligning with theological principles.

Ethical Decision-Making: Theological perspectives guide ethical decision-making within the criminal justice system, emphasizing fairness, compassion, and respect for the dignity of all individuals.

Advocacy for the Vulnerable: Many religious traditions advocate for the protection of the rights and dignity of vulnerable and marginalized populations within the criminal justice system.

Community Involvement: Theological perspectives often call for the involvement of communities in addressing issues of justice, fostering a sense of collective responsibility for upholding human dignity.

In summary, theological perspectives on dignity, rooted in various religious traditions, emphasize the sacredness of human life and the moral duty to protect human dignity. These perspectives influence attitudes and practices within the criminal justice system by promoting principles of justice, compassion, and personal transformation, with a focus on restoring the dignity of all individuals involved.

Dignity and Rehabilitation:

Recognizing the dignity of offenders is a crucial aspect of rehabilitation efforts within the criminal justice system. Here's a discussion of how this recognition informs rehabilitation efforts and an examination of programs and initiatives that prioritize the restoration of human dignity to promote reintegration and prevent recidivism:

1. Recognizing Dignity in Offenders:

Intrinsic Worth: Acknowledging the intrinsic worth and value of offenders, regardless of their past actions, is essential for fostering a sense of self-worth and motivating positive change.

Presumption of Potential: Recognizing that offenders have the potential for personal growth, transformation, and reintegration into society is a foundational principle of rehabilitation.

Human Rights: Upholding the human rights of offenders, including their right to be treated with dignity and respect, is a legal and ethical obligation.

2. Rehabilitation Programs and Initiatives:

Education and Skill Building: Providing access to educational programs, vocational training, and skill development opportunities within correctional facilities enables offenders to acquire valuable skills and qualifications, enhancing their prospects for reintegration.

Mental Health Services: Recognizing and addressing the mental health needs of offenders through counseling and therapy helps restore their emotional well-being and dignity.

Substance Abuse Treatment: Offering substance abuse treatment and support helps individuals overcome addiction, improve their mental health, and regain control over their lives.

Restorative Justice Practices: Implementing restorative justice practices, such as victim-offender dialogues, promotes self-reflection and empathy among offenders and fosters accountability and the restoration of dignity.

Reentry Programs: Comprehensive reentry programs that support individuals upon release from prison can help them access housing, employment, and social services, reducing the risk of reoffending.

Community Support: Engaging communities in the rehabilitation and reintegration process is vital. Community-based organizations and support networks can provide a sense of belonging and encourage pro-social behavior.

Counseling and Therapy: Access to counseling and therapy services, including anger management and conflict resolution programs, helps offenders address the underlying causes of their criminal behavior and develop healthier coping mechanisms.

3. Prevention of Recidivism:

Promoting Accountability: By holding offenders accountable for their actions and making amends to victims and the community, rehabilitation efforts align with restorative justice principles that aim to prevent recidivism.

Reducing Risk Factors: Rehabilitation programs often target risk factors associated with criminal behavior, such as substance abuse, unemployment, and lack of education, to reduce the likelihood of reoffending.

Personal Transformation: Recognizing the potential for personal transformation and character development promotes a sense of responsibility and encourages individuals to make positive choices.

Community Reintegration: Successful rehabilitation efforts prioritize the safe and supportive reintegration of offenders into their communities, where they can rebuild their lives and contribute positively.

Measuring Success: Effective rehabilitation programs measure success not only by reducing recidivism rates but also by assessing improvements in offenders' quality of life, emotional well-being, and social functioning.

Therefore, recognizing the dignity of offenders is integral to rehabilitation efforts within the criminal justice system. Rehabilitation programs and initiatives that prioritize the restoration of human dignity aim to promote personal growth, reintegration into society, and the prevention of recidivism. By addressing the underlying causes of criminal behavior and fostering a sense of self-worth and accountability, these efforts contribute to the restoration of dignity for individuals involved in the justice system.

Restorative Practices and Empathy:

Restorative justice practices, including victim-offender dialogues and circles, are important because they promote empathy and a deeper understanding of the human experience, contributing significantly to the restoration of human dignity in the aftermath of harm. Here's an exploration of why these practices and empathy are essential:

1. Empathy as a Foundation of Restorative Justice:

Restorative justice is grounded in principles of empathy, respect, and recognizing the humanity of all parties involved.

Empathy is at the core of understanding the pain and suffering experienced by victims and the reasons behind an offender's actions.

2. Victim-Offender Dialogues:

These dialogues provide a structured and safe space for victims and offenders to communicate directly.

Victims have the opportunity to express their emotions, ask questions, and seek answers, while offenders gain insights into the impact of their actions.

Dialogue fosters empathy as it requires both parties to listen to each other's perspectives and acknowledge the harm caused.

3. Perspective-Taking:

Restorative practices encourage participants to take on each other's perspectives. Victims may begin to understand the factors that led an offender to commit the harm, while offenders can appreciate the emotional consequences of their actions.

This perspective-taking contributes to a more comprehensive understanding of the human experience surrounding the harm.

4. Addressing Dehumanization:

Harm often dehumanizes both victims and offenders. Victims may feel reduced to the role of a passive victim, while offenders may be seen solely through the lens of their criminal actions.

Restorative practices humanize both parties by highlighting their shared experiences, emotions, and vulnerabilities.

5. Restoring Dignity Through Acknowledgment:

Victims often seek acknowledgment of their suffering and the harm done to them. Empathetic responses from offenders, such as sincere apologies and taking responsibility, are vital for restoring the dignity of victims.

For offenders, acknowledging the harm they caused and expressing remorse can be a transformative experience that aligns with the restoration of their own dignity.

6. Encouraging Accountability:

Empathy encourages offenders to take accountability for their actions and their impact on others. This accountability is not solely punitive but includes a commitment to making amends and preventing future harm.

Offenders recognize that their actions have consequences not only for victims but also for themselves and their communities.

7. Healing and Reconciliation:

Empathy is a key driver of healing and reconciliation. Victims may find a sense of closure and validation through empathetic interactions with offenders.

Genuine empathy from offenders can lead to a deeper commitment to making restitution and positive changes in their lives.

8. Preventing Recidivism:

Restorative practices that foster empathy can contribute to the prevention of recidivism. Offenders who understand the impact of their actions on victims are more likely to make efforts to avoid reoffending.

In summary, restorative justice practices, with their emphasis on empathy and understanding, play a crucial role in restoring human dignity in the aftermath of harm. They facilitate communication, acknowledgment of harm, and the humanization of both victims and offenders. Empathy is a powerful tool for promoting healing, accountability, and the prevention of future harm, ultimately contributing to the restoration of dignity for all parties involved.

CHAPTER 5

Shalom: God's Vision for a Restored World

Shalom:

Shalom is a Hebrew word with deep theological and cultural significance. While it is often translated as "peace," its meaning goes beyond mere absence of conflict. Shalom represents a state of holistic well-being, harmony, wholeness, and completeness. It encompasses not only the absence of violence but also the presence of justice, flourishing, and right relationships. Shalom reflects a vision of God's intended order for the world, where all aspects of life, including social, spiritual, and ecological, are in harmony.

Shalom as Divine Harmony:

Wholeness: Shalom embodies the idea of wholeness and completeness. It suggests that God's vision for creation includes the integration of all aspects of life—individual, communal, and environmental—into a harmonious whole.

Well-Being: Shalom is a state of well-being that extends to all living beings. It envisions a world where people live in health, prosperity, and mutual respect. This goes beyond physical health to encompass mental, emotional, and spiritual well-being.

Harmony with God: Shalom reflects the theological notion that God's intended order for the world is one in which humanity is in harmonious relationship with the divine. It implies a state of reconciliation and communion with God.

Justice and Righteousness: Shalom includes the presence of justice and righteousness. In this vision, injustice, oppression, and inequality have no place. Instead, it promotes equitable relationships and the fair distribution of resources.

Freedom from Brokenness: Shalom envisions a world free from brokenness, sin, and injustice. It represents a return to the original goodness of creation, where everything functions as it should, without distortion or corruption.

Community and Relationships: Shalom involves harmonious relationships within communities and between individuals. It emphasizes reconciliation, forgiveness, and the restoration of broken relationships.

Environmental Harmony: Shalom extends to the natural world, were ecological systems function in balance and sustainability. It reflects a deep respect for God's creation and a commitment to stewardship.

Eschatological Hope: Shalom is often associated with eschatological hope—the belief in the ultimate fulfillment of God's plan for restoration and peace. It points toward a future where all creation experiences perfect harmony and well-being.

Accordingly, Shalom is a profound theological concept that signifies more than just the absence of conflict. It represents divine harmony, wholeness, and well-being in all aspects of life. Shalom reflects the theological idea of God's intended order for the world, where creation is free from brokenness and injustice, and all beings live in harmony with one another and with the divine. It serves as a guiding vision for pursuing justice, reconciliation, and the restoration of human dignity.

Biblical Foundations of Shalom:

The Bible contains numerous passages and narratives that emphasize God's desire for Shalom—a vision of peace, justice, and restoration. These foundational elements can be found throughout the

Old Testament, particularly in prophetic writings and the Psalms. Here, we explore some of the key biblical foundations of Shalom:

Isaiah's Vision (Isaiah 2:4):

"They will beat their swords into plowshares and their spears into pruning hooks. Nation will not take up sword against nation, nor will they train for war anymore."

Isaiah's vision is a powerful image of Shalom, where weapons of war are transformed into tools for agriculture, symbolizing a world free from conflict and violence.

The Peaceable Kingdom (Isaiah 11:6-9):

"The wolf will live with the lamb, the leopard will lie down with the goat, the calf and the lion and the yearling together; and a little child will lead them."

Isaiah's depiction of animals living in harmony reflects the idea of Shalom extending to the natural world, where creation's predatory instincts are transformed into peaceful coexistence.

The Messianic Hope (Isaiah 9:6-7):

"For to us a child is born, to us a son is given, and the government will be on his shoulders. And he will be called Wonderful Counselor, Mighty God, Everlasting Father, Prince of Peace."

These verses anticipate the coming of the Messiah, who is described as the "Prince of Peace," bringing Shalom to the world through divine governance.

The Psalms of Peace (e.g., Psalm 85:10):

"Love and faithfulness meet together; righteousness and peace kiss each other."

Many Psalms express the connection between righteousness and peace, emphasizing that Shalom is intimately linked to justice and moral integrity.

Micah's Call for Justice (Micah 6:8):

"He has shown you, O mortal, what is good. And what does the Lord require of you? To act justly and to love mercy and to walk humbly with your God."

Micah's words underscore the importance of justice and mercy in the pursuit of Shalom, aligning righteousness with God's vision of peace.

The Restoration of Jerusalem (Jeremiah 33:6-9):

These verses speak of the restoration of Jerusalem and the return of joy, praise, and prosperity. They reflect the biblical theme of God's desire to restore what is broken and bring Shalom to the land.

The Covenant of Peace (Ezekiel 34:25):

"I will make a covenant of peace with them and rid the land of savage beasts so that they may live in the wilderness and sleep in the forests in safety."

This verse emphasizes the idea of a covenant of peace, where God's people are safe and protected in a world free from harm.

These biblical passages and narratives collectively paint a picture of God's desire for Shalom—a state of peace, justice, and restoration. They convey the theological idea that God's intended order for the world is one where humanity and creation live in harmony, free from brokenness and injustice. This vision of Shalom serves as a guiding principle for pursuing justice, reconciliation, and the restoration of human dignity in both religious and social contexts.

The Relationship between Shalom and Restorative Justice:

The pursuit of Shalom and restorative justice principles share a profound and harmonious relationship. Both concepts are deeply concerned with repairing harm, restoring relationships, promoting reconciliation, and upholding human dignity. Here's a discussion of how Shalom aligns with restorative justice and serves as a guiding vision for its practices:

1. Shared Vision of Wholeness:

Shalom: Shalom envisions wholeness and completeness in all aspects of life. It sees a world where individuals and communities are in harmony with one another, their environment, and the divine. This vision extends to social and spiritual well-being.

Restorative Justice: Restorative justice shares this vision of wholeness. It seeks to restore what has been broken or harmed, not just in a legal sense but in a holistic manner. It aims to repair the harm done to individuals, relationships, and communities.

2. Emphasis on Right Relationships:

Shalom: Shalom emphasizes the importance of right relationships—between people, with God, and with the natural world. It sees harmony in relationships as a fundamental aspect of well-being.

Restorative Justice: Restorative justice is centered on repairing relationships that have been damaged by harm or wrongdoing. It fosters dialogues and processes that allow victims, offenders, and communities to address the harm, express their needs, and work toward reconciliation.

3. Pursuit of Justice and Mercy:

Shalom: Shalom is often associated with justice and righteousness. It envisions a world where justice is not punitive but restorative, and where mercy is extended to those who seek reconciliation.

Restorative Justice: Restorative justice combines the pursuit of justice with mercy. It acknowledges the importance of accountability for offenders while emphasizing opportunities for personal growth, restitution, and healing.

4. Human Dignity and Healing:

Shalom: Shalom promotes human dignity by valuing the well-being and worth of all individuals. It recognizes the need for healing and restoration in the face of brokenness and harm.

Restorative Justice: Restorative justice places a strong emphasis on upholding human dignity for both victims and offenders. It provides a platform for victims to regain their sense of self-worth and for offenders to make amends and transform their lives.

5. Community and Reconciliation:

Shalom: Shalom extends to the community, emphasizing the need for communal harmony and well-being. It envisions societies where individuals and groups reconcile and work together for the common good.

Restorative Justice: Restorative justice practices often involve the broader community in the process of addressing harm and promoting reconciliation. Community support is seen as integral to the restoration of all parties involved.

6. Spiritual and Eschatological Hope:

Shalom: Shalom is often associated with spiritual and eschatological hope—a belief in the ultimate fulfillment of God's plan for restoration and peace.

Restorative Justice: Restorative justice aligns with this hope by providing practical avenues for pursuing reconciliation and healing, reflecting a commitment to realizing God's vision of Shalom on a human level.

Shalom and restorative justice are closely aligned in their shared emphasis on wholeness, right relationships, justice, mercy, human dignity, community, and the pursuit of a harmonious and restored world. Shalom serves as a guiding vision for restorative justice practices, inspiring individuals and communities to work toward reconciliation, healing, and the restoration of human dignity in the aftermath of harm.

Interfaith Perspectives on Shalom:

The concept of Shalom, while prominently associated with Judaism, is also found in various other religious traditions, including Christianity and Islam. Each tradition approaches the pursuit of divine harmony and peace in its unique way. Here's a consideration of interfaith perspectives on Shalom:

1. Judaism:

Shalom in Jewish Tradition: Shalom is a central concept in Judaism, symbolizing not only peace but also completeness, well-being, and wholeness. It's often used as a greeting and a blessing.

Pursuit of Justice: Judaism emphasizes the pursuit of justice (tzedek) as an essential aspect of Shalom. The pursuit of justice and righteousness is seen as integral to achieving peace and harmony within society.

Tikkun Olam: The Jewish concept of "Tikkun Olam" means "repairing the world." It reflects the responsibility to actively work for social justice, compassion, and healing in the world, aligning with the pursuit of Shalom.

2. Christianity:

Peace in Christianity: In Christianity, peace (eirene in Greek) is a prominent theme, and Jesus is often referred to as the "Prince of Peace." Christian teachings emphasize reconciliation, forgiveness, and the importance of peacemaking.

Biblical Emphasis: Christian scriptures, particularly the New Testament, contain numerous references to peace and reconciliation. Passages like the Beatitudes (Matthew 5) and the call to love one's neighbor highlight the pursuit of Shalom-like ideals.

Just War Theory: While Christianity emphasizes peace, it also developed the concept of "Just War Theory" to address situations when war might be deemed necessary for the greater good. This illustrates the complex interplay between peace and justice within the Christian tradition.

3. Islam:

Salaam in Islam: In Islam, "Salaam" is the Arabic word for peace. It's a common greeting among Muslims and signifies a desire for peace and well-being.

Justice and Mercy: Islam places a strong emphasis on justice and mercy. These principles are seen as essential for creating a just and peaceful society. The Quran contains numerous verses that promote justice, compassion, and reconciliation.

Conflict Resolution: Islamic teachings include guidelines for conflict resolution and reconciliation. The concept of "Sulh" refers to the settlement of disputes through peaceful means, fostering peace and harmony.

4. Interfaith Dialogue:

Interfaith dialogue often highlights the commonalities among these traditions regarding the pursuit of peace, justice, and reconciliation. It provides a platform for individuals from various faith backgrounds to collaborate in addressing social issues and promoting Shalom-like values.

Interfaith efforts may involve joint initiatives for peacebuilding, humanitarian work, and advocacy for social justice, reflecting the shared commitment to fostering divine harmony in the world.

In summary, Shalom is a concept with resonance in multiple religious traditions, each of which emphasizes the pursuit of divine harmony, peace, justice, and reconciliation. While the specific theological nuances and practices vary, there is a common thread of working toward a world where individuals and communities experience well-being, wholeness, and mutual respect—a world that reflects the divine vision of Shalom. Interfaith perspectives on Shalom underscore the potential for collaboration and dialogue among diverse religious communities to promote peace and justice globally.

Shalom in Action:

Shalom in action refers to tangible efforts by individuals and communities to pursue the principles of Shalom, which include peace, justice, reconciliation, and human dignity. Here are case studies and examples of how individuals and groups work towards Shalom through restorative justice initiatives, conflict resolution, and peacebuilding efforts:

1. Restorative Justice in Schools:

Case Study: In a school setting, restorative justice programs are implemented to address conflicts and disciplinary issues. Instead of punitive measures, students engage in restorative circles and dialogues to resolve conflicts and build relationships.

Impact: These initiatives reduce suspension rates, foster a sense of community, and empower students to take responsibility for their actions, aligning with the pursuit of Shalom in an educational context.

2. Truth and Reconciliation Commissions:

Example: South Africa's Truth and Reconciliation Commission (TRC) is a well-known example of pursuing Shalom after a history of apartheid. The TRC allowed victims and perpetrators to testify, seeking truth and forgiveness.

Impact: While not without controversies, the TRC contributed to national healing and reconciliation efforts, addressing historical injustices and promoting a sense of Shalom in a divided nation.

3. Interfaith Peacebuilding:

Case Study: Interfaith organizations worldwide work to bridge religious divides and promote peace. For instance, the Abraham Path Initiative encourages interfaith pilgrimage along the path of Abraham, fostering understanding among Jews, Christians, and Muslims.

Impact: These initiatives demonstrate that people from diverse faith backgrounds can collaborate to address conflict and promote the shared values of peace and human dignity.

4. Community Mediation Programs:

Example: Community-based mediation centers provide a space for neighbors to resolve disputes without resorting to legal action. Trained mediators facilitate dialogue and seek mutually agreeable solutions.

Impact: These programs reduce court backlogs, save resources, and empower communities to take an active role in resolving conflicts, contributing to a more peaceful and just society.

5. Grassroots Initiatives for Social Justice:

Case Study: Grassroots movements like the Civil Rights Movement in the United States or the anti-apartheid struggle in South Africa exemplify how individuals and communities can mobilize for systemic change.

Impact: These movements address entrenched injustices, advocate for equal rights, and challenge oppressive systems, ultimately contributing to greater societal Shalom.

6. Conflict Resolution in Post-Conflict Zones:

Example: Non-governmental organizations (NGOs) often work in post-conflict regions to facilitate dialogue, reconciliation, and conflict resolution. One such organization is the Peace and Reconciliation Trust in Zimbabwe.

Impact: These efforts help communities heal and rebuild after conflict, fostering an environment where Shalom can take root and flourish.

7. Humanitarian and Refugee Aid:

Case Study: Humanitarian organizations provide aid and support to refugees and displaced populations fleeing conflict and violence. Impact: These efforts alleviate suffering, protect vulnerable populations, and contribute to the pursuit of Shalom by upholding the dignity of those affected by crisis.

Shalom in action encompasses a wide range of initiatives and efforts aimed at promoting peace, justice, reconciliation, and human dignity. These examples demonstrate how individuals and communities can actively work towards these ideals in various contexts, from schools to conflict zones. The pursuit of Shalom inspires individuals and societies to address systemic injustices, heal wounds, and create environments where human dignity is upheld, aligning with the divine vision of a harmonious and restored world.

Theological Reflections:

Theological reflections on the pursuit of Shalom emphasize the role of human agency in realizing God's vision of peace, justice, and reconciliation. These reflections underscore the importance of active engagement in pursuing these ideals. Here are some key theological reflections:

Co-Creation with God:

Theological reflection acknowledges that humans are co-creators with God in bringing about Shalom. It emphasizes that God invites humanity to participate in the work of justice and reconciliation.

Moral Responsibility:

Theological perspectives emphasize the moral responsibility of individuals and communities to actively engage in addressing injustices and conflicts. This responsibility stems from the recognition of God's call to pursue righteousness and peace.

Image of God:

The belief that humans are created in the image of God underscores their capacity for empathy, compassion, and moral discernment. Theological reflection highlights that these qualities are essential for promoting Shalom.

Redemptive Work:

Theological reflection recognizes the redemptive nature of pursuing Shalom. It acknowledges that reconciliation and restoration are central themes in religious traditions, reflecting God's desire to redeem and heal a broken world.

Prophetic Witness:

Theological perspectives draw inspiration from the prophetic tradition within various religions. Prophets have historically called people to act justly, love mercy, and walk humbly with God, serving as models of active engagement for Shalom.

Solidarity with the Marginalized:

Theological reflection emphasizes the importance of solidarity with the marginalized and oppressed. It recognizes that pursuing Shalom often requires standing alongside those who are most affected by injustice.

Transformative Love:

Love, as a transformative force, is central in theological reflections on Shalom. Love is seen as the motivation for seeking reconciliation and justice, aligning with the divine command to love one's neighbor.

Repentance and Forgiveness:

Theological reflection acknowledges the role of repentance and forgiveness in the pursuit of Shalom. Recognizing one's own faults and seeking forgiveness is essential for fostering reconciliation and healing.

Prayer and Contemplation:

Theological perspectives recognize the role of prayer and contemplation in the pursuit of Shalom. These practices help individuals discern God's guidance and find the inner strength needed for active engagement.

Sacred Activism:

Theological reflection often encourages the concept of sacred activism—engaging in actions for justice and peace as a sacred duty. It views such activism as a form of worship and service to God.

Hence, theological reflections on Shalom highlight the inseparable connection between faith and action. They call upon individuals and communities to recognize their moral responsibility, draw inspiration from their religious traditions, and actively engage in the pursuit of justice, reconciliation, and human dignity. Theological reflections empower individuals to become agents of Shalom, working towards the realization of God's vision for a restored and harmonious world.

Understanding Restorative Justice

Restorative justice is a transformative approach to addressing harm, conflict, and wrongdoing that seeks to heal individuals and communities by emphasizing reconciliation, accountability, and restoration over punitive measures. At its core, restorative justice recognizes that harm affects not only the victim but also the offender and the broader community. It challenges the conventional punitive justice model, which often results in a cycle of retribution and further harm.

Instead, restorative justice offers a holistic perspective that addresses the emotional, psychological, and social consequences of wrongdoing.

In restorative justice processes, victims are given a voice and the opportunity to express their feelings, needs, and expectations for repair. Offenders are encouraged to take responsibility for their actions and make amends to those they have harmed. These encounters, often facilitated by trained mediators, allow for open dialogue, empathy, and the potential for reconciliation. The community also plays a vital role in holding offenders accountable and supporting both victims and offenders in their journey toward healing.

Restorative justice is not a one-size-fits-all approach but a flexible framework that can be applied in various settings, including schools, criminal justice systems, and communities. It acknowledges that each case is unique and requires tailored responses. By fostering a sense of ownership, empowerment, and collaboration among all parties involved, restorative justice aims to break the cycle of harm, promote human dignity, and contribute to the creation of a more just and compassionate society.

CHAPTER 6

The Principles of Restorative Justice

Voluntary Participation in Restorative Justice:

Voluntary participation is a foundational principle of restorative justice, highlighting the importance of individuals willingly engaging in the restorative process. Here's a closer look at what voluntary participation entails:

Informed Consent: In restorative justice, all parties involved, including victims, offenders, and sometimes community members, must provide informed and voluntary consent to participate. This means they fully understand the nature of the process, its goals, and the potential outcomes before choosing to take part.

Respecting Autonomy: Voluntary participation respects the autonomy and agency of individuals. It acknowledges that people have the right to decide whether they want to engage in the process or pursue other avenues, such as traditional criminal justice procedures.

Emphasis on Inclusivity: This principle ensures that no one is coerced or pressured into participating against their will. It promotes inclusivity by creating a space where all voices, particularly those of victims and offenders, are heard and respected.

Enhancing Ownership: When individuals voluntarily choose to participate in restorative justice, they are more likely to take ownership of the process and its outcomes. This sense of ownership can lead to a deeper commitment to addressing harm and finding resolution.

Creating Safe Spaces: By emphasizing voluntary participation, restorative justice processes aim to create safe and non-threatening spaces for dialogue. Participants are more likely to engage openly and honestly when they are there by choice, contributing to effective communication and understanding.

Respecting Human Rights: Voluntary participation aligns with the principles of human rights and ensures that individuals' rights are upheld. It respects their right to consent or decline involvement in the process, safeguarding their dignity and autonomy.

Ethical Foundation: This principle is rooted in ethics and moral considerations. It recognizes that the pursuit of justice and reconciliation should be based on the free will and consent of those directly affected by harm or conflict.

In essence, voluntary participation in restorative justice underscores the democratic and consent-based nature of the process. It is a fundamental aspect of ensuring that individuals have agency in addressing harm, healing relationships, and seeking resolution on their own terms. By respecting the principle of voluntary participation, restorative justice practices promote a sense of fairness, empowerment, and mutual respect among all parties involved.

Importance of Encounter and Dialogue in Restorative Justice:

Encounter and dialogue are fundamental to the practice of restorative justice, and their importance cannot be overstated. Here's why they play a crucial role in restorative justice processes:

Humanizing the Other:

Encounter and dialogue humanize both victims and offenders. These processes create opportunities for individuals to see each other as real people with feelings, experiences, and vulnerabilities. This recognition fosters empathy and understanding.

Facilitating Communication:

Effective communication is essential for resolving conflicts and addressing harm. Encounter and dialogue provide a structured platform where all parties can express themselves, share their perspectives, and be heard without interruption or judgment.

Sharing Impact and Needs:

Victims have the opportunity to share the impact of the harm on their lives, allowing offenders to fully grasp the consequences of their actions. Similarly, offenders can express remorse and convey their understanding of the harm they've caused. This exchange of information is crucial for resolution.

Building Trust:

Trust is a cornerstone of restorative justice. Encounter and dialogue enable participants to build trust through honest and respectful communication. Trust is essential for working collaboratively toward solutions and agreements.

Empowering Participants:

Encounter and dialogue empower participants by giving them agency in the process. Victims and offenders have a voice in shaping the outcomes and decisions, contributing to a sense of ownership and control over the resolution.

Conflict Transformation:

Through dialogue, conflicts are transformed from adversarial confrontations into opportunities for understanding and healing. Participants can explore the root causes of harm and work together to find mutually acceptable solutions.

Reparation and Amends:

Dialogue provides a space to discuss and agree upon measures of reparation and amends. Offenders can make concrete commitments to address the harm, and victims can express their needs and expectations regarding restitution and restoration.

Accountability and Responsibility:

Encounter and dialogue hold offenders accountable for their actions and encourage them to take responsibility. This is not only about acknowledging guilt but also committing to change and personal growth.

Conflict Prevention:

By addressing the underlying issues and grievances, encounter and dialogue help prevent future conflicts and harm. Participants learn problem-solving and communication skills that can be applied in other areas of their lives.

Healing and Closure:

Encounter and dialogue contribute to the healing process for victims and offenders alike. Sharing their experiences and emotions can be cathartic and provide a sense of closure, allowing individuals to move forward.

In summary, encounter and dialogue are the lifeblood of restorative justice. They create spaces for individuals to connect, communicate, and collaborate toward resolution and reconciliation. By emphasizing these processes, restorative justice promotes empathy, understanding, trust, and the transformative potential of human interaction in the aftermath of harm or conflict.

Empathy and Understanding in Restorative Justice:

Empathy and understanding are foundational principles of restorative justice that play a vital role in the healing and reconciliation process. Here's a closer look at their significance within restorative justice:

Seeing the Human Being: Restorative justice recognizes that both victims and offenders are human beings with complex emotions, experiences, and vulnerabilities. By fostering empathy, it encourages participants to look beyond labels and stereotypes and acknowledge the shared humanity of all involved.

Promoting Compassion: Empathy involves putting oneself in another person's shoes, understanding their emotions, and feeling a sense of compassion. In restorative justice, this compassionate understanding helps participants connect on a deeper level and relate to each other's pain and suffering.

Breaking Down Barriers: In many cases, harm and conflict create emotional and psychological barriers between victims and offenders. Empathy and understanding help break down these barriers by creating a space where individuals can express their emotions and be heard without judgment.

Facilitating Communication: Empathy and understanding are essential for effective communication. They enable participants to listen actively, validate each other's feelings, and respond with empathy. This open and respectful communication is key to resolving conflicts and addressing harm.

Building Trust: Trust is a fragile element in the aftermath of harm or conflict. Restorative justice processes, by emphasizing empathy and understanding, help rebuild trust among participants. When individuals feel heard and valued, they are more likely to trust in the process and in each other's commitment to resolution.

Empowering Victims: Empathy empowers victims by validating their experiences and emotions. It acknowledges the pain and suffering they have endured, giving them a sense of agency and control over the process. This empowerment contributes to their healing.

Fostering Accountability: Understanding the impact of one's actions on others is a crucial aspect of accountability. Restorative justice encourages offenders to develop empathy by hearing directly from victims about the harm caused. This personal connection often leads to genuine remorse and a commitment to making amends.

Transformation and Healing: Empathy and understanding are transformative forces. They can lead to personal growth, healing, and positive change in both victims and offenders. Participants may develop a heightened awareness of the consequences of their actions, motivating them to prevent future harm.

Long-Term Impact: The empathy and understanding cultivated in restorative justice processes can have long-term effects. Participants may carry these skills into other aspects of their lives, contributing to improved relationships, conflict resolution, and community cohesion.

In essence, empathy and understanding are at the heart of restorative justice's ability to mend relationships, promote healing, and pave the way for resolution. They remind participants that even in the aftermath of harm or conflict, there is an opportunity for connection, growth, and the restoration of human bonds.

Benefits of Accountability and Responsibility in Restorative Justice:

Accountability and responsibility are core principles of restorative justice, and they bring forth numerous benefits within this context:

Acknowledgment of Wrongdoing: By taking responsibility, offenders acknowledge their actions and admit wrongdoing. This acknowledgment is a crucial step in the healing process for victims and the community.

Empowering Victims: Accountability validates the experiences of victims by confirming that harm was done. This acknowledgment empowers victims, providing them with a sense of justice and closure.

Restitution and Reparation: Offenders taking responsibility often involves making amends. This may include restitution to the victim or contributing to the restoration of the community. These actions directly address the tangible consequences of the harm.

Personal Growth: Accountability fosters personal growth and self-awareness in offenders. They are encouraged to reflect on their actions, understand the impact on others, and develop empathy and remorse.

Reducing Recidivism: Restorative justice processes that emphasize accountability have been linked to lower rates of reoffending. Offenders who take responsibility and actively engage in making amends are less likely to commit further crimes.

Community Healing: Accountability extends to the community affected by the harm. When offenders take responsibility and contribute to the community's well-being, it helps in healing collective wounds and restoring trust.

Positive Social Reintegration: Offenders who have taken responsibility and made amends are more likely to be reintegrated into society successfully. This reintegration benefits not only the offender but also the community.

Transformative Justice: Accountability is a key aspect of transformative justice. It shifts the focus from punishment to personal growth and transformation, emphasizing that individuals can change and learn from their mistakes.

Rebuilding Relationships: In cases where relationships have been strained or broken due to harm, offenders' accountability can be a crucial step in rebuilding trust and repairing the relationship with victims and the community.

Deterrence: The accountability aspect of restorative justice can serve as a deterrent to potential offenders. Knowing that they will be held accountable for their actions and expected to make amends may discourage individuals from engaging in harmful behavior.

Cultural Sensitivity: Restorative justice processes can be culturally sensitive, allowing offenders to take responsibility in a manner that aligns with their cultural values and practices. This promotes inclusivity and respect for diverse backgrounds.

Personal Satisfaction: Offenders who take responsibility often report a sense of personal satisfaction and closure. They know they have done everything within their power to address the harm they caused.

In summary, accountability and responsibility are not punitive measures but transformative elements of restorative justice. They provide opportunities for offenders to learn, grow, and contribute positively to the well-being of victims and the community. By emphasizing personal responsibility, restorative justice seeks to repair harm and prevent future wrongdoing, ultimately promoting a sense of justice and reconciliation.

Importance of Reparation and Amends in Restorative Justice:

The principle of making reparation and amends holds significant importance in restorative justice, and here are the key reasons why:

Restoring Equity: Reparation and amends seek to restore a sense of equity and balance. When offenders take tangible actions to address the harm they caused, it symbolizes their commitment to rectifying the imbalance they created.

Addressing Tangible Consequences: Wrongdoing often results in concrete, tangible consequences for victims and the community, such as financial losses or damage to property. Reparation and amends directly address these practical aspects of harm.

Validation of Victim's Experience: Victims often suffer financial or material losses in addition to emotional harm. Reparation validates the victim's experience by recognizing and addressing these losses, demonstrating empathy and understanding.

Personal Responsibility: Making amends requires offenders to take personal responsibility for their actions. This process can lead to self-reflection and a deeper understanding of the impact of their behavior on others.

Restoring Trust: When offenders fulfill their commitments to make amends, it can help rebuild trust with the victim and the community. Trust is a critical component of restorative justice, and reparation contributes to its restoration.

Community Benefit: Reparative actions may benefit the community at large. For example, community service undertaken by offenders can have positive effects on neighborhoods and organizations, strengthening community bonds.

Learning from Consequences: Offenders gain a firsthand understanding of the real-life consequences of their actions when they actively participate in reparation. This learning can be a catalyst for personal growth and change.

Preventing Recidivism: By actively engaging in making amends, offenders may be less likely to repeat their harmful behavior. This preventive aspect contributes to the reduction of recidivism.

Educational Value: Reparation and amends can be educational for both offenders and the community. They highlight the broader implications of harmful actions and promote a culture of responsibility and accountability.

Victim Satisfaction: Victims often express a sense of satisfaction and closure when they see offenders taking concrete steps to repair the harm. This satisfaction can contribute to their healing and well-being.

Conflict Resolution: In cases where conflicts arise due to harm, reparation and amends can be a practical means of resolving those conflicts and finding mutually acceptable solutions.

Long-Term Impact: Reparation and amends can have long-term positive impacts on the lives of victims, offenders, and the community. They provide a sense of justice, closure, and the opportunity for everyone involved to move forward.

In summary, reparation and amends are essential components of restorative justice that focus on addressing the practical consequences of wrongdoing. They promote personal responsibility, healing, and reconciliation while ensuring that victims receive compensation and recognition for their losses. This principle reinforces the idea that restorative justice seeks not only to mend relationships but also to rectify the tangible harm caused by offenses.

Inclusivity and Community in Restorative Justice:

The principles of inclusivity and community in restorative justice emphasize the importance of involving the broader community in the process of healing, accountability, and reintegration. Here's why they are vital:

Collective Responsibility: Inclusivity and community underscore the idea that addressing harm is not solely the responsibility of victims, offenders, and facilitators but also of the entire community. This collective responsibility promotes a sense of shared accountability for the well-being of all community members.

Support for Victims: Victims often find solace and support in their communities. Inclusivity ensures that victims receive the backing of their community, which can contribute significantly to their healing and recovery.

Community Voice: Communities have a voice in restorative justice processes. They can express their concerns, expectations, and needs, influencing the outcomes of the process and ensuring that community interests are taken into account.

Holding Offenders Accountable: Inclusivity encourages communities to actively engage in holding offenders accountable. Community members may play roles in monitoring and supporting offenders as they fulfill their commitments to make amends.

Reintegration: Communities play a key role in the successful reintegration of offenders. Their support, acceptance, and guidance can help offenders reintegrate into society in a positive and constructive manner.

Preventing Isolation: Inclusivity prevents the isolation of offenders and victims. It emphasizes that they remain part of the broader community despite the harm or conflict, reducing the likelihood of stigmatization or marginalization.

Learning Opportunity: Restorative justice processes that involve the community provide a learning opportunity for all members. They can gain a deeper understanding of the consequences of harm, the importance of empathy, and the value of community cohesion.

Conflict Resolution: Communities may experience internal conflicts or divisions due to harm or conflict. Restorative justice processes that engage the community can address these conflicts, fostering unity and resolution.

Building Social Capital: Inclusivity and community-building in restorative justice contribute to the development of social capital within communities. Social bonds and trust are strengthened as community members actively participate in processes of accountability and restoration.

Cultural Sensitivity: Different communities may have unique cultural norms and values. Inclusivity ensures that restorative justice processes are culturally sensitive and respectful of diverse perspectives and practices.

Preventative Measures: By involving the community in addressing harm and promoting accountability, restorative justice processes can act as preventive measures, discouraging future wrongdoing and conflicts.

Sustainable Change: Community involvement fosters a sense of ownership over the restorative justice process and its outcomes, promoting lasting, sustainable change in community dynamics and conflict resolution practices.

Inclusivity and community engagement in restorative justice reinforce the idea that healing and accountability are not isolated events but processes that involve the entire community. By recognizing the role of the community, restorative justice seeks to restore not only individual relationships but also the social fabric of the community itself, promoting harmony, unity, and justice for all.

Safety and Well-Being in Restorative Justice:

Safety and well-being are foundational principles in restorative justice, emphasizing the physical, emotional, and psychological safety of all participants. Here's why these principles are crucial:

Preventing Harm: Restorative justice processes aim to address harm and conflict while preventing further harm. Ensuring the safety of all participants is essential in achieving this goal.

Emotional and Psychological Safety: Harm and conflict often result in emotional and psychological distress. Prioritizing emotional safety means creating an environment where individuals can express their feelings without fear of judgment or retribution.

Rebuilding Trust: Victims and offenders may have deep-seated concerns about their safety and well-being. By guaranteeing safety, restorative justice processes can help rebuild trust and confidence in the process itself.

Encouraging Participation: Participants are more likely to engage openly and honestly when they feel safe. Emotional safety enables them to share their experiences, emotions, and perspectives, contributing to effective communication and understanding.

Re-Victimization Prevention: Victims should not experience re-victimization during restorative justice processes. Safety measures are in place to protect victims from further harm or distress during encounters with offenders.

Minimizing Retraumatization: Some victims may have experienced trauma related to the harm they suffered. Restorative justice processes must take steps to minimize retraumatization and promote healing.

Promoting Accountability: Ensuring the safety of all participants is instrumental in promoting accountability. Offenders are more likely to take responsibility for their actions in an environment where they feel safe and supported.

Ethical Responsibility: Restorative justice practitioners have an ethical responsibility to prioritize safety and well-being. This commitment reinforces the ethical foundation of restorative justice, which aims to promote justice without causing harm.

Community Confidence: Ensuring safety and well-being builds community confidence in restorative justice processes. When community members know that participants are protected, they are more likely to support and engage in these processes.

Respect for Human Dignity: Respecting the safety and well-being of all individuals involved is a fundamental aspect of upholding human dignity. It reaffirms the principle that every person deserves to be treated with respect and care.

Conflict Prevention: By addressing safety concerns and minimizing re-victimization, restorative justice processes contribute to preventing future conflicts and harm within communities.

Promoting Healing: Emotional and psychological safety are essential for the healing process. Participants who feel safe are more likely to engage in meaningful dialogue, express their needs, and work toward resolution and reconciliation.

In summary, safety and well-being are essential principles in restorative justice that prioritize the physical and emotional safety of all participants. By creating a secure and supportive environment, restorative justice processes promote effective communication, accountability, healing, and the prevention of further harm or re-traumatization. These principles reinforce the ethical and human-centered nature of restorative justice.

Cultural Sensitivity in Restorative Justice:

Cultural sensitivity in restorative justice is a principle that recognizes and respects the diverse cultural perspectives, values, and practices of individuals and communities involved in the restorative process. Here's why cultural sensitivity is important in restorative justice:

Respect for Diversity: Cultural sensitivity acknowledges the rich tapestry of cultures and backgrounds that exist within society. It respects the uniqueness of each culture and the diverse ways in which people may view and address harm and conflict.

Inclusivity: Cultural sensitivity promotes inclusivity by ensuring that restorative justice processes are accessible and respectful of all cultural groups. It prevents the exclusion or marginalization of individuals based on their cultural backgrounds.

Avoiding Cultural Insensitivity: Cultural insensitivity can unintentionally cause harm or misunderstandings during restorative processes. Being culturally sensitive helps practitioners avoid inadvertently disrespecting or misinterpreting cultural practices.

Effective Communication: Restorative justice relies on effective communication and understanding. Cultural sensitivity enhances communication by considering cultural nuances, languages, and communication styles.

Building Trust: Acknowledging and respecting cultural differences builds trust among participants. When individuals feel that their culture is understood and valued, they are more likely to engage openly in the process.

Conflict Resolution: Cultural sensitivity can facilitate conflict resolution by recognizing that cultural factors may contribute to conflicts.

By addressing these factors with cultural competence, practitioners can find more effective solutions.

Customized Approaches: Restorative justice processes can be customized to align with cultural values and preferences. This flexibility ensures that the process remains relevant and meaningful to participants from diverse backgrounds.

Reducing Stigmatization: Cultural sensitivity helps prevent stigmatization or stereotyping of individuals based on their cultural identity. It ensures that participants are treated as unique individuals rather than representatives of a particular culture.

Community Engagement: Communities are more likely to engage in restorative justice processes when they feel their cultural values and traditions are respected and integrated into the process.

Learning Opportunity: Cultural sensitivity is an opportunity for participants and practitioners to learn about different cultures, fostering cultural competency and mutual understanding.

Promoting Equity: Cultural sensitivity promotes equity by ensuring that all participants have equal access to restorative justice processes regardless of their cultural background.

Legal and Ethical Considerations: In some cases, cultural practices may intersect with legal and ethical considerations. Cultural sensitivity helps navigate these intersections while upholding the principles of justice and accountability.

In essence, cultural sensitivity in restorative justice ensures that the process is inclusive, respectful, and responsive to the cultural diversity of participants. It acknowledges that culture plays a significant role in how individuals perceive and address harm and conflict and strives to integrate cultural competence into restorative practices, fostering a sense of justice and reconciliation that resonates with diverse communities.

Importance of Continual Learning and Improvement in Restorative Justice:

Continual learning and improvement are fundamental in the field of restorative justice for several compelling reasons:

Adaptation to Changing Needs: Society's understanding of harm, conflict, and justice continually evolves. Restorative justice must adapt to these changing needs and challenges to remain relevant and effective.

Enhancing Effectiveness: Reflecting on past experiences and outcomes allows practitioners to identify areas for improvement. By making necessary adjustments, restorative justice processes can become more effective in achieving their goals.

Cultural Competence: Cultural sensitivity and competence are essential in restorative justice. Continual learning ensures that practitioners are aware of and can respond to the diverse cultural perspectives of participants.

Community Engagement: Communities play a central role in restorative justice. Learning from community feedback and experiences helps build trust and engagement, fostering a sense of ownership over the process.

Strengthening Ethical Foundations: Restorative justice processes are guided by ethical principles. Continual learning helps practitioners deepen their understanding of these principles and ensures that they are consistently applied.

Preventing Harm: The goal of restorative justice is to address harm while preventing further harm. Learning from past cases can help identify practices that unintentionally cause harm and find ways to mitigate these risks.

Innovation: Continual learning encourages innovation in restorative justice practices. It provides opportunities to experiment with new approaches, technologies, and methodologies to enhance the effectiveness of the process.

Increasing Accountability: By regularly evaluating and improving processes, restorative justice practitioners and communities can hold themselves accountable for delivering justice and achieving meaningful outcomes.

Professional Development: Continual learning supports the professional development of practitioners, ensuring that they remain well-informed and skilled in their roles. This benefits both practitioners and the participants they serve.

Building a Knowledge Base: Restorative justice benefits from a growing body of knowledge and research. Continual learning contributes to this knowledge base, allowing the field to draw on evidence-based practices.

Evaluation and Measurement: Learning and improvement facilitate the evaluation of restorative justice processes. By assessing outcomes and impacts, practitioners can refine their methods and measure their effectiveness.

Community Trust: A commitment to continual learning and improvement builds community trust. When participants see that restorative justice is a dynamic and responsive process, they are more likely to engage with confidence.

Conflict Prevention: Learning from past cases and continually improving processes can contribute to conflict prevention by addressing root causes and patterns of harm.

Therefore, continual learning and improvement are essential for the ongoing success and relevance of restorative justice. By embracing a culture of learning, practitioners, communities, and the field as a whole can adapt to changing circumstances, refine their practices, and better serve the principles of justice, reconciliation, and healing.

Non-Discrimination and Equity in Restorative Justice:

Non-discrimination and equity are foundational principles in restorative justice that emphasize fairness, inclusivity, and the elimination of biases or prejudices. Here's why these principles are of utmost importance:

Equal Access to Justice: Non-discrimination and equity ensure that everyone, regardless of their background, has equal access to restorative justice processes. This levels the playing field and prevents systemic barriers that may hinder certain groups from seeking justice.

Social Justice: Restorative justice is deeply rooted in principles of social justice. Non-discrimination and equity align with these principles by addressing structural inequalities and disparities within society.

Victim-Centered Approach: Victims of harm or crime come from diverse backgrounds. Non-discrimination and equity ensure that the needs and experiences of victims from marginalized or underrepresented groups are equally recognized and respected.

Addressing Bias: Bias and prejudice can undermine the effectiveness of restorative justice. These principles require practitioners to be aware of and address any biases they may have, ensuring that all participants are treated fairly.

Community Involvement: Communities often have diverse populations. Non-discrimination and equity encourage the active involvement of all community members, promoting a sense of belonging and shared responsibility.

Cultural Competence: Restorative justice processes must be culturally competent. These principles ensure that practitioners are sensitive to the cultural norms, values, and practices of diverse participants.

Preventing Revictimization: Discrimination or bias within the process can lead to revictimization, particularly for marginalized individuals. Non-discrimination and equity aim to prevent any form of revictimization.

Building Trust: Trust is a crucial element in restorative justice. Non-discrimination and equity build trust by assuring participants that they will be treated fairly and respectfully, regardless of their background.

Conflict Resolution: Addressing systemic injustices and disparities is often a root cause of conflict. Non-discrimination and equity contribute to conflict resolution by promoting a more just and inclusive society.

Legal and Ethical Standards: Non-discrimination and equity align with legal and ethical standards related to human rights, civil rights, and social justice. They reinforce the ethical foundations of restorative justice.

Community Healing: Communities affected by harm may include members from various backgrounds. Non-discrimination and equity contribute to community healing by ensuring that the restoration process is inclusive and just for all.

Positive Outcomes: When participants perceive that restorative justice processes are non-discriminatory and equitable, they are more likely to engage positively, leading to more effective outcomes.

Human Dignity: These principles uphold the inherent dignity of every individual, reinforcing the idea that every person deserves to be treated with respect, regardless of their identity or circumstances.

In summary, non-discrimination and equity are critical principles in restorative justice that underpin its commitment to justice, inclusivity, and fairness. By addressing systemic injustices and disparities, restorative justice seeks to create a more just and equitable society where all individuals have access to fair and meaningful processes for addressing harm and conflict.

CHAPTER 7

The Role of Forgiveness and Repentance

The Role of Forgiveness and Repentance

In the realm of restorative justice, forgiveness and repentance play pivotal roles in the process of healing, reconciliation, and the restoration of relationships. Forgiveness, often regarded as an act of grace and mercy, holds the power to liberate victims from the shackles of resentment and anger. It offers victims the opportunity to release the burden of their suffering and embark on a journey towards emotional and psychological healing. This act of forgiveness is not merely the absence of revenge but a profound act of courage, empathy, and transcendence.

On the other side of the coin, repentance emerges as a transformative force for offenders. It goes beyond mere remorse; it signifies a sincere acknowledgment of wrongdoing and a commitment to making amends. Repentance requires individuals to confront the consequences of their actions and take responsibility for the harm they have caused. In restorative justice, repentance is not coerced but emerges as a genuine desire for personal growth and ethical transformation. It is an invitation for offenders to reintegrate into society as responsible, empathetic individuals.

The dynamic interplay between forgiveness and repentance within restorative justice processes fosters an environment where healing and reconciliation become achievable. This process is not linear but complex, marked by genuine emotions and cathartic moments. It challenges participants to confront the depths of their humanity, where vulnerability, empathy, and the possibility of redemption reside. By embracing these profound aspects, restorative justice seeks to transcend punitive paradigms and pave the way for the restoration of human dignity, harmony, and justice.

Understanding forgiveness is crucial within the context of restorative justice for several significant reasons:

Clarity of Purpose: Forgiveness is a central aspect of restorative justice processes. Understanding what forgiveness means and entails provides clarity of purpose for both victims and offenders as they engage in these processes.

Emotional Healing: Forgiveness is a potent tool for emotional healing. Victims who comprehend the concept of forgiveness may be more willing to explore it as a path toward healing and letting go of the emotional burden of resentment, anger, and pain.

Conflict Resolution: Forgiveness is often a key element in resolving conflicts and repairing relationships. Understanding how forgiveness functions can guide participants toward reconciliation and the restoration of broken bonds.

Psychological Well-Being: Research indicates that forgiveness can lead to improved psychological well-being. Knowing the potential benefits of forgiveness may motivate individuals to embrace it as a means of personal growth and emotional health.

Cultural Sensitivity: Different cultures may have varying interpretations of forgiveness. Understanding these cultural nuances is essential to ensure that restorative justice processes are culturally sensitive and respectful of diverse perspectives.

Theological Significance: Forgiveness holds profound theological significance in many religious traditions. Understanding these theological aspects can enrich the spiritual dimension of restorative justice and foster a deeper sense of meaning for participants.

Ethical Considerations: Forgiveness is intertwined with ethical considerations related to justice, mercy, and compassion. Participants in restorative justice processes may find it easier to navigate these ethical complexities when they have a clear understanding of forgiveness.

Conflict Prevention: Understanding forgiveness can also contribute to conflict prevention. By addressing the root causes of conflicts and harm, forgiveness can help prevent future disputes and harm within communities.

Promoting Empathy: Forgiveness often involves empathizing with the experiences and perspectives of others. Understanding forgiveness can foster empathy among participants, which is essential for effective communication and reconciliation.

Rebuilding Trust: Forgiveness is a trust-building process. When participants understand how forgiveness can contribute to rebuilding trust, they may be more willing to engage in restorative justice processes with openness and honesty.

In essence, understanding forgiveness is vital within restorative justice because it informs participants about its significance, benefits, and potential outcomes. It empowers individuals to make informed choices about whether to embark on the transformative journey of forgiveness, ultimately contributing to the overarching goals of justice, healing, and reconciliation.

Forgiveness in Restorative Justice:

Forgiveness within the context of restorative justice is a complex and transformative process that holds profound significance. Here's why it is essential and how it operates within restorative justice:

Healing and Liberation: Forgiveness is a powerful tool for victims to heal emotionally and psychologically. It liberates them from the burden of anger, resentment, and the desire for revenge, allowing them to regain a sense of control over their lives.

Reconciliation and Restoration: Forgiveness paves the way for reconciliation between victims and offenders. It opens a door for dialogue and understanding, allowing both parties to seek resolution and rebuild broken relationships.

Empathy and Understanding: Forgiveness encourages empathy, as it often requires victims to consider the perspective and experiences of the offender. This process fosters a deeper understanding of the root causes of harm and conflict.

Conditions for Forgiveness: Forgiveness is not automatic and requires certain conditions to be met. These may include genuine remorse from the offender, accountability for their actions, and a commitment to making amends.

Empowerment: Forgiveness empowers victims by giving them agency in the process. It allows them to choose whether, when, and how to forgive, putting them in control of their own healing journey.

Transformation: Forgiveness can transform both victims and offenders. It can lead to personal growth, empathy, and a commitment to avoiding harmful behaviors in the future. For offenders, it can be a turning point in their lives.

Community Healing: Forgiveness extends beyond individual healing; it contributes to the healing of communities as well. When victims and offenders find a path to forgiveness, it sets an example for others, fostering a sense of collective healing and unity.

Challenges and Opportunities: Forgiveness is not without its challenges. Victims may struggle with forgiving, and offenders may find it difficult to express genuine remorse. However, these challenges present opportunities for growth and transformation.

Spiritual and Ethical Dimensions: Forgiveness often has deep spiritual and ethical dimensions. It aligns with principles of mercy, compassion, and grace found in various religious traditions, enriching the spiritual aspect of restorative justice.

Alternatives to Retribution: Forgiveness offers an alternative to retribution and punitive justice. It replaces a cycle of harm and punishment with a path of healing, accountability, and reconciliation.

Accordingly, forgiveness in restorative justice is not just an emotional act but a profound process that contributes to healing, reconciliation, and transformation. It empowers victims, transforms offenders, and fosters a sense of empathy and understanding among all participants. By embracing forgiveness, restorative justice seeks to move beyond punitive paradigms and toward a more just, compassionate, and reconciled society.

Repentance and Accountability in Restorative Justice:

Repentance and accountability are integral components of restorative justice, contributing to the transformative power of this approach. Here's a closer look at these concepts and their importance within restorative justice:

Repentance Defined: Repentance signifies more than just feeling sorry for one's actions; it represents a profound change of heart and mind. It involves acknowledging wrongdoing, feeling genuine remorse, and committing to making amends and avoiding future harm.

Genuine Remorse: In restorative justice, offenders are encouraged to express genuine remorse for the harm they have caused. This goes beyond superficial apologies and requires a deep understanding of the impact of their actions on victims and the community.

Taking Responsibility: Repentance entails taking full responsibility for one's actions. Offenders must understand that they are accountable for the harm they have caused and be willing to face the consequences of their behavior.

Conditions for Repentance: Restorative justice processes create conditions that encourage repentance. These may include victim-offender dialogues, where offenders have the opportunity to directly engage with victims, hear their perspectives, and express their remorse.

Accountability as a Pillar: Accountability is a fundamental pillar of restorative justice. Offenders are held accountable not just through punitive measures but through active participation in the restoration process, which includes making amends and taking steps to prevent future harm.

Personal Growth: Repentance and accountability often lead to personal growth and transformation for offenders. They have the opportunity to reflect on their actions, develop empathy for victims, and commit to positive change.

Rebuilding Trust: Accountability and repentance contribute to rebuilding trust between victims and offenders. Victims are more likely to trust that offenders will follow through on their commitments to make amends and avoid further harm.

Preventing Recidivism: Repentance is a significant factor in preventing recidivism. Offenders who genuinely repent and undergo personal growth are less likely to engage in harmful behavior in the future.

Community Reintegration: Repentance and accountability support the successful reintegration of offenders into the community. When offenders take responsibility for their actions and seek to make amends, it fosters a sense of accountability within the community.

Healing and Closure: Repentance and accountability contribute to the healing and closure of victims. Victims often find solace in knowing that offenders have acknowledged their wrongdoing and are actively working to make things right.

In essence, repentance and accountability are essential components of restorative justice because they align with the principles of personal growth, responsibility, and reconciliation. They empower offenders to face the consequences of their actions, foster empathy and understanding, and contribute to the overarching goals of healing and restoration within the context of restorative justice.

The Impact of Forgiveness on Victims:

Forgiveness within the context of restorative justice can have a profound and transformative impact on victims. Here's an exploration of the various ways in which forgiveness influences victims:

Healing Journey: Forgiveness often marks the beginning of a healing journey for victims. It allows them to release the heavy burden of anger, resentment, and emotional pain that may have consumed them after experiencing harm. Through forgiveness, victims can start to mend the emotional wounds caused by the wrongdoing.

Liberation from Emotional Chains: Forgiveness liberates victims from the emotional chains that tie them to the offender and the traumatic event. It offers them a sense of freedom and empowerment, allowing them to regain control over their lives and emotions.

Emotional Well-Being: Victims who choose to forgive often experience improved emotional well-being. They may find relief from symptoms of anxiety, depression, and post-traumatic stress disorder (PTSD) as they let go of the negative emotions associated with the harm.

Restored Self-Esteem: Forgiveness can contribute to the restoration of a victim's self-esteem and self-worth. It reminds them that they are not defined by the harm they've experienced and that they have the strength to transcend it.

Rebuilding Trust: In cases where victims engage in restorative justice processes and forgiveness leads to reconciliation, trust between victims and offenders can be rebuilt. This renewed trust can be a powerful step toward healing.

Empowerment: Forgiveness empowers victims by giving them agency over their own healing process. It allows them to decide when and how to forgive, putting them in control of their emotional recovery.

Enhanced Resilience: Victims who forgive often exhibit greater resilience in the face of adversity. They demonstrate the ability to bounce back from trauma and continue with their lives in a healthy and constructive manner.

Closure and Moving Forward: Forgiveness can provide a sense of closure for victims, allowing them to move forward with their lives. It signifies a willingness to leave the past behind and embrace a future free from the burdens of the harm.

Contribution to Community Healing: When victims forgive and engage in restorative justice processes, it can contribute to the healing of the broader community. It sets an example of forgiveness, resilience, and the possibility of redemption.

Transformation of the Offender: In cases where forgiveness leads to the transformation of the offender, victims may find solace in knowing that their forgiveness has contributed to positive change, preventing further harm to others.

It's important to note that forgiveness is a deeply personal and individual choice for victims. Not all victims may choose to forgive, and that choice should always be respected. However, for those who do embark on the path of forgiveness, it can be a powerful means of reclaiming their emotional well-being, finding closure, and contributing to the broader goals of restorative justice, which include healing and reconciliation.

The Transformation of Offenders:

Within the framework of restorative justice, the transformation of offenders is a central objective, and it is often facilitated through the processes of repentance and seeking forgiveness. Here's a closer look at how these processes can bring about the transformation of offenders:

Genuine Remorse: Repentance involves genuine remorse for one's actions. Offenders must confront the consequences of their wrongdoing and experience a deep sense of regret and responsibility. This emotional response is the first step toward transformation.

Taking Responsibility: Offenders taking full responsibility for their actions is a crucial aspect of repentance. Acknowledging that they have caused harm and accepting accountability for their behavior is a fundamental shift in their mindset.

Personal Growth: Repentance often leads to personal growth for offenders. As they reflect on their actions and the impact on others, they may undergo a process of self-examination and self-improvement. This can include developing better impulse control, decision-making skills, and empathy.

Empathy Development: Seeking forgiveness requires offenders to empathize with their victims and understand the pain and suffering they have caused. This development of empathy can lead to a heightened sense of compassion and understanding for others.

Restitution and Making Amends: Offenders committed to transformation actively seek ways to make amends for the harm they've caused. This can include restitution to victims, community service, or other forms of reparation. These actions demonstrate a genuine commitment to righting their wrongs.

Commitment to Avoiding Harm: Transformed offenders commit to avoiding harmful behavior in the future. They recognize that their actions have consequences not only for victims but for themselves and their communities as well. This commitment is a key aspect of their transformation.

Reduced Recidivism: Research indicates that offenders who engage in restorative justice processes, undergo personal growth, and commit to making amends are less likely to reoffend. This reduction in recidivism benefits not only the offenders but also society at large.

Reintegration into the Community: Transformed offenders can successfully reintegrate into their communities. Their commitment to personal growth, accountability, and making amends often allows them to rebuild trust within their social networks.

Positive Role Models: Transformed offenders can become positive role models for others who are at risk of engaging in harmful behavior. Their stories of personal growth and transformation serve as examples of redemption and change.

Contributing to Healing: By undergoing a genuine transformation, offenders contribute to the healing of victims and communities. Their willingness to change and take responsibility can provide a sense of closure and justice for those they have harmed.

The transformation of offenders is a testament to the potential for growth and change within individuals, even in the wake of serious wrongdoing. Restorative justice recognizes this potential and provides a framework for offenders to embark on a journey of personal transformation, accountability, and making amends for their actions. Ultimately, this transformation benefits not only the offenders themselves but also the broader community by reducing harm and promoting healing and reconciliation.

Challenges and Complexities in Forgiveness and Repentance:

Forgiveness and repentance, while transformative, are intricate processes within restorative justice. They come with their own set of challenges and complexities that participants may encounter:

1. Emotional Hurdles: Both victims and offenders may struggle with intense emotions during the forgiveness and repentance process. Victims may grapple with anger, grief, and fear, while offenders may face shame, guilt, and remorse. Managing these emotions can be challenging.

2. Timing: Forgiveness and repentance may not happen immediately. It takes time for victims to heal and for offenders to genuinely understand the impact of their actions. Rushing these processes can hinder their effectiveness.

3. Unwilling Participants: Not all victims are willing or able to forgive, and not all offenders are genuinely remorseful. Coercing forgiveness or repentance can be counterproductive and may retraumatize victims or lead to insincere apologies.

4. Degrees of Harm: Forgiveness and repentance can be more challenging in cases of severe harm or violent crimes. The greater the harm, the more complex the process may become, as victims and offenders grapple with the enormity of the wrongdoing.

5. Power Dynamics: Power imbalances between victims and offenders can complicate forgiveness and repentance. Victims may feel pressured to forgive, while offenders may struggle to express genuine remorse if they perceive themselves as powerless.

6. Cultural and Religious Differences: Cultural and religious beliefs can influence attitudes toward forgiveness and repentance. Participants from diverse backgrounds may have varying interpretations of these concepts, making it crucial to respect cultural nuances.

7. Lack of Accountability: For forgiveness to be meaningful, offenders must take responsibility for their actions. In cases where

offenders deny wrongdoing or refuse accountability, the forgiveness process may stall.

8. Repeat Offenders: Forgiving repeat offenders can be particularly challenging. Victims may question the sincerity of an offender's remorse if they have a history of harmful behavior.

9. Reconciliation vs. Forgiveness: It's important to distinguish between forgiveness and reconciliation. While forgiveness can occur independently, reconciliation may not always be feasible or appropriate, especially if the harm is severe or trust cannot be rebuilt.

10. Community Expectations: In tight-knit communities, there may be external pressure on victims to forgive or on offenders to seek forgiveness. This external influence can hinder the authenticity of the process.

11. Legal Implications: In some cases, forgiveness and repentance within a restorative justice context may raise legal questions, especially if criminal charges are involved. Balancing restorative justice with legal proceedings can be complex.

12. Emotional Impact on Facilitators: Facilitators of restorative justice processes may also face emotional challenges, as they navigate the intense emotions and complexities of forgiveness and repentance within their roles.

Navigating these challenges and complexities requires a delicate and nuanced approach within restorative justice. It's essential to prioritize the well-being and agency of victims, encourage genuine remorse in offenders, and provide the necessary support and guidance throughout the process. In cases where forgiveness is not feasible or appropriate, other forms of resolution and healing may be explored to address the harm caused.

Theological Perspectives on Forgiveness and Repentance:

Forgiveness and repentance hold profound theological significance in various religious traditions. Here's an overview of how different faiths view these concepts and their relevance within the context of restorative justice:

1. Christianity:

Forgiveness: In Christianity, forgiveness is central to the faith. Christians are encouraged to forgive others as they have been forgiven by God. The parable of the prodigal son illustrates God's unconditional forgiveness and the possibility of reconciliation. Within restorative justice, Christian perspectives emphasize the transformative power of forgiveness and the importance of seeking reconciliation.

Repentance: Repentance is a core concept in Christianity, signifying a turning away from sin and a commitment to follow God's path. It involves acknowledging wrongdoing, feeling genuine remorse, and seeking forgiveness from God and others. In restorative justice, Christian theology underscores the potential for offenders to experience repentance and transformation through accountability and making amends.

2. Islam:

Forgiveness: Islam teaches the importance of forgiveness as a means of attaining God's mercy. Forgiving others is seen as a virtuous act, and God's forgiveness is sought through sincere repentance. Islamic perspectives within restorative justice emphasize the opportunity for offenders to seek forgiveness and make restitution for their actions.

Repentance: Repentance (Tawbah) in Islam involves recognizing one's sins, feeling genuine remorse, and making a commitment to avoid wrongdoing in the future. It is viewed as a way to cleanse one's soul and seek God's forgiveness. Restorative justice from an Islamic perspective focuses on the potential for offenders to experience genuine repentance and make amends to victims and society.

3. Judaism:

Forgiveness: Forgiveness is encouraged in Judaism as a path to healing and reconciliation. Jewish tradition emphasizes the importance of seeking forgiveness from both God and others. Restorative justice within Judaism emphasizes the role of restitution and acts of kindness as a means of seeking forgiveness and restoring relationships.

Repentance: In Judaism, repentance (Teshuvah) involves sincere remorse, confession of wrongdoing, and a commitment to change. Restitution and making amends are central to the process of Teshuvah. Within restorative justice, Jewish perspectives highlight the transformative potential of Teshuvah for offenders and the importance of repairing harm to victims.

4. Buddhism:

Forgiveness: Buddhism teaches the importance of compassion and forgiveness as a means of liberating oneself from suffering. Forgiveness is viewed as a way to let go of negative emotions and cultivate inner peace. Restorative justice within a Buddhist context emphasizes the role of forgiveness and compassion in addressing harm and promoting reconciliation.

Repentance: In Buddhism, repentance involves acknowledging one's actions, feeling remorse, and making a commitment to change. It is seen as a way to purify the mind and cultivate positive qualities.

Restorative justice from a Buddhist perspective focuses on the potential for offenders to undergo transformation through genuine repentance and making amends.

These theological perspectives offer insights into the significance of forgiveness and repentance within different faith traditions and how these concepts align with the goals of restorative justice, which include healing, reconciliation, and personal transformation. They demonstrate the universal value of forgiveness and repentance as pathways to spiritual growth and societal harmony.

Importance of Case Studies:

Case studies play a crucial role in highlighting the practical application and impact of forgiveness and repentance within restorative justice processes. Here's why they are important:

Concrete Examples: Case studies provide tangible, real-world examples of how forgiveness and repentance work in practice. They offer readers a clear understanding of how these concepts are applied and their effects on individuals and communities.

Illustrating Complexity: Forgiveness and repentance can be complex and emotionally charged processes. Case studies capture the nuances and challenges involved, allowing readers to appreciate the depth of these experiences.

Personal Stories: Case studies often feature the personal stories of victims, offenders, and facilitators. These narratives humanize the concepts, making them relatable and empathetic.

Evidence of Transformation: They offer evidence of personal transformation. Readers can witness how individuals, including offenders, undergo change through the forgiveness and repentance process, fostering hope and belief in the power of restorative justice.

Impact on Communities: Case studies reveal the broader impact of forgiveness and repentance on communities. They show how healing and reconciliation ripple out from individual interactions to benefit society at large.

Cross-Cultural Insights: Case studies can provide cross-cultural insights, demonstrating how forgiveness and repentance manifest in different cultural and religious contexts. This promotes cultural sensitivity and understanding.

Learning from Successes and Challenges: By examining both successful and challenging cases, readers can learn valuable lessons about what works and what doesn't in restorative justice processes involving forgiveness and repentance.

Inspiration for Practitioners: Case studies can inspire practitioners of restorative justice, including facilitators, counselors, and community leaders, by showcasing the positive outcomes that can be achieved through these processes.

Research and Evaluation: Case studies contribute to the body of research and evaluation in restorative justice. They provide data and narratives that researchers can analyze to better understand the effectiveness of forgiveness and repentance within this framework.

Promoting Dialogue: Case studies stimulate dialogue and discussion among readers. They invite reflection on the ethical, moral, and theological dimensions of forgiveness and repentance.

In essence, case studies bring the principles and concepts of forgiveness and repentance within restorative justice to life. They demonstrate that these processes are not just theoretical ideals but practical tools for healing, transformation, and reconciliation in real-world situations.

CHAPTER 8

The Power of Empathy and Compassion

The Power of Empathy and Compassion:

In the realm of restorative justice, the power of empathy and compassion is nothing short of transformative. These qualities serve as the bedrock of healing, understanding, and reconciliation, as they bridge the emotional chasm that often separates victims and offenders. Empathy, the capacity to feel and understand the emotions of others, allows individuals to step into the shoes of those they have harmed or been harmed by. Compassion, the desire to alleviate suffering and offer support, propels individuals toward acts of kindness and healing. Together, these forces unleash a profound potential for positive change.

Within the restorative justice framework, empathy serves as the compass guiding participants toward deeper understanding. Victims, often plagued by anger and pain, find solace in knowing that their suffering is acknowledged and validated. Offenders, on the other hand, experience the weight of their actions as they comprehend the real impact on another human being. Through structured practices like victim-offender dialogues and circles, empathy paves the way for honest, open, and transformative conversations.

Compassion emerges as the catalyst for healing and reconciliation.

It encourages individuals to extend kindness and support to one another, even in the face of harm. Acts of compassion can range from sincere apologies and reparations to acts of service within the community. These gestures of goodwill not only help victims heal but also contribute to the moral and emotional growth of offenders. Compassion becomes the driving force behind accountability and the motivation to make amends.

The power of empathy and compassion extends beyond individual interactions. Research has shown that restorative justice processes rooted in these qualities have the potential to reduce recidivism, offering a path toward rehabilitation rather than punitive retribution. Furthermore, empathy and compassion align with the moral and theological imperatives found in various religious traditions, emphasizing the importance of loving thy neighbor, offering forgiveness, and fostering reconciliation. In essence, the power of empathy and compassion illuminates a path toward healing, transformation, and the restoration of human dignity within the realm of restorative justice.

Understanding empathy and compassion is pivotal within the context of restorative justice for several key reasons:

Foundation for Communication: Empathy and compassion serve as the building blocks for effective communication. They enable victims and offenders to connect on an emotional level, fostering an environment where genuine dialogue can occur. Without these qualities, meaningful conversations about harm, responsibility, and reconciliation may be hindered.

Humanizing Participants: Empathy and compassion humanize both victims and offenders. They remind us that every individual involved in a restorative justice process is a person with emotions, experiences, and vulnerabilities. This recognition is fundamental for treating each party with dignity and respect.

Emotional Healing: In cases of harm and conflict, emotional wounds run deep. Understanding empathy and compassion helps participants recognize the emotional pain experienced by victims and the remorse felt by offenders. This understanding lays the groundwork for emotional healing and catharsis.

Promoting Understanding: Empathy enables individuals to step into the shoes of others and see the world from their perspective. This perspective-taking is crucial for victims to feel heard and validated and for offenders to grasp the full impact of their actions. Compassion then motivates action to alleviate suffering and make amends.

Conflict Resolution: Restorative justice aims at resolving conflicts and repairing harm. Empathy and compassion are essential tools for achieving these goals. They foster an environment where conflicts can be addressed constructively, and solutions can be found that satisfy the needs and interests of all parties involved.

Preventing Retaliation: Without empathy and compassion, victims may be more inclined to seek revenge or retribution, perpetuating a cycle of harm. Understanding these qualities can help victims explore alternatives to retaliation, promoting a more peaceful resolution.

Long-Term Impact: Empathy and compassion have long-term effects. They contribute to the personal growth of both victims and offenders, fostering empathy in offenders and aiding victims in their healing journey. These qualities can extend their positive influence beyond the specific restorative justice process.

Ethical and Theological Alignment: Understanding empathy and compassion aligns with the ethical and theological principles found in various religious traditions. Many faiths emphasize the importance of empathy, compassion, and forgiveness as paths toward reconciliation and moral growth. Recognizing these principles within restorative justice reinforces their universal value.

Accordingly, understanding empathy and compassion is paramount because they set the tone for restorative justice processes. They create an atmosphere of empathy, respect, and understanding, enabling victims and offenders to engage in transformative conversations that promote healing, accountability, and reconciliation. These qualities are not just abstract concepts but practical tools that lead to meaningful change and restoration.

The Empathy Gap:

The "empathy gap" is a phenomenon that occurs within the context of restorative justice and refers to the emotional disconnect or lack of understanding between victims and offenders. This gap can manifest due to several factors, including fear, anger, and a perception of the other party as dehumanized or as the "enemy." Here, we delve into the concept of the empathy gap and strategies for bridging it:

1. Fear and Anger: In cases of harm or wrongdoing, victims often experience intense emotions such as fear, anger, and resentment. These emotions can create a barrier to empathy, making it difficult for victims to empathize with the experiences or motivations of offenders. Similarly, offenders may feel defensive or hostile, hindering their ability to empathize with the pain and suffering of victims.

2. Dehumanization: The empathy gap can widen when one party dehumanizes the other. Victims might view offenders as irredeemable or inherently evil, while offenders may see victims as merely obstacles or inconveniences. This dehumanization can make it challenging for both parties to recognize each other's humanity and suffering.

3. Stereotypes and Prejudices: Pre-existing stereotypes and prejudices can exacerbate the empathy gap. These biases can cloud perceptions and prevent individuals from seeing each other as individuals with unique stories and struggles.

4. Communication Barriers: Victims and offenders may struggle to communicate effectively due to the emotional turmoil and negative emotions associated with the harm. This breakdown in communication can further widen the empathy gap.

5. Power Dynamics: Power imbalances between victims and offenders can contribute to the empathy gap. Victims may feel powerless or vulnerable, making it difficult for them to empathize with offenders. Similarly, offenders may perceive themselves as powerless or unfairly treated.

Strategies for Bridging the Empathy Gap:

Structured Dialogue: Restorative justice processes often involve structured dialogues between victims and offenders. These dialogues provide a safe and controlled environment for both parties to express their emotions, perspectives, and needs. Facilitators play a crucial role in guiding these conversations and ensuring that empathy is fostered.

Humanizing Narratives: Encouraging victims and offenders to share their personal stories can humanize both parties. Listening to each other's narratives can help break down stereotypes and prejudices, allowing empathy to emerge.

Empathy Education: Providing participants with education on the nature of empathy, its importance, and how it can be cultivated can be beneficial. Understanding the science and psychology of empathy can motivate individuals to make an effort to bridge the gap.

Restorative Circles: Restorative circles are community-based processes that encourage open dialogue and the sharing of emotions. These circles can help participants connect on a deeper level and see each other as fellow community members rather than adversaries.

Facilitator Guidance: Skilled facilitators play a pivotal role in bridging the empathy gap. They guide participants through the process, ensuring that emotions are managed, and empathy is actively encouraged.

Recognition of Common Humanity: Encouraging participants to recognize their common humanity and shared experiences of pain, suffering, or regret can help bridge the gap. This recognition emphasizes that both victims and offenders are fundamentally human.

Support Networks: Providing victims and offenders with support networks and resources can help them navigate the emotional challenges of restorative justice processes, making it easier to develop empathy.

Bridging the empathy gap is an essential aspect of restorative justice, as it enables victims and offenders to engage in meaningful dialogue, foster understanding, and work toward healing and reconciliation. By addressing the factors that contribute to this gap and implementing strategies to overcome them, restorative justice processes can become more effective in achieving their goals.

Restorative Practices:

Restorative Practices refer to a set of structured and intentional approaches used within the framework of restorative justice. These practices are designed to promote understanding, empathy, and communication among individuals involved in harm, conflict, or wrongdoing. Restorative practices aim to repair harm, build relationships, and facilitate accountability and reconciliation. They include various processes such as victim-offender dialogues, circles, and conferencing. Here's why restorative practices are important:

Healing and Repairing Harm: Restorative practices provide a structured and safe space for victims to express their feelings, share the impact of the harm, and seek answers to their questions. Offenders are given the opportunity to understand the consequences of their actions and take responsibility. This leads to the healing of emotional wounds and the repair of harm, which may not occur in traditional punitive approaches.

Building Empathy and Understanding: Restorative practices actively encourage participants, both victims and offenders, to engage in empathetic listening and sharing. Through facilitated dialogues, individuals can better understand each other's perspectives, emotions, and motivations. This fosters empathy, which is essential for reconciliation and conflict resolution.

Promoting Accountability: Restorative practices hold offenders accountable for their actions in a constructive manner. Instead of punishment, they are asked to take responsibility, make amends, and contribute to the restoration process. This approach encourages offenders to recognize the impact of their actions on others and society.

Preventing Recidivism: Research has shown that restorative practices have the potential to reduce recidivism rates. When offenders engage in meaningful dialogues and take steps to repair harm, they are less likely to repeat their offenses. This benefits both the individuals involved and the community.

Community Involvement: Restorative practices often involve the broader community, including family members, friends, and community leaders. This community involvement reinforces the idea that harm and conflict affect not just the immediate parties but also the larger social fabric. Communities play a role in supporting the healing and reintegration of offenders.

Conflict Resolution: Restorative practices offer an alternative approach to conflict resolution. Instead of escalating disputes through punitive measures, restorative practices seek to address the underlying causes of conflict and find solutions that satisfy the needs and interests of all parties involved.

Education and Skill Development: Participants in restorative practices develop essential life skills such as active listening, communication, conflict resolution, and emotional intelligence. These skills can have a positive impact on their personal lives and interactions beyond the restorative justice context.

Ethical and Theological Alignment: Restorative practices align with ethical and theological principles found in various religious traditions. Many faiths emphasize forgiveness, reconciliation, and the restoration of relationships. Restorative practices provide a practical means of putting these principles into action.

Restorative practices are important because they offer a constructive and compassionate approach to addressing harm, conflict, and wrongdoing. By prioritizing healing, empathy, accountability, and community involvement, these practices contribute to the overall well-being of individuals and communities, promote reconciliation, and align with moral and ethical values

Who are the facilitators?

Facilitators in the context of restorative justice are trained professionals or individuals who play a central role in guiding and overseeing the restorative processes involving victims and offenders. Their role is pivotal for several reasons:

1. Neutral Mediators: Facilitators are neutral third parties who do not have a vested interest in the outcome of the process. This neutrality ensures that participants perceive the facilitator as an unbiased mediator who is there to assist rather than take sides.

2. Creating a Safe Environment: Facilitators are responsible for creating a safe and structured environment for dialogue. This is crucial because victims and offenders may have strong emotions, including fear and anger. Facilitators help set ground rules and ensure that all participants feel physically and emotionally safe.

3. Guiding the Process: Facilitators guide the restorative process, ensuring that it follows a structured format. They initiate and steer discussions, ask questions to facilitate dialogue, and ensure that participants adhere to the agreed-upon guidelines and objectives.

4. Encouraging Empathy and Active Listening: A key role of facilitators is to promote empathy and active listening among participants. They encourage individuals to genuinely understand each other's experiences and perspectives. This fosters a deeper sense of connection and empathy.

5. Managing Emotions: Restorative processes can evoke strong emotions, and facilitators are trained to help manage these emotions constructively. They assist participants in expressing their feelings in a healthy way and prevent conflicts from escalating.

6. Ensuring Fair Participation: Facilitators ensure that all participants, including victims, offenders, and community members, have an equal opportunity to speak and be heard. They prevent one party from dominating the conversation.

7. Conflict Resolution Skills: Facilitators possess conflict resolution skills and techniques that help de-escalate tensions and address conflicts that may arise during the process. They guide participants toward finding solutions and reaching agreements.

8. Maintaining Focus on Objectives: Restorative justice processes have specific objectives, such as repairing harm, promoting accountability,

and achieving reconciliation. Facilitators keep participants focused on these objectives and steer conversations toward productive outcomes.

9. Cultural Sensitivity: In diverse settings, facilitators need to be culturally sensitive and aware of the unique needs and perspectives of participants from different backgrounds. This helps ensure that the process is inclusive and respectful of cultural differences.

10. Post-Process Support: Facilitators may provide post-process support, helping participants access resources, counseling, or further assistance as needed. This support contributes to the long-term success of the restorative justice process.

The role of facilitators is crucial because they serve as skilled guides who enable participants to navigate the complex emotional and interpersonal terrain of restorative justice. They help create an environment where empathy, compassion, and meaningful dialogue can flourish, ultimately contributing to the healing, accountability, and reconciliation of all parties involved. Facilitators are instrumental in ensuring that the restorative justice process remains fair, safe, and effective.

The Healing Power of Compassion:

The concept of "The Healing Power of Compassion" embodies the idea that compassion, as an empathetic and benevolent response to the suffering of others, possesses the capacity to facilitate profound healing and transformation, particularly within the context of restorative justice.

Here's a deeper exploration of its meaning:

1. Healing Emotional Wounds: Compassion plays a pivotal role in healing emotional wounds, both for victims and offenders. Victims often experience deep emotional pain as a result of harm or wrongdoing. When they receive compassion from others, it validates their suffering and helps in the process of emotional healing. Similarly, offenders can undergo a transformation when they feel compassion from others, leading to remorse and a desire to make amends.

2. Restoring Trust: Acts of compassion can help rebuild trust between victims and offenders. Trust is often shattered in the aftermath of harm or conflict, and compassion serves as a bridge that enables

individuals to reconnect. When victims and offenders perceive genuine compassion from each other, it can pave the way for restored relationships and the rebuilding of trust.

3. Encouraging Accountability: Compassion is not a substitute for accountability, but it can be a catalyst for it. Offenders who experience compassion are more likely to take responsibility for their actions and seek ways to make amends. Compassion can motivate offenders to be accountable and actively participate in the restoration process.

4. Transformative Potential: Compassion has the power to bring about transformation in both victims and offenders. Victims who receive compassion may find the strength to move forward and heal. Offenders who experience compassion may undergo a process of personal growth, empathy development, and a commitment to preventing harm in the future.

5. Promoting Reconciliation: Compassion is an essential element in the reconciliation process. It softens hearts and opens doors to dialogue and understanding. When victims and offenders extend compassion to each other, it can lead to a genuine desire for reconciliation and the restoration of damaged relationships.

6. Moral and Ethical Foundation: Compassion aligns with the moral and ethical principles found in various religious and philosophical traditions. It embodies the idea of loving one's neighbor, forgiving others, and showing kindness. Recognizing the healing power of compassion reinforces these universal values.

7. Community and Social Healing: Compassion is not limited to individuals; it can also extend to communities and society at large. Acts of compassion within the context of restorative justice can contribute to the healing of broader social wounds and the prevention of future harm.

"The Healing Power of Compassion" signifies that compassion is not only a benevolent response to suffering but also a potent force for transformation, healing, and reconciliation. Within the realm of restorative justice, it serves as a guiding principle that fosters understanding, empathy, and the restoration of human dignity for victims, offenders, and communities. Compassion is an essential component of restorative justice processes, as it helps individuals move from pain and conflict toward healing, accountability, and the restoration of relationships.

What is empathy?

Empathy is the ability to understand and share the feelings, thoughts, and experiences of another person. It involves putting oneself in another's shoes, imagining their emotions, and responding with care and understanding. Empathy is a fundamental human capacity that allows individuals to connect with one another on a deep emotional level. In the context of restorative justice, empathy plays a crucial role in facilitating healing, accountability, and reconciliation, particularly concerning offenders. Here's how empathy's impact on offenders can influence their accountability:

Recognition of Harm: Empathy enables offenders to recognize the harm they've caused on a personal and emotional level. When they genuinely understand the suffering and pain experienced by victims, it becomes more challenging for them to minimize or dismiss the consequences of their actions. This recognition is a critical first step toward accountability.

Emotional Connection: Empathy fosters an emotional connection between offenders and victims. Offenders begin to see victims as real people with feelings and experiences, rather than abstract entities or adversaries. This emotional connection can be a powerful motivator for offenders to take responsibility for their actions.

Remorse and Regret: Empathy often leads to feelings of remorse and regret in offenders. They may genuinely feel sorry for the pain they've caused to another human being. This emotional response can be a catalyst for taking ownership of their actions and seeking ways to make amends.

Desire for Reconciliation: When offenders experience empathy and recognize the humanity of victims, they may develop a sincere desire for reconciliation. They understand the importance of restoring the relationship and making things right. This desire can drive them to actively participate in the restorative justice process.

Increased Accountability: Empathy contributes to a heightened sense of personal accountability. Offenders who empathize with victims are more likely to acknowledge their responsibility for the harm and take proactive steps to address it. This includes cooperating in restitution, community service, or other forms of reparation.

Prevention of Recidivism: The empathy-driven accountability process can also serve as a deterrent to future offending. When offenders grasp the impact of their actions and the harm they've caused to others, they may be more motivated to avoid engaging in harmful behavior in the future.

Empathetic Dialogue: Restorative justice processes often involve structured dialogues between victims and offenders, guided by facilitators.

These dialogues encourage empathetic listening and the sharing of emotions and perspectives. Through these dialogues, empathy is actively nurtured and reinforced.

Support for Rehabilitation: Empathy can contribute to the rehabilitation and personal growth of offenders. When they acknowledge the harm caused and take steps to make amends, they are more likely to transform their behavior and develop a stronger sense of empathy toward others in the future.

Accordingly, empathy's impact on offenders' accountability is profound. It leads to the recognition of harm, emotional connection, remorse, a desire for reconciliation, and a heightened sense of personal responsibility. Empathy-driven accountability processes within restorative justice play a pivotal role in achieving the goals of healing, reconciliation, and the prevention of future harm.

Recidivism:

Research indicates that restorative justice processes rooted in empathy and compassion can be effective in reducing recidivism. We present case studies and evidence to support this claim.

Compassion is a deep feeling of empathy and sympathy for the suffering, misfortune, or challenges of others, often accompanied by a desire to alleviate their pain or distress. It involves a genuine concern for the well-being of others and a willingness to offer support and understanding.

Recidivism, on the other hand, refers to the tendency of individuals to reoffend or engage in criminal behavior after they have previously been convicted and served a sentence for a crime. It is a critical issue within the criminal justice system because it represents a cycle of criminal behavior that can be harmful to individuals, communities, and society as a whole.

The relationship between compassion and reducing recidivism within the context of restorative justice is significant:

Emotional Rehabilitation: Compassionate approaches within restorative justice processes often prioritize the emotional and psychological rehabilitation of offenders. This can include providing emotional support, counseling, and opportunities for offenders to confront the emotional impact of their actions. Emotional rehabilitation is essential for addressing the underlying causes of criminal behavior.

Empathy and Understanding: Compassion fosters empathy and understanding among all parties involved, including victims, offenders, and the community. When offenders experience empathy and compassion from others, they are more likely to understand the consequences of their actions and the impact on victims and communities. This understanding can motivate them to change their behavior.

Accountability and Responsibility: Compassion does not negate accountability but rather encourages it in a constructive manner. Offenders who feel compassion from others may be more willing to take responsibility for their actions and actively participate in the process of making amends. This sense of accountability can reduce the likelihood of reoffending.

Restorative Justice Practices: Restorative justice processes, which often emphasize compassion and empathy, provide opportunities for offenders to make reparations and amends to victims and the community.

These processes can be transformative for offenders, as they actively engage in addressing the harm they've caused.

Community Support: Compassionate restorative justice approaches involve the broader community in the process. Communities can play a supportive role in the reintegration of offenders, offering resources, encouragement, and social connections that can reduce the risk of recidivism.

Personal Growth: Compassionate approaches encourage offenders to undergo personal growth and development. When they experience compassion and support, they are more likely to seek positive changes in their lives, including addressing the factors that contributed to their criminal behavior.

Conflict Resolution Skills: Restorative justice processes teach valuable conflict resolution skills, including communication, active listening, and problem-solving. These skills can equip offenders with more effective ways of dealing with conflicts and challenges, reducing the likelihood of resorting to criminal behavior.

Research and case studies have shown that restorative justice practices rooted in empathy and compassion can be effective in reducing recidivism rates. By addressing the underlying causes of criminal behavior, promoting accountability, and fostering personal growth and community support, these practices contribute to breaking the cycle of reoffending and promoting long-term positive change among offenders.

Challenges and Barriers:

Fostering empathy and compassion within the context of restorative justice can indeed face several challenges and barriers.

These challenges may include:

Emotional Resistance: Offenders, victims, and even facilitators may initially resist engaging in empathetic and compassionate dialogues.

Strong emotions, such as anger, fear, or shame, can make it difficult to open up to understanding and forgiveness.

Power Dynamics: Power imbalances between victims and offenders can hinder the development of empathy. Victims may feel vulnerable or powerless, while offenders may feel defensive. These power dynamics can impede open and honest communication.

Cultural Differences: Cultural backgrounds and beliefs can impact the way individuals perceive and express empathy and compassion. Misunderstandings or misinterpretations may arise due to cultural differences in communication styles and norms.

Lack of Trust: Trust is essential for empathy and compassion to flourish. Participants may lack trust in one another or in the restorative justice process itself, making it challenging to build the necessary emotional connections.

Resistance to Change: Offenders may resist acknowledging the harm they've caused or may be resistant to the idea of personal transformation. Overcoming this resistance to change can be a significant barrier.

External Pressure: External pressures, such as societal expectations, legal requirements, or community judgment, can influence participants' willingness to engage in empathetic and compassionate interactions.

Trauma and Mental Health: Both victims and offenders may have experienced trauma or have mental health issues that can complicate their ability to engage in restorative justice processes effectively.

Strategies for addressing these challenges and barriers may include:

Building Trust: Establishing trust is essential. Facilitators can work to create a safe and supportive environment where participants feel comfortable sharing their experiences and emotions.

Cultural Sensitivity: Recognizing and respecting cultural differences is crucial. Facilitators should receive training in cultural competence to navigate diverse perspectives effectively.

Managing Emotions: Developing strategies for managing strong emotions, such as anger or fear, can help participants engage in more constructive dialogues. This may include mindfulness techniques or emotional regulation skills.

Education and Preparation: Providing participants with information and preparation for the restorative justice process can help set appropriate expectations and reduce resistance.

Addressing Power Imbalances: Facilitators can actively work to address power imbalances and ensure that all participants have an equal voice and agency in the process.

Trauma-Informed Practices: Employing trauma-informed practices can help participants, especially victims, navigate the process more effectively while considering their trauma-related needs.

Flexibility: Recognizing that not all participants will progress at the same pace is essential. Facilitators should be flexible and patient, allowing individuals to engage in the process at their own comfort level.

External Support: Participants may benefit from external support, such as counseling or therapy, to address trauma, mental health issues, or emotional resistance.

Community Involvement: Engaging the broader community can provide additional support and encouragement, helping participants overcome barriers.

By addressing these challenges and implementing strategies to foster empathy and compassion, restorative justice processes can become more effective in achieving their goals of healing, accountability, and reconciliation. Facilitators and practitioners play a critical role in navigating these complexities to create an environment where empathy and compassion can flourish.

Theological and Ethical Dimensions:

Theological and ethical dimensions of empathy and compassion within restorative justice draw upon the teachings and principles of various religious traditions, shedding light on the moral imperative of these virtues. Here are some insights from different faith perspectives:

Christianity: In Christianity, empathy and compassion align with the teachings of Jesus, who emphasized love for one's neighbor and forgiveness of wrongs. The Parable of the Good Samaritan illustrates the importance of showing mercy and empathy to others, even to those from different backgrounds. The act of forgiveness, rooted in compassion, is central to Christian ethics and serves as a model for restorative justice.

Judaism: Judaism places a strong emphasis on compassion, often expressed as "rachamim." The Hebrew Bible calls for empathy toward the vulnerable and oppressed, reminding believers that they were once strangers in Egypt. The concept of "Tikkun Olam" encourages individuals to repair the world through acts of compassion and justice, aligning with restorative justice principles.

Islam: Islam teaches the importance of empathy and compassion through the concept of "Rahma" (mercy) and "Sadaqah" (charity). The Quran encourages believers to be kind, merciful, and just, particularly to those who have wronged them. Restorative justice processes that promote empathy and reconciliation align with these Islamic principles.

Buddhism: Buddhism emphasizes compassion ("Karuna") as one of its core virtues. The practice of metta (loving-kindness) meditation aims to cultivate empathy and compassion toward all sentient beings, including those who have caused harm. Restorative justice processes that prioritize understanding and transformation align with Buddhist values.

Hinduism: Hinduism's teachings on empathy and compassion are rooted in the concept of "Ahimsa," which is non-violence and compassion toward all living beings. Restorative justice practices that seek to heal and restore rather than harm align with this ethical principle.

Sikhism: Sikhism teaches compassion and selflessness ("Daya" and "Nimrata"). The Sikh tradition encourages individuals to serve and support others, particularly those in need. Restorative justice, which seeks to repair harm and promote healing, resonates with these values.

Native Spirituality: Indigenous spiritual traditions often emphasize interconnectedness and empathy toward all living beings and the Earth. Restorative justice processes that consider the broader community and seek harmony align with these indigenous values.

From a theological and ethical standpoint, these religious traditions underscore the moral imperative of empathy and compassion within restorative justice. They emphasize the inherent worth and dignity of all individuals, the importance of reconciliation and forgiveness, and the healing power of compassion. By drawing from these traditions, restorative justice can find a strong ethical foundation that supports its goals of healing, accountability, and reconciliation.

Personal Stories and Testimonies:

Personal stories and testimonies have a profound impact on individuals' lives, especially when it comes to restorative justice processes rooted in empathy and compassion. Here's how personal stories and testimonies can influence and inspire:

Emotional Connection: Personal stories and testimonies create an emotional connection between readers or participants and the experiences being shared. They allow individuals to relate on a human level, fostering empathy and compassion.

Inspiration: Hearing about real-life experiences of transformation and healing can inspire others who may be going through similar challenges. These stories offer hope and demonstrate that change is possible.

Understanding Complexity: Personal stories often reveal the complexity of human experiences, including the motivations behind wrongdoing and the deep emotional impact of harm. They help individuals understand the multifaceted nature of crime and its aftermath.

Reducing Stigma: Testimonies can reduce the stigma associated with both victims and offenders. They humanize those involved in restorative justice processes, challenging stereotypes and preconceived notions.

Validation: Personal stories validate the importance of restorative justice practices. When individuals share how these processes have positively impacted their lives, it reinforces the value of such approaches.

Learning Opportunities: Hearing about the challenges and successes of others can provide valuable learning opportunities for practitioners, policymakers, and communities interested in implementing restorative justice programs.

Promoting Dialogue: Personal stories and testimonies encourage open dialogue and discussion about the role of empathy and compassion in justice processes. They can lead to meaningful conversations and the sharing of best practices.

Policy Advocacy: Personal stories often serve as powerful advocacy tools for policy changes and the expansion of restorative justice programs. They provide real-world evidence of the effectiveness of these approaches.

Encouraging Participation: Individuals who hear stories of transformation may be more inclined to participate in restorative justice processes, either as victims, offenders, or community members.

Building Trust: Personal stories can help build trust in the restorative justice process. When individuals see the positive impact on others, they may be more willing to engage in these processes themselves.

In the context of restorative justice, personal stories and testimonies serve as living examples of the principles and values at the heart of these practices. They remind us of the potential for healing, reconciliation, and personal growth that can be achieved through empathy and compassion.

CHAPTER 9

Accountability and Responsibility

Accountability and Responsibility:

Accountability and responsibility are foundational principles within the realm of restorative justice, guiding the transformative process of addressing harm, fostering healing, and rebuilding relationships. At their core, these principles emphasize acknowledgment, ownership, and amends-making, but their significance extends far beyond these actions.

First and foremost, accountability involves acknowledging one's actions and their impact on others. This acknowledgment is not merely a legal formality but a genuine recognition of the harm caused. It requires individuals, particularly offenders, to confront the consequences of their behavior on a deeply personal level. This acknowledgment serves as the initial step in the journey toward accountability and is essential for fostering empathy and understanding between victims and offenders.

Taking responsibility within a restorative justice framework goes beyond accepting blame; it involves a profound commitment to making amends and repairing the harm inflicted. Responsibility is rooted in the understanding that actions have consequences, and it requires individuals to actively engage in the process of restitution and restoration. This commitment to addressing the tangible and emotional consequences of wrongdoing is a transformative force that can lead to personal growth, empathy, and the restoration of damaged relationships.

The concept of accountability extends beyond the individual level to encompass communities and society as a whole. Communities have a role in holding offenders accountable and supporting the healing process. This collective accountability reinforces the idea that addressing harm is not solely the responsibility of the victim and offender but of the broader community. It acknowledges that harm has a ripple effect, impacting not only individuals but also the social fabric.

One of the unique aspects of restorative justice is its emphasis on accountability as a means of addressing harm while also promoting the reintegration of offenders into society. By actively taking responsibility for their actions and participating in the restoration process, offenders have an opportunity for personal transformation. This transformation can lead to a reduced likelihood of reoffending, contributing to a safer and more just society.

In essence, accountability and responsibility within restorative justice offer a path toward healing and growth for all parties involved, ultimately facilitating the restoration of individuals, relationships, and communities.

Setting the stage for the importance of accountability and responsibility within restorative justice.

Briefly summarizing the key principles of restorative justice. Introduction:

In the world of justice and conflict resolution, there exists a profound paradigm shift that has been quietly reshaping the way societies respond to wrongdoing and harm. This transformation is embodied in the principles of restorative justice—a philosophy that transcends punitive measures and embraces accountability and responsibility as the cornerstones of healing and reconciliation. As we embark on this journey through the heart of restorative justice, it is imperative to recognize the pivotal roles that accountability and responsibility play in this transformative approach.

Restorative justice is grounded in a set of principles that seek not only to address the immediate aftermath of harm but also to mend the deep-seated fractures within individuals, relationships, and communities. At its core, this approach recognizes the interconnectedness of all parties involved, emphasizing that harm reverberates far beyond the immediate act. It challenges the punitive status quo by shifting the focus from punitive measures to a process that encourages individuals to confront their actions, make amends, and ultimately find the path to redemption.

Understanding Accountability:

Understanding accountability is of paramount importance within the context of restorative justice because it reshapes our perception of justice itself. In the conventional punitive system, accountability is often equated with punishment—imposing penalties on offenders to balance the scales of justice. However, in restorative justice, accountability takes on a more profound and transformative meaning.

Restorative accountability centers on acknowledging the harm caused, recognizing the ripple effects of one's actions, and actively participating in the process of making amends. It shifts the focus from retribution to repair, from punitive consequences to personal responsibility. This understanding of accountability is essential because it paves the way for healing, reconciliation, and restoration rather than perpetuating cycles of harm and retribution.

A critical distinction between punitive and restorative accountability lies in their objectives. Punitive accountability seeks to punish and incapacitate offenders, often neglecting the needs and voices of victims. In contrast, restorative accountability aims to address the needs of all parties involved—victims, offenders, and communities. It prioritizes understanding, empathy, and the restoration of relationships, ultimately striving for a sense of closure that goes beyond punitive measures.

By grasping the transformative power of accountability within restorative justice, individuals can recognize that justice is not merely about assigning blame and penalties. It is a profound journey toward acknowledging wrongdoing, taking responsibility, and actively participating in the process of repairing what has been broken. This understanding is pivotal in our exploration of how restorative justice principles reshape the way we approach harm, conflict, and justice itself.

Taking Responsibility for Harm:

Taking responsibility for harm is a pivotal concept within restorative justice, signifying a profound shift away from denial and defensiveness toward accountability and personal growth. This principle holds immense significance in transforming the lives of offenders and facilitating the restoration of harmed individuals and communities.

At its core, taking responsibility for harm means that offenders are not only acknowledging their actions but also recognizing the profound impact of those actions on others. It involves a deep, honest, and often introspective acknowledgment of the harm inflicted—whether it be physical, emotional, or psychological. This acknowledgment is not driven by external pressures but stems from a genuine desire to confront the consequences of one's behavior.

The act of taking responsibility carries significant psychological and emotional weight. It involves confronting guilt, remorse, and shame—powerful emotions that can be difficult to face. However, it is through this process that offenders can begin to understand the gravity of their actions and their consequences on both victims and themselves. This understanding can lead to a sense of empathy, as offenders come to grasp the pain they have caused and the need for healing and reconciliation.

Taking responsibility is not merely a legal or procedural step; it is a transformative journey toward personal growth and accountability. It allows offenders to actively engage in making amends and seeking redemption. Moreover, it plays a crucial role in the restorative justice process, as it lays the foundation for meaningful dialogues between victims and offenders, fosters empathy, and ultimately contributes to the healing and restoration of all parties involved. In the chapters to come, we will explore how this transformative principle unfolds within the broader context of restorative justice.

What is Reparation?

Reparation, within the framework of restorative justice, refers to the actions taken by offenders to make amends for the harm they have caused. It goes beyond mere acknowledgment and involves concrete efforts to repair the damage inflicted on victims, communities, and relationships. The role of reparation is pivotal within restorative justice because it not only signifies an offender's commitment to accountability but also actively contributes to the healing and restoration process.

The importance of the role of reparation lies in its ability to translate words into actions. It demonstrates the sincerity of an offender's commitment to righting their wrongs and actively participating in the restoration of those they have harmed. Reparation is a tangible way for offenders to take responsibility for their actions and to address the concrete consequences of their wrongdoing.

Restitution is one form of reparation that involves offenders compensating victims for tangible losses, such as property damage or financial harm. For example, an offender who stole a valuable item may be required to return it or provide financial compensation equivalent to its value. This act not only repairs the material harm but also sends a powerful message that the offender is willing to make things right.

Amends-making, on the other hand, focuses on the emotional and relational aspects of harm. It might involve sincere apologies, community service, or other actions that demonstrate an offender's commitment to repairing the harm caused to victims and communities. For instance, an offender who vandalized a community space might engage in activities to restore and beautify that space, actively contributing to its well-being.

In essence, the role of reparation underscores the transformative potential of restorative justice. It allows offenders to move beyond remorse and actively engage in actions that promote healing, reconciliation, and the restoration of trust and dignity. Through concrete acts of reparation, offenders demonstrate their commitment to being accountable for their actions, contributing to a sense of closure and a path toward redemption for all parties involved.

Accountability and Empathy:

The relationship between accountability and empathy is symbiotic within the context of restorative justice. They are interconnected and mutually reinforcing, playing pivotal roles in transforming individuals and fostering genuine reconciliation.

Accountability, at its core, involves offenders taking responsibility for their actions and the harm caused. However, this acknowledgment goes beyond mere words or legal formalities. It requires offenders to engage in a deep, honest reflection on the consequences of their behavior. This introspective process often leads to a heightened awareness of the suffering and pain their actions have inflicted on victims and communities.

Empathy enters the equation as the bridge that connects this newfound understanding with meaningful accountability. When offenders genuinely grasp the impact of their actions on a human level, they are more likely to feel empathy toward the victims. This empathy is not a mere intellectual understanding but an emotional connection—a recognition of the suffering and trauma experienced by others.

This interplay between empathy and accountability fosters a profound transformation in offenders. It shifts their perspective from self-centeredness to a focus on the well-being and dignity of those they have harmed. This transformation is key to genuine accountability because it propels offenders to actively engage in actions that contribute to the healing and restoration of victims and communities.

In essence, empathy fuels the engine of accountability within restorative justice. It is the emotional catalyst that propels offenders to take meaningful steps toward making amends and repairing the harm. The relationship between accountability and empathy underscores the transformative potential of restorative justice, as it invites all parties involved to not only seek justice but also to cultivate understanding, empathy, and the possibility of redemption.

Accountability for Communities:

Expanding the concept of accountability to include communities.

How communities can hold offenders accountable and support restoration.

Accountability for communities is a crucial extension of the restorative justice paradigm because it recognizes that harm and wrongdoing have broader implications beyond individual victims and offenders. Communities play an integral role in the restorative justice process, both in holding offenders accountable and in supporting the restoration of individuals and relationships.

Communities are not passive bystanders in cases of harm or wrongdoing. They are directly affected by the consequences of these actions, which can disrupt the social fabric and create fear and mistrust. Therefore, it is vital for communities to actively engage in holding offenders accountable for their actions. This can involve supporting restorative justice practices, participating in community conferences, or simply providing a platform for dialogue between offenders and community members.

Community accountability extends beyond punitive measures and instead focuses on rehabilitation and reintegration. By holding offenders accountable in a restorative sense, communities encourage personal growth and transformation. This approach recognizes that offenders are often members of the same community and have the potential to reintegrate as responsible and contributing individuals.

Furthermore, communities can provide essential support for the healing and restoration of victims. The sense of belonging and connection that communities offer can be instrumental in helping victims recover and rebuild their lives. When communities actively participate in the restorative justice process, they send a message that they are committed to addressing harm, seeking justice, and restoring a sense of safety and well-being.

Therefore, accountability for communities in the context of restorative justice recognizes the interconnectedness of individuals within a society. It emphasizes the collective responsibility for addressing harm, fostering healing, and promoting the reintegration of offenders. By actively engaging in the restorative process, communities play a vital role in reshaping the way society responds to wrongdoing, ultimately contributing to safer, more resilient, and more compassionate communities.

Challenges in Taking Responsibility:

Taking responsibility for one's actions, particularly within the framework of restorative justice, can be a challenging and complex process. Offenders may face various obstacles and barriers when attempting to confront their wrongdoing and actively engage in the restoration of harmed parties and communities. It is essential to recognize these challenges and explore strategies for overcoming them.

Emotional Resistance: One of the primary challenges offenders may encounter is emotional resistance. Confronting the harm, they've caused can evoke feelings of guilt, shame, and fear. These emotions can be overwhelming and may lead to a reluctance to take responsibility.

Overcoming emotional resistance often requires a supportive and empathetic environment that allows offenders to express and process these emotions.

Denial and Defensiveness: Some offenders may initially deny or downplay their actions, adopting a defensive stance. This can hinder the accountability process, as it creates barriers to open and honest communication. Overcoming denial and defensiveness often involves creating a safe and nonjudgmental space for offenders to reflect on their behavior and its consequences.

Lack of Awareness: Offenders may not fully grasp the extent of the harm they've caused or the ripple effects of their actions. Increasing awareness of the impact of their behavior is crucial for fostering genuine accountability. Restorative justice processes often include opportunities for victims to share their experiences, helping offenders better understand the consequences of their actions.

External Pressures: Offenders may feel pressured by external factors, such as legal proceedings or societal expectations, to take responsibility in a certain way. These external pressures can sometimes lead to insincere or coerced admissions of guilt. Overcoming this challenge involves ensuring that accountability is voluntary and genuinely driven by a desire to make amends.

Cultural and Contextual Factors: Cultural differences and the specific context of the offense can also pose challenges. Offenders from different cultural backgrounds may have varying understandings of accountability and restitution. Cultural sensitivity and flexibility are essential in addressing these challenges.

Strategies for overcoming these challenges include providing emotional support and counseling for offenders, facilitating open and nonjudgmental dialogues, and tailoring restorative justice processes to suit the specific needs and circumstances of each case. Ultimately, fostering genuine accountability is a complex but essential aspect of the restorative justice approach, as it paves the way for personal growth, empathy, and the restoration of relationships and communities.

Restorative Justice and Legal Accountability:

The relationship between restorative justice and legal accountability is intricate and dynamic, reflecting the evolving landscape of justice systems worldwide. While these two approaches have distinct principles and goals, they can intersect and complement each other in several ways.

Complementary Approaches: Restorative justice and legal accountability are not mutually exclusive. In many cases, they can work together to achieve a more holistic form of justice. Legal accountability, through criminal proceedings, establishes that a violation of the law has occurred and assigns legal consequences to offenders. Restorative justice, on the other hand, focuses on addressing the harm caused by these violations and facilitating healing and reconciliation. In this sense, restorative processes can complement the legal system by providing a space for dialogue, understanding, and restoration alongside the legal penalties.

Reparative and Transformative: Restorative justice is inherently reparative and transformative. It emphasizes repairing the harm done to victims and communities and aims to transform offenders into responsible and empathetic individuals. This focus on personal growth and rehabilitation can complement the punitive aspects of legal accountability, which primarily seek to establish guilt and impose penalties. Restorative processes can contribute to an offender's rehabilitation, reducing the risk of recidivism.

Victim-Centered Approach: Restorative justice places a strong emphasis on meeting the needs of victims and involving them in the decision-making process. This contrasts with traditional legal systems, where victims often have limited participation and voice. Restorative processes allow victims to express their concerns, seek answers to their questions, and actively participate in determining outcomes. Legal accountability, while necessary for upholding the rule of law, may not always provide victims with the same level of engagement and restoration.

Community Involvement: Restorative justice actively engages the community in addressing harm and wrongdoing. Community members can play roles as facilitators, supporters, and witnesses in restorative processes. In contrast, legal accountability tends to be a more formal and centralized process. Restorative justice acknowledges the community's stake in the well-being of its members and leverages this collective responsibility to promote healing and reconciliation.

Balancing Punishment and Restoration: The legal system primarily focuses on punishment as a means of accountability. Restorative justice introduces a balance by emphasizing restoration, reconciliation, and personal responsibility. While legal accountability assigns penalties for violations, restorative processes provide opportunities for offenders to take responsibility, make amends, and actively contribute to repairing the harm they've caused.

In essence, the relationship between restorative justice and legal accountability is one of potential synergy. Restorative justice processes can complement the legal system by addressing the human and relational aspects of harm, promoting rehabilitation, and involving victims and communities in the pursuit of justice. While both approaches have their distinct roles, they can work in tandem to create a more comprehensive and inclusive system of accountability and justice.

Accountability and the Victim's Perspective:

Accountability from the victim's perspective holds significant importance within the context of restorative justice. It encompasses several key aspects that address victims' needs and contribute to their healing and recovery:

Acknowledgment of Harm: One of the fundamental needs of victims is the acknowledgment of the harm they have suffered. Legal accountability may establish that an offense occurred, but restorative justice goes further by providing a platform for offenders to acknowledge the specific harm inflicted on individual victims. This acknowledgment validates the victim's experience and offers a sense of validation and recognition.

Empowerment and Participation: Victims often express a desire for a greater voice and participation in the justice process. Restorative justice prioritizes victim engagement, allowing them to actively participate in meetings or conferences with offenders. This involvement gives victims the opportunity to express their feelings, ask questions, and directly contribute to decision-making, helping to restore their sense of agency and control.

Apology and Amends: Many victims seek a genuine apology from offenders as a means of accountability. Restorative justice processes provide a structured environment for offenders to offer sincere apologies.

These apologies are not coerced but emerge from a genuine understanding of the harm caused. Apologies can be profoundly healing for victims, as they signify remorse and a willingness to take responsibility.

Restitution and Repair: Accountability within restorative justice often includes concrete actions by offenders to repair the harm they've caused. This may involve restitution, community service, or other forms of reparation that directly benefit victims. Victims may have practical needs arising from the harm, and these actions help address those needs, contributing to their sense of justice and restoration.

Closure and Emotional Healing: Accountability contributes to a sense of closure and emotional healing for victims. When offenders take responsibility and actively engage in making amends, victims may experience a sense of resolution and relief. This process can help victims move forward from the trauma and pain caused by the offense.

Preventing Future Harm: Victims often express concern about the prevention of future harm. Accountability within restorative justice includes an emphasis on personal growth and rehabilitation for offenders. By addressing the root causes of offending behavior and promoting understanding, restorative processes can contribute to reducing the risk of reoffending, providing victims with a sense of safety and security.

In essence, accountability from the victim's perspective in restorative justice is about recognizing the multidimensional needs of victims beyond mere punishment. It focuses on healing, restoration, and the reparation of harm in ways that empower victims, validate their experiences and contribute to their overall well-being. It acknowledges that true accountability goes beyond legal consequences; it involves taking meaningful steps to address the emotional, psychological, and practical needs of victims, fostering a path toward healing and reconciliation.

Cultural and Ethical Dimensions of Accountability:

The cultural and ethical dimensions of accountability within the context of restorative justice are multifaceted, reflecting the diversity of perspectives and values across different cultures and belief systems. Understanding and navigating these dimensions are essential for ensuring that restorative justice practices are respectful, inclusive, and ethically sound.

Cultural Variations in Accountability:

Cultural diversity influences how individuals and communities perceive accountability and the methods used to achieve it. Here are some cultural variations in accountability:

Collectivism vs. Individualism: Collectivist cultures often prioritize community harmony and collective responsibility.

Accountability may be framed in terms of restoring group cohesion rather than individual retribution. In contrast, individualistic cultures may emphasize personal responsibility and autonomy.

Communication Styles: Cultural norms regarding communication and conflict resolution may impact how accountability is expressed. Some cultures may value direct communication, while others may prefer indirect or mediated approaches.

Restitution Practices: Cultural differences may influence the forms of restitution or amends-making deemed appropriate. What constitutes a meaningful act of reparation can vary significantly across cultures.

Religious and Spiritual Beliefs: Religious and spiritual beliefs play a substantial role in shaping cultural values and attitudes toward accountability. For example, forgiveness and redemption may be central themes in some religious traditions, influencing how accountability is approached.

Traditional Justice Systems: Indigenous and traditional justice systems in various cultures often have their own mechanisms for accountability and conflict resolution, which may differ from Western legal paradigms.

Ethical Considerations in Accountability:

Ethical dimensions of accountability within restorative justice include principles that guide fair and just practices. Here are some ethical considerations:

Fair Process: Restorative justice processes should adhere to principles of fairness, transparency, and impartiality. All parties involved should have an equal opportunity to participate and be heard.

Voluntariness: Participation in restorative processes should be voluntary, and no one should be coerced or pressured into admitting guilt or accepting responsibility.

Respect for Rights: Restorative justice should respect the legal and human rights of all participants, including the rights of victims and offenders. Ethical accountability does not entail violating these rights.

Inclusivity: Restorative justice should be inclusive and accessible to individuals from diverse backgrounds, ensuring that cultural and linguistic differences are respected.

Restorative Intent: The primary goal of accountability in restorative justice is to repair harm and promote healing, not to seek revenge or perpetuate harm. Ethical accountability focuses on restoration and transformation.

Consent: All parties involved should provide informed consent to participate in restorative processes, understanding the nature and purpose of the proceedings.

Confidentiality: Ethical accountability respects the confidentiality and privacy of participants, safeguarding sensitive information shared during the process.

Navigating the cultural and ethical dimensions of accountability requires a nuanced and culturally sensitive approach. Practitioners of restorative justice should be mindful of these dimensions, adapt their processes to respect cultural values, and uphold ethical principles that prioritize justice, healing, and the well-being of all involved parties.

Accountability in Action:

"Accountability in Action" is a section within the book or chapter that provides real-life case studies and examples to illustrate how accountability is implemented and experienced within restorative justice processes. These case studies serve as practical examples of how accountability principles are put into practice and how they impact individuals, victims, offenders, and communities.

In this section, you may find narratives, interviews, or detailed accounts of specific restorative justice cases, highlighting various aspects of accountability, such as:

Acknowledgment of Harm: Stories where offenders genuinely acknowledge the harm they've caused to victims and express remorse.

Apologies and Amends: Instances where offenders offer sincere apologies and take concrete actions to make amends or restitution to victims.

Victim Involvement: Examples of how victims actively participate in the accountability process, including their role in decision-making and shaping outcomes.

Community Engagement: Cases that showcase the involvement of the community in holding offenders accountable and supporting the restoration of individuals and relationships.

Personal Transformation: Stories of offenders who undergo personal growth and transformation as a result of accountability processes, reducing the likelihood of reoffending.

Cultural and Ethical Considerations: Instances where cultural and ethical dimensions are taken into account in designing and conducting restorative justice processes.

These real-life examples help readers grasp the practical implications of accountability within restorative justice. They demonstrate the impact of restorative practices on individuals, highlight the potential for healing and reconciliation, and underscore the role of accountability in the restoration of well-being for victims and the reintegration of offenders into the community.

Ultimately, "Accountability in Action" provides tangible evidence of how restorative justice principles can be applied in diverse situations, offering insights into the transformative potential of accountability within the justice system.

Theological and Spiritual Perspectives on Accountability:

Theological and spiritual perspectives on accountability draw from the teachings and values of various religious traditions to provide insights into the moral and ethical dimensions of holding individuals accountable within restorative justice. These perspectives emphasize the importance of accountability as a means of promoting justice, reconciliation, and personal transformation while aligning with the spiritual and ethical principles of each tradition.

Here are some examples of how theological and spiritual perspectives from different religious traditions can contribute to the understanding of accountability within restorative justice:

Christianity: In Christian theology, the concept of accountability is closely linked to the notions of repentance and redemption. Accountability involves acknowledging one's sins, seeking forgiveness, and making amends. The Christian perspective highlights the transformative power of accountability, as it can lead to spiritual growth and reconciliation with both God and fellow humans.

Islam: Islamic ethics emphasize personal responsibility and accountability before God. In restorative justice, the Islamic perspective underscores the importance of admitting wrongdoing, seeking forgiveness from both the victim and God, and making reparations to rectify harm. Accountability is seen as a means of purifying the soul and seeking God's mercy.

Buddhism: Buddhist teachings emphasize the interdependence of all beings and the importance of personal accountability for one's actions (karma). In restorative justice, the Buddhist perspective emphasizes acknowledging the harm caused, expressing remorse, and taking steps to make amends. Accountability aligns with the Buddhist principle of right action and contributes to inner peace and the cessation of suffering.

Judaism: Jewish ethics emphasize the importance of accountability, repentance (teshuvah), and restitution. Restorative justice aligns with the Jewish tradition's focus on repairing relationships and seeking forgiveness. Accountability involves recognizing the harm done, offering apologies, and taking actions to rectify the situation in accordance with Jewish legal and ethical principles.

Indigenous Spiritual Traditions: Many Indigenous spiritual traditions emphasize accountability as a means of restoring balance and harmony within the community and the natural world. Accountability involves acknowledging the harm done to both human and non-human entities, making restitution, and seeking reconciliation with the community and the land.

Interfaith Dialogues: Interfaith perspectives on accountability encourage dialogue and mutual understanding among diverse religious traditions. These discussions often highlight commonalities in the moral imperatives of accountability, forgiveness, and reconciliation, fostering a shared commitment to restorative justice principles.

Incorporating theological and spiritual perspectives into restorative justice practices enriches the ethical foundation of these processes. It emphasizes the interconnectedness of individuals, their moral responsibilities, and the potential for spiritual growth and transformation through accountability. These perspectives encourage practitioners to approach accountability with a sense of reverence for the sacredness of life and the shared values that underpin diverse religious traditions.

Accountability and Personal Growth:

Accountability and personal growth are closely intertwined within the context of restorative justice. When individuals take responsibility for their actions in a restorative manner, it can lead to profound personal growth and transformation. Here's how this process unfolds:

Acknowledgment of Wrongdoing: The first step in accountability is acknowledging the harm one has caused. This acknowledgment goes beyond a mere admission of guilt; it involves a genuine recognition of the impact of one's actions on others, especially on victims. This introspective step encourages individuals to confront their behavior honestly.

Remorse and Empathy: Accountability often involves experiencing genuine remorse for the harm inflicted on others. This remorse is not driven by fear of punishment but by a deep understanding of the suffering caused. It fosters empathy as individuals begin to see the world through the eyes of those they have harmed.

Taking Responsibility: Taking responsibility means more than admitting fault; it means actively participating in the restoration process. This may include offering sincere apologies to victims, engaging in dialogue, and making amends in meaningful ways. Individuals learn that they have agency in repairing the harm they've caused.

Personal Reflection and Growth: As individuals engage in the accountability process, they engage in self-reflection. They confront their actions, motivations, and values. This self-examination can lead to personal growth as they strive to align their behavior with their values and develop a stronger sense of moral responsibility.

Commitment to Change: Accountability often involves a commitment to change one's behavior and make better choices in the future. Offenders may seek rehabilitative programs, counseling, or support to address underlying issues that contributed to their actions. This commitment to change is a critical aspect of personal growth and transformation.

Empowerment: Taking responsibility empowers individuals to address the consequences of their actions head-on. This sense of empowerment comes from recognizing that they have the capacity to make amends and positively impact the lives of others. It shifts the focus from passivity to active engagement in the healing process.

Reduced Likelihood of Reoffending: Through accountability and personal growth, individuals can reduce the likelihood of reoffending. They gain insight into the root causes of their behavior and develop coping strategies to avoid repeating harmful actions. This benefits both the individual and the community.

Restored Relationships: Accountability can lead to the restoration of relationships with victims, loved ones, and the broader community. When offenders take responsibility and actively work to repair harm, it can rebuild trust and pave the way for healthier, more constructive relationships.

In essence, accountability within restorative justice is a transformative process. It challenges individuals to confront their actions, fosters empathy and remorse, and empowers them to actively participate in the restoration of relationships and communities. Personal growth and transformation emerge from this journey of self-reflection, responsibility, and the commitment to making amends and positive changes in one's life. Intersection of Accountability and Forgiveness:

The intersection of accountability and forgiveness within restorative justice is a complex and nuanced space where these two principles can coexist and mutually reinforce each other. Here's an exploration of how accountability and forgiveness intersect:

Accountability as a Prerequisite for Forgiveness:

In many restorative justice processes, accountability is often seen as a necessary precursor to forgiveness. Victims and the community often require offenders to take responsibility for their actions, acknowledge the harm caused, and actively work toward making amends.

Accountability demonstrates a genuine commitment on the part of offenders to right their wrongs, which can create a foundation of trust necessary for victims to consider forgiveness as a possibility.

Accountability Fosters Empathy and Understanding:

The accountability process, which includes acknowledging harm and taking responsibility, can foster empathy and understanding between offenders and victims.

When offenders truly understand the pain and suffering, they've caused, it can evoke feelings of remorse and empathy, which are key emotional components of forgiveness.

Forgiveness as a Catalyst for Personal Growth:

Forgiveness, when extended by victims, can serve as a catalyst for personal growth and transformation for offenders. When they are forgiven, offenders may experience relief, gratitude, and a sense of responsibility to ensure they do not repeat their harmful actions. Knowing they have been forgiven can motivate offenders to actively engage in the accountability process and make amends.

Restitution and Reparation as Acts of Accountability and Restoration:

Part of accountability often involves making restitution or amends to victims. These actions are not only about taking responsibility but also about actively working to repair the harm done.

From the perspective of victims, accepting restitution or amends can be seen as an act of grace and a willingness to move toward forgiveness.

The Healing Power of Forgiveness:

Forgiveness can have a profound healing effect on victims. It can release them from the emotional burden of anger and resentment, allowing them to move forward with their lives.

This healing power of forgiveness is a testament to the potential for restoration and transformation within the restorative justice process.

Balancing Accountability and Compassion:

The intersection of accountability and forgiveness requires a delicate balance. While offenders are held accountable for their actions, there is also room for compassion and understanding.

Restorative justice practitioners often emphasize the importance of both accountability and compassion in creating a space where healing and reconciliation can occur.

In essence, the intersection of accountability and forgiveness in restorative justice represents a dynamic interplay between justice, healing, and reconciliation. Accountability sets the stage for forgiveness by creating the conditions for genuine remorse and responsibility. Forgiveness, in turn, can facilitate personal growth, healing, and the restoration of relationships. These two principles work together within restorative justice to promote transformation and the reparation of harm.

Conclusion:

In conclusion, this chapter has illuminated the pivotal role of accountability and responsibility within the framework of restorative justice. We've explored the intricate relationship between these principles and their profound impact on achieving restoration and healing. Here are the key takeaways:

Accountability as a Cornerstone: Accountability stands as a cornerstone of restorative justice, emphasizing the importance of individuals taking responsibility for their actions. It involves acknowledging the harm caused, demonstrating genuine remorse, and actively participating in the restoration process.

Path to Empathy and Understanding: Accountability fosters empathy and understanding, not only for victims but also for offenders. It provides an opportunity for offenders to grasp the emotional and psychological consequences of their actions, creating a foundation for meaningful dialogue.

Personal Growth and Transformation: Accountability often leads to personal growth and transformation. Offenders who genuinely engage in the accountability process may undergo profound changes, which can reduce the likelihood of reoffending and contribute to their rehabilitation.

Reparation and Amends: Taking responsibility includes making restitution and amends to victims. This act of repair goes beyond mere words, demonstrating a commitment to righting the wrongs and addressing the tangible consequences of harm.

Community Involvement: Accountability extends to communities as well. Communities play a vital role in holding offenders accountable and supporting the restoration process. Their engagement reinforces the collective responsibility for justice.

Restoration of Relationships: The accountability process often paves the way for the restoration of relationships. Victims, offenders, and communities may find a path toward healing and reconciliation, rebuilding trust and forging stronger, more constructive connections.

Intersection with Forgiveness: Accountability and forgiveness intersect in a powerful way. While accountability is often a prerequisite for forgiveness, the two principles can mutually reinforce each other, creating a space where healing, transformation, and restoration can flourish.

In essence, accountability and responsibility are not just mechanisms of punishment but essential components of a justice system rooted in healing and reconciliation. They empower individuals to confront their actions, make amends, and contribute to the restoration of well-being for victims and offenders alike. Through this chapter, we have witnessed how these principles, when carefully applied within the context of restorative justice, can lead to profound personal growth, community restoration, and the mending of broken relationships.

CHAPTER 10

The Importance of Community

The Importance of Community:

Community is not just a backdrop in the realm of restorative justice; it plays a pivotal and active role in the pursuit of healing, reconciliation, and justice. Within the context of restorative justice, community takes on multifaceted significance, and its importance cannot be overstated.

First and foremost, community serves as a supportive network for individuals impacted by crime and wrongdoing. Victims find solace in knowing that their community stands with them, offering emotional and practical support during challenging times. Similarly, offenders benefit from a supportive community that encourages them to take responsibility for their actions and embark on a path of personal growth and transformation.

Community accountability is another critical facet. In restorative justice, the community collectively holds individuals accountable, emphasizing the idea that harm to one is harm to all. This approach fosters a sense of responsibility among community members to address the root causes of crime and work collaboratively to prevent further harm. It highlights the interconnectedness of individuals within a community and their shared commitment to promoting justice.

Restorative justice programs and initiatives are often implemented within communities. These programs create structured spaces for dialogue, reconciliation, and accountability. They empower communities to actively participate in the resolution of conflicts and the restoration of relationships, reinforcing the idea that justice is a communal endeavor.

Moreover, community involvement is instrumental in preventing recidivism. By providing a supportive and rehabilitative environment for offenders upon their reintegration, communities reduce the likelihood of reoffending and contribute to the overall safety and well-being of society. Communities that embrace restorative justice approaches understand the importance of addressing the root causes of criminal behavior and are dedicated to fostering a sense of belonging and purpose among all their members.

In essence, the importance of community within restorative justice cannot be overstated. It is the cornerstone upon which healing, reconciliation, and justice are built. As active participants in the restorative process, communities reaffirm their commitment to promoting well-being, unity, and harmony, making strides toward a more just and compassionate society.

Community as the Supportive Network:

Community as the Supportive Network is of paramount importance within the realm of restorative justice for several compelling reasons.

Firstly, communities offer a vital source of emotional support to individuals impacted by crime and wrongdoing. Victims often face immense emotional turmoil, ranging from fear and anger to grief and trauma. Communities provide a safe and empathetic space for victims to express their feelings and receive comfort from others who have experienced similar hardships. This sense of solidarity can be profoundly healing, assuring victims that they are not alone in their journey toward recovery.

Secondly, for offenders, community support can be a linchpin in their process of personal growth and transformation. Acknowledging one's actions and taking responsibility for wrongdoing can be emotionally challenging. Communities that provide guidance and encouragement help offenders navigate this process and find constructive ways to make amends. By offering a sense of belonging and acceptance, communities can motivate offenders to actively engage in the accountability and restitution process.

Thirdly, community support fosters a sense of agency and empowerment for all involved. It reinforces the idea that justice is not solely the responsibility of the criminal justice system but is a communal endeavor. This communal aspect encourages individuals to actively participate in creating safer and more harmonious communities. It instills a sense of responsibility for preventing future harm and addressing the root causes of criminal behavior.

Ultimately, community as the supportive network amplifies the impact of restorative justice by creating a web of relationships that extends beyond individual cases. It promotes empathy, understanding, and unity, reinforcing the interconnectedness of individuals within a community. Through this collective support, communities become catalysts for healing, reconciliation, and the restoration of well-being for victims, offenders, and society as a whole.

Community Accountability:

Community Accountability within restorative justice is of profound significance as it redefines the concept of responsibility and justice within a collective context. Here's why it holds such importance:

Shared Responsibility: In restorative justice, accountability extends beyond individual wrongdoers; it encompasses the entire community. This shared responsibility highlights that harm to one member affects the entire community. Therefore, when community members actively engage in the accountability process, they collectively address the roots of wrongdoing and work together to create safer and more resilient communities.

Prevention of Recidivism: Community accountability creates an environment where individuals are not only held responsible for their actions but are also guided toward personal growth and transformation. This proactive approach reduces the likelihood of reoffending, contributing to safer neighborhoods and a decrease in the cycle of harm.

Restorative Justice Culture: Encouraging community accountability nurtures a restorative justice culture within a society. This culture prioritizes open communication, empathy, and healing over punitive measures. As individuals and communities embrace restorative practices, they collectively promote a more compassionate and just society.

Community Empowerment: When communities actively participate in the accountability process, they gain a sense of empowerment. They recognize their agency in addressing crime and conflict, rather than relying solely on punitive legal systems. This empowerment can lead to more resilient and self-sufficient communities.

Healing and Restoration: Community accountability emphasizes not only punitive measures but also the restoration of relationships and well-being. This holistic approach acknowledges that true justice encompasses healing and reconciliation. By working together, communities can support victims in their healing journey and facilitate the rehabilitation of offenders.

Prevention of Systemic Issues: By collectively addressing harm and wrongdoing, communities have the potential to identify and rectify systemic issues that may contribute to crime. This proactive stance allows communities to advocate for changes in policies, practices, and environments that may be conducive to criminal behavior.

In essence, community accountability reframes justice as a shared responsibility and fosters an environment where individuals and communities actively engage in promoting well-being and preventing harm. It empowers communities to play a proactive role in the restoration of justice, emphasizing the interconnectedness of individuals within a society. Through this collective accountability, communities move toward a more compassionate, resilient, and just future.

Restorative Justice Programs

Restorative justice programs hold great importance within communities for several compelling reasons:

Healing and Reconciliation: Restorative justice programs provide structured processes for victims, offenders, and community members to come together and address harm. These programs prioritize healing and reconciliation, allowing those affected by wrongdoing to express their feelings, share their perspectives, and work toward resolution. This emphasis on healing contributes to a sense of closure and relief for victims and supports the rehabilitation of offenders.

Community Engagement: These programs actively involve community members, emphasizing that justice is a communal endeavor. Community members participate as facilitators, supporters, or observers, reinforcing the idea that everyone has a role to play in addressing harm and preventing future offenses. This engagement fosters a sense of shared responsibility within the community.

Empowerment: Restorative justice programs empower individuals and communities to take an active role in shaping the outcomes of cases. Participants have a say in the terms of amends, restitution, and reconciliation, which can be more satisfying and meaningful than punitive measures imposed by the criminal justice system. This empowerment instills a sense of agency and self-determination.

Conflict Resolution: Beyond addressing criminal offenses, restorative justice programs are effective tools for resolving conflicts and disputes within communities. They provide a non-adversarial approach that promotes understanding and problem-solving. By offering alternatives to litigation, these programs can reduce the burden on the traditional legal system.

Preventing Recidivism: Restorative justice programs contribute to preventing recidivism by focusing on rehabilitation and reintegration. They offer support and guidance to offenders, helping them understand the consequences of their actions and providing opportunities for personal growth. This approach reduces the likelihood of repeat offenses and promotes community safety.

Community Well-Being: Implementing restorative justice programs enhances community well-being by addressing the root causes of harm and conflict. By fostering a culture of empathy, understanding, and accountability, these programs create more harmonious and resilient communities where individuals feel safer and supported.

Examples of restorative justice programs in communities include victim-offender dialogues, community conferencing, and restorative circles. These programs vary in structure and application but share a common goal: to promote justice that is focused on repairing harm, restoring relationships, and nurturing community bonds. Their positive impact on community well-being reinforces the notion that restorative justice is not merely an alternative to punitive measures but a proactive and transformative approach to addressing harm and conflict within societies.

How can we Prevent Recidivism?

Preventing recidivism is a complex but critical goal that communities can actively contribute to. Here are several ways in which communities can support the reintegration of offenders and reduce the likelihood of reoffending:

Community-Based Rehabilitation Programs: Communities can establish and support rehabilitation programs that address the underlying causes of criminal behavior, such as substance abuse, mental health issues, and lack of education or job opportunities. These programs provide essential resources and support for offenders to rebuild their lives.

Employment and Education: Access to stable employment and education are key factors in preventing recidivism. Communities can collaborate with local businesses and educational institutions to create opportunities for offenders to gain job skills and education while also addressing potential barriers to employment, such as criminal records.

Mentorship and Support: Providing mentorship programs where individuals who have successfully reintegrated into society mentor those who are reentering the community can be highly effective. This support system offers guidance, encouragement, and a sense of belonging for offenders seeking a fresh start.

Housing Assistance: Securing stable housing is a significant challenge for many ex-offenders. Communities can work to provide affordable housing options and support services that help offenders find safe and stable places to live.

Community Supervision: Restorative justice programs often involve a form of community supervision or monitoring. These programs enable offenders to stay connected with supportive community members who can offer guidance and hold them accountable for their actions.

Conflict Resolution and Communication Skills: Teaching conflict resolution and communication skills to offenders equips them with tools to navigate interpersonal challenges without resorting to harmful behavior. These skills are valuable for personal growth and reducing the likelihood of reoffending.

Access to Social Services: Communities can ensure that offenders have access to essential social services, including mental health counseling, addiction treatment, and support for victims. Addressing underlying issues contributes to offenders' rehabilitation.

Restorative Justice Initiatives: Communities can embrace restorative justice initiatives that prioritize healing, reconciliation, and accountability. These programs provide a structured framework for offenders to make amends and address the harm they've caused, reducing the risk of reoffending.

Community Reintegration Planning: Collaborative reintegration planning involving offenders, community members, and service providers can help create a personalized roadmap for each individual's successful reintegration into society. These plans can address the unique needs and challenges faced by each offender.

Public Awareness and Education: Raising awareness within the community about the challenges faced by offenders upon reentry and the importance of support and rehabilitation can foster empathy and reduce stigma. Informed communities are more likely to provide a welcoming environment for ex-offenders.

Preventing recidivism requires a multifaceted approach that acknowledges the complexity of the issue. Communities play a pivotal role in providing the support, resources, and opportunities needed for offenders to rebuild their lives and become productive members of society.

By investing in these strategies, communities contribute to safer neighborhoods and promote the long-term well-being of both individuals and society as a whole.

Community Healing:

Community healing is a necessary and transformative process for several compelling reasons:

Collective Trauma: When a crime occurs within a community, it can create a sense of collective trauma. Community members may feel violated, unsafe, and emotionally affected by the incident. Acknowledging and addressing this trauma is essential for the overall well-being of the community.

Restoring Trust: Crimes within a community can erode trust among its members. Restorative justice processes provide a structured way for community members to rebuild trust by facilitating open communication and understanding among those affected.

Community Cohesion: Healing within a community strengthens its cohesion. By collectively addressing harm and working toward reconciliation, community members forge stronger bonds and a sense of solidarity, which contributes to social stability.

Breaking the Cycle: Community healing through restorative justice can break the cycle of retaliation and revenge. By providing non-punitive avenues for addressing harm, these processes discourage further violence or retribution.

Preventing Vigilantism: In the absence of restorative justice practices, communities may seek their own forms of justice, sometimes resorting to vigilante actions. Community healing supported by restorative justice offers a peaceful and lawful alternative to vigilantism.

Empowerment: Engaging in the healing process empowers community members. It allows them to actively participate in addressing harm, shaping the outcome, and contributing to a safer and more harmonious community.

Resilience: Community healing fosters resilience. It equips communities with the tools and knowledge to respond to harm and conflict in a way that promotes recovery and growth.

Restoring a Sense of Safety: Community members often experience heightened feelings of insecurity following a crime. Engaging in healing processes reassures them that efforts are being made to restore safety and well-being.

Addressing Underlying Issues: Restorative justice encourages communities to address the underlying issues that may contribute to crime, such as social inequality, poverty, or lack of access to resources. By tackling these root causes, communities can work toward long-term prevention.

Creating a Supportive Environment: Healing processes create a supportive environment for victims, offenders, and the broader community. They emphasize that everyone is valued and has a role in promoting restoration and justice.

Incorporating restorative justice principles into community healing processes allows communities to collectively address the harm caused by crime, rebuild trust and cohesion, and create a more resilient and compassionate social fabric. It shifts the focus from punitive measures to healing, reconciliation, and the well-being of all community members.

Ultimately, community healing is not only necessary but also transformative, contributing to safer, more harmonious, and empowered communities.

Conflict Resolution:

Conflict resolution is of paramount importance within communities for various reasons:

Preserving Community Cohesion: Conflicts, if left unresolved, can escalate and lead to divisions within a community. Effective conflict resolution preserves the unity and cohesion that are essential for a community's well-being.

Enhancing Communication: Conflict resolution processes encourage open and honest communication among community members. By addressing underlying issues and concerns, these processes improve communication skills and promote a culture of dialogue.

Preventing Escalation: Unresolved conflicts can escalate into larger, more destructive issues. Timely and effective conflict resolution prevents minor disputes from growing into more significant problems that can harm the community's stability.

Fostering Understanding: Conflict resolution encourages individuals to consider different perspectives and empathize with others. This fosters mutual understanding and helps community members appreciate the diversity of viewpoints within the community.

Promoting Equity and Fairness: Restorative justice approaches emphasize fairness and equity in conflict resolution. These processes ensure that all parties have a voice in finding solutions, rather than one party dominating or imposing decisions on others.

Conflict Prevention: By addressing conflicts promptly and fairly, communities can create a culture of conflict prevention. Community members become more skilled at identifying potential conflicts and addressing them before they escalate.

Building Trust: Effective conflict resolution builds trust within the community. When individuals see that conflicts are handled fairly and justly, they are more likely to trust their neighbors and community leaders.

Community Empowerment: Conflict resolution processes empower community members to actively participate in resolving issues and shaping the future of their community. This sense of agency contributes to a stronger and more resilient community.

Setting a Positive Example: Communities that embrace restorative justice principles for conflict resolution set a positive example for their members. They demonstrate that disputes can be resolved peacefully and constructively, encouraging individuals to adopt similar approaches in their personal lives.

Creating a Safer Environment: When conflicts are effectively resolved, the community becomes a safer and more peaceful place to live. Residents can go about their daily lives with reduced fear of disputes turning violent or causing harm.

Long-Term Well-Being: Sustainable community well-being is closely tied to effective conflict resolution. Communities that can navigate conflicts with respect, fairness, and understanding are better equipped to address ongoing challenges and promote positive social development.

By incorporating restorative justice approaches into conflict resolution, communities can build stronger foundations for harmony, unity, and resilience. These approaches prioritize communication, understanding, and fairness, creating a culture where conflicts are seen as opportunities for growth and community development rather than as sources of division and harm.

Community Decision-Making:

Community decision-making circles are indeed important within the context of restorative justice for several reasons:

Inclusivity: Decision-making circles ensure that a wide range of community members have a voice in the resolution of issues. They promote inclusivity by allowing diverse perspectives to be heard and considered.

Transparency: These circles often operate with transparency, making the decision-making process visible to all participants. This transparency builds trust and confidence in the decisions made.

Community Ownership: When community members collectively participate in making decisions, they take ownership of the outcomes. This sense of ownership fosters a greater commitment to implementing decisions and addressing issues effectively.

Conflict Resolution: Decision-making circles can address not only specific issues but also underlying conflicts or tensions within the community. By creating a structured space for dialogue, they help communities navigate complex problems.

Community Building: The process of coming together in decision-making circles can be a community-building experience. It encourages relationships, dialogue, and collaboration among community members, strengthening community bonds.

Problem-Solving: Decision-making circles are problem-solving tools. They provide a structured framework for identifying issues, exploring solutions, and reaching consensus on how to address challenges within the community.

Empowerment: These circles empower community members to actively participate in shaping the direction of their community. This empowerment can lead to a greater sense of agency and engagement among residents.

Conflict Prevention: By addressing issues proactively, decision-making circles contribute to conflict prevention. Communities can address potential sources of conflict before they escalate into larger problems.

Customized Solutions: Decision-making circles allow for solutions that are tailored to the specific needs and circumstances of the community. This customization increases the likelihood of successful outcomes.

Learning Opportunities: Community members involved in decision-making circles have the opportunity to learn from one another, exchange ideas, and build skills in conflict resolution and consensus-building.

Sustainable Solutions: Decisions reached through these circles tend to be more sustainable because they are supported by the collective will of the community. This can lead to lasting positive changes.

Restorative Justice Principles: Decision-making circles align with restorative justice principles, emphasizing dialogue, accountability, and the restoration of relationships. They provide a structured framework for applying these principles at the community level.

In essence, community decision-making circles are a valuable tool for promoting community cohesion, resolving conflicts, and making decisions that reflect the collective wisdom and aspirations of community members. They facilitate a collaborative and inclusive approach to addressing challenges and building stronger, more resilient communities.

Cultural and Diversity Considerations:

Cultural and diversity considerations are of utmost importance in the implementation of restorative justice practices within communities for several compelling reasons:

Respect for Cultural Differences: Communities are often comprised of individuals from various cultural backgrounds, each with their own beliefs, values, and norms. Recognizing and respecting these differences is essential to ensure that restorative justice processes are culturally sensitive and relevant.

Inclusivity: Cultural diversity considerations promote inclusivity by making sure that all community members, regardless of their cultural background, have equal access to restorative justice practices. This inclusivity fosters a sense of belonging and ownership in the community.

Customized Approaches: Different cultural groups may have unique ways of addressing harm and conflict. Cultural sensitivity allows restorative justice practitioners to adapt their approaches to align with the preferences and practices of specific cultural communities, increasing the effectiveness of these processes.

Avoiding Harmful Stereotypes: Cultural awareness helps prevent the perpetuation of harmful stereotypes or biases within restorative justice practices. It ensures that decisions and actions are based on an accurate understanding of individuals from diverse backgrounds.

Effective Communication: Effective communication is at the heart of restorative justice. Cultural diversity considerations emphasize the importance of clear and respectful communication, especially when language barriers or cultural differences may be present.

Conflict Resolution Strategies: Different cultures may have distinct approaches to conflict resolution and reconciliation. Recognizing these variations allows restorative justice practitioners to draw upon culturally appropriate strategies for resolving disputes.

Trust Building: Trust is a fundamental element of restorative justice processes. Cultural sensitivity helps build trust by demonstrating a genuine respect for cultural identities and a commitment to understanding and honoring cultural practices.

Community Engagement: Culturally sensitive restorative justice practices encourage greater community engagement. When community members see that their cultural values and perspectives are respected, they are more likely to actively participate in the resolution of issues.

Preventing Harm: Cultural diversity considerations can help prevent further harm during the restorative justice process. By understanding and addressing potential cultural sensitivities or misunderstandings, practitioners can ensure that the process does not inadvertently cause harm.

Strengthening Community Bonds: Embracing cultural diversity within restorative justice processes can strengthen community bonds. It sends a message that the community values and celebrates its rich tapestry of cultures, which can enhance social cohesion.

Interfaith and Intersecting Identities: Communities may also be diverse in terms of religious beliefs, gender identities, and other intersecting identities. Cultural and diversity considerations extend to these dimensions, recognizing the importance of respecting and accommodating these aspects of individual and community identity.

In summary, cultural and diversity considerations are integral to the successful implementation of restorative justice practices within communities. They ensure that these practices are inclusive, respectful, and effective, reflecting the values and identities of all community members. By embracing cultural diversity, restorative justice processes become more adaptable, equitable, and capable of fostering reconciliation and healing across a broad spectrum of cultural backgrounds.

Challenges and Opportunities:

Certainly, exploring both the challenges and opportunities in adopting restorative justice approaches within communities is crucial for a comprehensive understanding of the process. Here are some key points to consider:

Challenges:

Resistance to Change: Communities may resist adopting restorative justice practices due to a long-standing reliance on punitive approaches. Overcoming this resistance requires education and awareness-building.

Resource Constraints: Implementing restorative justice programs can require resources, such as training, facilitators, and support services. Communities with limited resources may face challenges in establishing these programs.

Cultural Sensitivity: Ensuring that restorative justice practices are culturally sensitive can be challenging, particularly in diverse communities. It requires a deep understanding of various cultural norms and practices.

Community Engagement: Engaging all community members in restorative justice processes can be challenging, as some individuals may be skeptical or disengaged. Building trust and participation is an ongoing effort.

Addressing Power Imbalances: Restorative justice aims to address power imbalances between parties involved. Recognizing and addressing these imbalances can be complex, especially in cases involving systemic inequality.

Opportunities:

Community Empowerment: Restorative justice empowers communities to take an active role in addressing issues and conflicts. It encourages individuals to be agents of change within their own communities.

Conflict Prevention: By addressing conflicts and harm proactively, restorative justice can prevent future issues from arising, contributing to a more harmonious community environment.

Building Trust: Successful restorative justice processes build trust within communities, fostering stronger relationships and a sense of safety among residents.

Reconciliation: Restorative justice provides opportunities for reconciliation and healing, allowing communities to mend relationships and move forward from conflict or harm.

Customization: Restorative justice practices can be tailored to fit the unique needs and circumstances of each community, ensuring that solutions are contextually relevant.

Community Resilience: Communities that embrace restorative justice practices tend to be more resilient in the face of challenges. They develop skills and processes for addressing issues effectively.

Social Change: Restorative justice can be a catalyst for broader social change, as it challenges punitive systems and encourages a shift towards more humane and community-oriented approaches to justice.

Learning and Growth: Communities that adopt restorative justice approaches often experience personal and collective growth. They learn from their experiences and develop skills in communication, empathy, and conflict resolution.

Reducing Recidivism: Restorative justice can contribute to lower rates of recidivism by addressing the root causes of offending behavior and promoting personal growth among offenders.

Cultural Exchange: Communities that embrace diversity and cultural sensitivity as part of restorative justice practices have an opportunity to engage in cultural exchange and promote cross-cultural understanding.

In summary, while there are challenges to overcome in adopting restorative justice approaches within communities, there are also significant opportunities for personal, communal, and societal growth. Addressing these challenges through education, community engagement, and ongoing dialogue can help communities fully realize the potential benefits of restorative justice.

Case Studies:

Case studies play a vital role in understanding and appreciating the practical applications and benefits of restorative justice within communities. Here's how case studies can help:

Illustrating Success Stories: Case studies provide concrete examples of communities that have effectively implemented restorative justice practices. These success stories serve as inspiration and proof that restorative justice can work in various contexts.

Learning from Real Experiences: By examining real-life cases, communities can learn from the experiences of others. They can gain insights into the challenges faced, strategies employed, and outcomes achieved, helping them make informed decisions about implementing restorative justice.

Highlighting Diverse Approaches: Case studies often showcase a diversity of approaches to restorative justice. Communities can explore different models and methods and adapt them to suit their unique needs and circumstances.

Demonstrating Impact: Case studies provide evidence of the positive impact of restorative justice on individuals and communities. They can show how these practices contribute to healing, reconciliation, and reduced recidivism.

Inspiring Community Engagement: Success stories can inspire community members to actively participate in restorative justice initiatives. When people see the tangible benefits of these practices, they may be more inclined to get involved.

Building Trust: Case studies that highlight restored relationships and improved community cohesion demonstrate the trust-building potential of restorative justice. Trust is a key element in the success of these processes.

Highlighting Challenges: While case studies often focus on successes, they may also address challenges and obstacles encountered during the implementation of restorative justice. This provides a realistic view of what communities may face and helps in planning for potential challenges.

Informing Policy and Practice: Policymakers, community leaders, and practitioners can draw insights from case studies to inform the development of restorative justice programs and policies. Successful examples can serve as models for replication.

Promoting Accountability: Case studies can show how restorative justice processes hold individuals accountable for their actions while providing opportunities for growth and transformation.

Encouraging Peer-to-Peer Learning: Communities can learn from other communities that have navigated the path toward restorative justice. They can engage in peer-to-peer learning, seeking advice and guidance from those with similar experiences.

Measuring Progress: Case studies often include data on the outcomes of restorative justice programs. This data can be used to measure progress and evaluate the effectiveness of these initiatives.

In essence, case studies are invaluable tools for communities interested in adopting restorative justice practices. They provide tangible evidence of the benefits and challenges, helping communities make informed decisions, develop effective strategies, and build a strong foundation for restorative justice within their own contexts.

PART II
Implementing Restorative Justice

Part II of the book, "Implementing Restorative Justice," delves into the practical aspects of applying restorative justice principles and processes.

Here are four key aspects explored in this section:

Restorative Justice Models: This section introduces various models and approaches to restorative justice, such as conferencing, circles, and victim-offender dialogues. It explains how these models work, their benefits, and their applicability in different contexts. Readers gain insights into the mechanics of restorative justice processes and how to choose the most suitable model for specific situations.

Community Engagement: Implementing restorative justice requires active engagement from community members, practitioners, and stakeholders. The book discusses strategies for engaging and mobilizing communities to embrace restorative justice principles. It emphasizes the importance of community buy-in, participation, and support to ensure the success of restorative initiatives.

Practical Guidelines: This section offers practical guidelines for conducting restorative justice processes effectively. It covers topics such as facilitation skills, creating safe spaces for dialogue, and addressing power imbalances. Readers learn how to navigate the complexities of restorative justice encounters and facilitate meaningful conversations between victims and offenders.

Measuring Success: Implementing restorative justice involves measuring its impact and success. The book explores methods for evaluating the outcomes of restorative processes, including assessing changes in relationships, satisfaction among participants, and recidivism rates. It emphasizes the importance of ongoing evaluation to continually improve restorative justice practices.

Overall, Part II provides readers with the tools and knowledge needed to put restorative justice into action. It equips them with practical guidance on selecting appropriate models, engaging communities, conducting restorative processes, and assessing their effectiveness. This section empowers individuals and communities to take proactive steps in implementing restorative justice and realizing its transformative potential.

CHAPTER 11

Restorative Justice in the Criminal Justice System

What is Restorative Justice as Complement?

Restorative justice as a complement within the criminal justice system means that it works alongside and complements traditional punitive approaches, rather than replacing them. It acknowledges that punitive measures, such as incarceration, have their place in responding to crime but recognizes their limitations in achieving comprehensive justice.

Here's a closer look at what this concept entails:

Balancing Punishment and Restoration: Restorative justice seeks to balance punitive consequences with a focus on repairing the harm caused by the offense. While punitive measures aim to punish offenders, restorative justice aims to make them accountable for their actions, facilitate victim healing, and address the underlying issues that led to the offense.

Reducing Recidivism: By addressing the root causes of offending behavior and involving offenders in the restoration process, restorative justice can contribute to reducing recidivism rates. Offenders may gain a better understanding of the impact of their actions, which can lead to personal growth and a decreased likelihood of reoffending.

Victim-Centered Approach: Restorative justice places a strong emphasis on meeting the needs of victims and empowering them in the justice process. This focus on victim satisfaction and well-being can lead to greater victim cooperation and a sense of closure.

Community Engagement: Restorative justice often involves the broader community in the process, encouraging community members to actively participate in addressing crime and its consequences. This can strengthen community bonds and provide a sense of collective responsibility for justice.

Addressing Underlying Issues: Restorative justice recognizes that many offenders have unmet needs or underlying issues, such as substance abuse or mental health issues, that contribute to their criminal behavior. By addressing these needs within a restorative framework, it aims to break the cycle of crime.

Restorative justice as a complement to traditional punitive approaches aims to enhance the effectiveness of the criminal justice system by incorporating restorative practices. It seeks to achieve a more holistic form of justice that considers the needs of victims, holds offenders accountable, and addresses the broader social and community context in which crime occurs. This approach is viewed as a way to improve the overall outcomes of the justice system while maintaining a role for punitive measures when necessary.

Diversion Programs:

Diversion programs are alternative approaches within the criminal justice system designed to redirect certain cases away from traditional court proceedings and into restorative justice processes or other rehabilitative interventions. These programs are important for several reasons:

Reducing Court Overload: Diversion programs help alleviate the burden on overcrowded court systems by diverting low-risk and non-violent offenders away from the formal legal process. This allows courts to focus on more serious cases and ensures that resources are allocated more efficiently.

Addressing Root Causes: Diversion programs aim to address the underlying causes of criminal behavior rather than simply applying punitive measures. They provide opportunities for offenders to engage in interventions such as counseling, therapy, or community service, which can address issues like substance abuse, mental health, or socioeconomic challenges.

Promoting Rehabilitation: Diversion programs align with the rehabilitation philosophy of the criminal justice system. By providing offenders with the chance to participate in restorative justice practices or receive needed support and services, these programs focus on helping individuals become law-abiding citizens rather than punishing them.

Empowering Victims: Victims may have a say in the diversion process and the type of restitution or reparative actions they believe would be most meaningful. This empowers victims by giving them a voice in the resolution of their cases and can contribute to their healing and satisfaction.

Reducing Recidivism: Many diversion programs aim to reduce recidivism by addressing the factors that contribute to reoffending.

Through counseling, education, and support, offenders may gain the tools and insights needed to avoid future criminal behavior.

Community Engagement: Diversion programs often involve the community in the restorative justice process. This engagement can build trust, foster a sense of responsibility among community members, and create a more supportive environment for rehabilitation and reintegration.

Cost-Effective: Diversion programs can be cost-effective compared to the expenses associated with traditional court proceedings, incarceration, and long-term supervision.

Hence, diversion programs are important within the criminal justice system because they offer an alternative to punitive measures, focusing on rehabilitation, victim empowerment, and community involvement. They contribute to the overall goals of the criminal justice system by addressing the root causes of offending behavior, reducing recidivism, and promoting a more balanced and effective approach to justice.

Victim-Offender Mediation:

Victim-offender mediation (VOM), also known as victim-offender dialogue or conferencing, is a restorative justice practice that brings together the victim of a crime and the offender in a facilitated, structured conversation. This mediation is important for several reasons:

Facilitating Communication: VOM provides a safe and controlled environment for victims and offenders to communicate directly. This direct communication can lead to a deeper understanding of each other's perspectives and experiences related to the crime.

Empowering Victims: Victims often have a strong desire to have their voices heard and to express the impact of the crime on their lives. VOM empowers victims by allowing them to share their feelings, ask questions, and seek answers from the offender. This can contribute to their emotional healing and sense of closure.

Offender Accountability: VOM holds offenders accountable by requiring them to take responsibility for their actions and face the impact of their behavior on the victim. Offenders are encouraged to express remorse and make amends, which can lead to personal growth and the development of empathy.

Restitution and Amends: VOM discussions can lead to agreements on restitution and amends. Offenders may agree to compensate victims for financial losses or engage in actions that repair the harm caused. This process aligns with the restorative justice principle of addressing the tangible consequences of wrongdoing.

Reducing Recidivism: VOM has been associated with lower rates of recidivism, as offenders who engage in meaningful dialogue with their victims are more likely to understand the impact of their actions and commit to positive changes in their lives.

Enhancing Victim Satisfaction: Victims who participate in VOM often report higher levels of satisfaction with the justice process compared to traditional court proceedings. They appreciate the opportunity to have a say in the resolution of their cases and to receive direct responses from offenders.

Rebuilding Trust: In some cases, VOM can contribute to the rebuilding of trust between victims and offenders. While not all cases result in reconciliation, the process can lay the groundwork for future understanding and forgiveness.

Emphasizing Restorative Principles: VOM embodies key restorative justice principles, including victim-centeredness, offender accountability, and community involvement. It exemplifies how restorative practices can transform the justice process.

Victim-offender mediation is important within restorative justice because it provides a structured and empathetic platform for victims and offenders to engage in direct communication. It serves as a means of healing for victims, a vehicle for offender accountability, and a path toward reducing recidivism and promoting positive change.

Restitution and Community Service:

Restitution and community service are imperative restorative justice practices within the criminal justice system for several reasons:

Addressing Tangible Harm: Restitution requires offenders to compensate victims for financial losses resulting from the crime. This addresses the concrete and tangible harm suffered by victims, such as property damage or stolen goods. It aligns with the restorative justice principle of repairing harm.

Victim-Centered Approach: Restitution is victim-centered, as it directly benefits victims by reimbursing them for their losses. It empowers victims by holding offenders accountable for the financial consequences of their actions.

Promoting Accountability: Restitution and community service hold offenders accountable for their behavior. Offenders are required to take responsibility for the harm they caused, which can contribute to their personal growth and understanding of the impact of their actions.

Making Amends: These practices provide a means for offenders to make amends to both their victims and the community. By fulfilling their restitution obligations and engaging in community service, offenders actively contribute to repairing the harm they caused.

Community Involvement: Community service involves offenders in activities that benefit the community. This engagement can be restorative for both the offender and the community, as it encourages a sense of responsibility and civic participation.

Alternative to Incarceration: Restitution and community service can serve as alternatives to incarceration for non-violent offenders. This can reduce the strain on the prison system and allow offenders to remain in the community while making amends.

Positive Outcomes: Research has shown that restitution and community service programs can lead to positive outcomes, including victim satisfaction, reduced recidivism rates, and the restoration of community trust.

Restorative Justice Principles: These practices embody key restorative justice principles by emphasizing victim needs, offender accountability, and community involvement in the justice process.

In summary, restitution and community service are imperative within restorative justice because they provide concrete means for addressing the harm caused by offenders, promoting accountability, and actively involving offenders in repairing the harm they've done to victims and communities. These practices contribute to the broader goals of restorative justice by fostering healing, personal growth, and community restoration.

Restorative Sentencing:

Restorative sentencing is an approach within the criminal justice system that considers restorative justice principles when determining the appropriate sentences for offenders. It focuses on rehabilitation, community reintegration, and victim restoration, rather than solely punitive measures. Here are key aspects of restorative sentencing:

Individualized Sentencing: Restorative sentencing seeks to tailor sentences to the specific needs and circumstances of each offender. It takes into account factors such as the nature of the offense, the offender's level of responsibility, and the harm caused to victims and the community.

Rehabilitation: One of the central goals of restorative sentencing is the rehabilitation of offenders. Rather than solely punitive measures, it aims to address the underlying causes of criminal behavior and support offenders in making positive changes in their lives.

Community Reintegration: Restorative sentencing encourages the reintegration of offenders into the community. It recognizes that offenders are part of the community and that their successful reintegration benefits both the individual and society as a whole.

Victim Restoration: Victim restoration is a key component of restorative sentencing. It involves efforts to repair the harm caused to victims, including restitution, victim-offender mediation, and opportunities for victims to have a say in the sentencing process.

Accountability: Restorative sentencing holds offenders accountable for their actions. Offenders are encouraged to take responsibility for the harm they've caused, acknowledge the impact on victims, and work towards making amends.

Community Involvement: Restorative sentencing may involve the community in the process. Community members, including victims, may participate in decision-making regarding the appropriate sentencing options for offenders.

Alternatives to Incarceration: Restorative sentencing explores alternatives to incarceration, especially for non-violent offenders. These alternatives may include probation, community service, restitution, or restorative justice programs.

Reducing Recidivism: By focusing on rehabilitation and addressing the root causes of criminal behavior, restorative sentencing aims to reduce recidivism rates, contributing to safer communities.

Restorative Justice Principles: Restorative sentencing aligns with key restorative justice principles, such as victim-centeredness, offender accountability, and community involvement in the justice process.

In summary, restorative sentencing is an approach that seeks to balance the interests of justice, rehabilitation, and community well-being. It recognizes that the traditional punitive model of sentencing may not always be the most effective way to address the complex issues surrounding criminal behavior and seeks to promote healing and restoration for all parties involved.

Challenges and Criticisms:

Integrating restorative justice into the criminal justice system is not without its challenges and criticisms. Some of the common challenges and criticisms include:

Consistency: Critics argue that restorative justice practices may lack consistency in sentencing and outcomes compared to traditional punitive approaches. The level of restitution or amends-making can vary depending on the participants and the nature of the offense.

Due Process: Restorative justice processes may be seen as less formal and structured than traditional court proceedings, leading to concerns about due process and the protection of individuals' rights, particularly for offenders.

Victim Participation: While victim participation is a core principle of restorative justice, some victims may be reluctant or unwilling to engage in restorative processes, potentially limiting the applicability of these practices.

Resource Intensive: Implementing restorative justice programs within the criminal justice system can require additional resources, including trained facilitators and mediators, which some jurisdictions may struggle to provide.

Offender Accountability: Critics argue that restorative justice may not always hold offenders sufficiently accountable for their actions, especially in cases where offenders do not take responsibility or make meaningful amends.

Risk Assessment: Determining which cases are suitable for restorative justice processes can be challenging. Assessing the risk posed by offenders and ensuring the safety of all participants is crucial.

Resistance to Change: Resistance to change within the criminal justice system, both among practitioners and the public, can hinder the widespread adoption of restorative justice practices.

To address these challenges and criticisms, it is important to:

Develop Clear Guidelines: Establish clear guidelines and standards for restorative justice processes to ensure consistency, fairness, and due process.

Provide Training: Train criminal justice professionals, including judges, lawyers, and probation officers, in restorative justice principles and practices.

Offer Victim Support: Ensure that victims are provided with adequate support and information to make informed decisions about participating in restorative processes.

Monitor Outcomes: Continuously evaluate the effectiveness of restorative justice programs and processes in achieving their intended goals, including reducing recidivism and improving victim satisfaction.

Promote Public Awareness: Educate the public about the benefits and limitations of restorative justice and address misconceptions or misunderstandings.

Tailor Approaches: Recognize that restorative justice is not a one-size-fits-all solution and tailor approaches to the specific needs and circumstances of each case.

In summary, while there are challenges and criticisms associated with integrating restorative justice into the criminal justice system, these can be addressed through careful planning, training, and ongoing evaluation. Restorative justice offers the potential for more victim-centered, rehabilitative, and community-oriented approaches to addressing crime and its impact.

Training and Education:

Training and education in restorative justice principles and practices are critically important for several reasons:

Awareness and Understanding: Training programs provide criminal justice professionals with a deep understanding of the principles and philosophy of restorative justice. This awareness helps them appreciate the potential benefits of restorative approaches and how they differ from traditional punitive methods.

Appropriate Application: Education ensures that criminal justice professionals can accurately assess cases and determine when restorative justice processes are suitable. This prevents inappropriate or ineffective use of restorative practices.

Legal Framework: Training helps professionals understand the legal framework and standards associated with restorative justice, ensuring that restorative processes comply with legal requirements and due process.

Communication Skills: Restorative justice often involves direct communication between victims and offenders. Training equips professionals with the necessary communication and mediation skills to facilitate these dialogues effectively.

Cultural Competency: Cultural sensitivity and competency are crucial in restorative justice, as participants may come from diverse backgrounds. Training programs teach professionals how to navigate cultural differences and ensure inclusivity.

Victim-Centered Approach: Restorative justice places victims at the center of the process. Training helps criminal justice professionals adopt a victim-centered mindset, ensuring that victims' needs, concerns, and rights are respected.

Reducing Recidivism: By understanding the underlying causes of criminal behavior and how restorative practices address these causes, professionals can contribute to reducing recidivism rates in their communities.

Community Engagement: Criminal justice professionals play a role in engaging the community in restorative justice initiatives. Training equips them with the skills to collaborate with community organizations and promote the benefits of restorative justice.

Conflict Resolution: Restorative justice is fundamentally about resolving conflicts and repairing harm. Training in conflict resolution techniques is essential for professionals to effectively navigate the restorative justice process.

Ethical Considerations: Restorative justice involves complex ethical considerations. Education helps professionals navigate these ethical dilemmas and make decisions that prioritize justice and fairness.

Continuous Improvement: The field of restorative justice is continually evolving. Ongoing training and education ensure that professionals stay informed about new developments, best practices, and emerging research in the field.

In summary, training and education are essential components of integrating restorative justice into the criminal justice system. They equip professionals with the knowledge, skills, and ethical awareness needed to apply restorative principles effectively, ultimately contributing to more just and healing outcomes for victims, offenders, and communities.

CHAPTER 12

Restorative Practices in Education

Restorative Practices in Education refers to an approach to school discipline and community-building that focuses on repairing harm, building relationships, and fostering a sense of belonging within the educational environment. It aims to transform the traditional punitive disciplinary methods used in schools into a more restorative and relationship-centered approach.

Key aspects of Restorative Practices in Education include:

1. Conflict Resolution: Restorative practices provide strategies for resolving conflicts and addressing incidents of harm in a constructive manner. This often involves bringing together those affected by an issue, including students, teachers, and sometimes parents, in a facilitated dialogue to discuss the impact of the behavior, find solutions, and promote understanding.

2. Community-Building: Restorative practices aim to create a positive and inclusive school culture where all members feel valued and connected. Activities such as community circles, restorative meetings, and peer support programs help build strong relationships among students, teachers, and staff.

3. Accountability: Rather than simply punishing students for rule violations, restorative practices encourage students to take responsibility for their actions and make amends. This accountability is typically achieved through meaningful dialogue and restitution to those affected.

4. Empathy and Active Listening: Restorative processes prioritize empathy and active listening, helping individuals understand one another's perspectives and feelings. This fosters greater compassion and better communication within the school community.

5. Prevention of Harm: Restorative practices seek to prevent harm by addressing underlying issues and conflicts before they escalate. By providing a platform for open communication, schools can identify and resolve issues proactively.

6. Alternatives to Punitive Measures: Restorative practices offer alternatives to traditional punitive measures like suspension and expulsion. These alternatives focus on rehabilitation, reintegration, and skill-building rather than exclusionary punishment.

7. Data-Driven Improvement: Many schools that implement restorative practices use data and assessments to measure their impact. This data can help track improvements in behavior, school climate, and academic performance.

8. Professional Development: Educators and school staff often receive training in restorative practices to effectively implement them within the school community. This training helps build a restorative justice mindset among staff members.

Overall, Restorative Practices in Education are designed to create a safe and supportive learning environment where conflicts are addressed constructively, relationships are nurtured, and students are encouraged to take responsibility for their actions. It promotes a sense of belonging and aims to improve overall school culture and the well-being of both students and educators.

Understanding Restorative Practices in Education is crucial for several reasons:

1. Promotes Positive School Culture: Restorative practices are instrumental in creating a positive and inclusive school culture. They help students and staff feel a sense of belonging and connectedness within the school community, which contributes to a healthier learning environment.

2. Effective Conflict Resolution: Restorative practices provide schools with effective tools for resolving conflicts and addressing incidents of harm. By understanding these practices, educators can facilitate constructive dialogues that lead to better conflict resolution and reduced disciplinary issues.

3. Reduces Exclusionary Discipline: Traditional punitive discipline measures like suspension and expulsion often lead to students' disengagement and increased likelihood of future misbehavior. Restorative practices offer an alternative approach that reduces the reliance on exclusionary discipline, keeping students connected to the educational system.

4. Fosters Empathy and Communication: Restorative practices prioritize empathy and active listening. When educators understand and implement these principles, they can teach students valuable skills in communication, empathy, and conflict resolution, which are beneficial in both academic and personal life.

5. Enhances Teacher-Student Relationships: Restorative practices can improve teacher-student relationships. When teachers use restorative methods to address conflicts, students perceive them as more approachable and supportive, fostering a more positive teacher-student dynamic.

6. Prevents Escalation of Issues: Restorative practices emphasize the prevention of harm and the early resolution of conflicts. By recognizing the importance of these preventative measures, schools can reduce the escalation of issues and create a safer learning environment.

7. Promotes Accountability: Restorative practices encourage students to take responsibility for their actions and make amends.

Understanding these practices helps educators instill a sense of accountability in students, a valuable life skill.

8. Supports Academic Success: A positive school culture and effective conflict resolution contribute to a conducive learning environment. When students feel safe, connected, and valued, they are more likely to engage in their studies and achieve academic success.

9. Reduces Disparities: Restorative practices have been shown to reduce discipline disparities among different student groups, particularly marginalized communities. Understanding and implementing these practices can contribute to more equitable educational outcomes.

In summary, understanding restorative practices in education is essential for educators, administrators, and students alike. It not only promotes a more positive and inclusive school culture but also equips individuals with valuable skills for conflict resolution, communication, and personal growth.

Building a positive school culture through restorative practices is of paramount importance for several reasons:

1. Enhanced Student Engagement: Restorative practices create an environment where students feel heard and valued. When students are engaged and feel a sense of belonging, they are more motivated to participate actively in their learning and extracurricular activities.

2. Improved Teacher-Student Relationships: Restorative practices emphasize open communication, empathy, and active listening. When teachers use these practices, it fosters stronger teacher-student relationships. Students are more likely to approach teachers with questions or concerns, creating a supportive learning atmosphere.

3. Conflict Resolution: Restorative practices provide effective conflict resolution tools. When conflicts arise, these practices offer a structured and constructive way to address them. This not only resolves issues but also teaches students how to handle disagreements in a healthy manner.

4. Reduced Behavior Problems: By focusing on the underlying causes of misbehavior and addressing them through restorative processes,

schools can reduce behavior problems. Punitive approaches may suppress behavior temporarily, but restorative practices aim to get to the root of the issue, leading to long-term behavior improvement.·

5. Positive Peer Relationships: Restorative practices also promote positive peer relationships. When students learn to communicate, empathize, and resolve conflicts restoratively, they build stronger bonds with their peers. This reduces bullying and fosters a sense of community.

6. Safe Learning Environment: A positive school culture created through restorative practices contributes to a safe learning environment. When students feel safe emotionally and physically, they are better able to focus on their studies and personal growth.

7. Increased Teacher Satisfaction: Teachers who implement restorative practices often report higher job satisfaction. These practices provide teachers with tools to manage classroom conflicts and create a more enjoyable teaching experience.

8. Parental Engagement: Restorative practices can extend beyond the classroom to involve parents and caregivers. When parents see the positive impact of restorative practices on their children's education, they may become more engaged in school activities and support their child's learning journey.

9. Holistic Development: Restorative practices align with the holistic development of students. They teach valuable life skills such as empathy, active listening, and conflict resolution, which are not only applicable in school but also in various aspects of students' lives.

In summary, building a positive school culture through restorative practices contributes to a nurturing and supportive educational environment. It enhances student engagement, strengthens relationships, and fosters holistic development while reducing behavior problems and conflicts. Ultimately, it creates a space where students can thrive academically and personally.

Implementing restorative circles in education is important for several reasons:

1. Open Communication: Restorative circles create a safe space for open and honest communication. They provide students and teachers with a structured format to share their thoughts, feelings, and experiences. This open dialogue is essential for building trust and resolving conflicts.

2. Conflict Resolution: Restorative circles are a powerful tool for resolving conflicts. When conflicts arise among students or between students and teachers, these circles offer a structured process to address the issues constructively. Instead of punitive measures, students are encouraged to understand each other's perspectives and find mutually agreeable solutions.

3. Community-Building: Restorative circles foster a sense of community within the classroom. They allow students to get to know each other on a deeper level, promoting empathy and understanding. As students share their stories and experiences, they build stronger connections with their peers and teachers.

4. Improved Relationships: By facilitating restorative circles, teachers can improve their relationships with students. It demonstrates that teachers are willing to listen, understand, and support their students. This, in turn, can lead to more positive teacher-student relationships.

5. Social and Emotional Learning: Restorative circles align with social and emotional learning (SEL) goals. They help students develop important SEL skills such as active listening, empathy, self-awareness, and responsible decision-making. These skills are valuable not only in the classroom but also in students' lives outside of school.

6. Conflict Prevention: By regularly using restorative circles, educators can create a proactive approach to conflict prevention. When students become accustomed to open communication and conflict resolution, they are more likely to address issues before they escalate into larger problems.

7. Increased Participation: Restorative circles encourage participation from all students. In a traditional classroom setting, some students may be hesitant to speak up or share their thoughts. Restorative circles provide an inclusive platform where every voice is heard and valued.

8. Cultural Sensitivity: Restorative circles can be adapted to respect and honor various cultural perspectives. This makes them an inclusive practice that recognizes and values diversity within the classroom.

9. Positive School Culture: When implemented consistently, restorative circles contribute to a positive school culture. They create an environment where students feel valued, respected, and heard, which is essential for a healthy and thriving learning community.

10. Conflict Resolution Skills: Restorative circles teach students essential conflict resolution skills that they can carry with them throughout their lives. These skills are applicable in personal relationships, the workplace, and broader society.

In summary, implementing restorative circles in education is essential for promoting open communication, conflict resolution, community-building, and positive relationships within the classroom. It aligns with social and emotional learning goals and equips students with valuable life skills. Additionally, it contributes to a more inclusive and culturally sensitive school environment.

Addressing conflicts and harm within the school community is of significant importance for several reasons:

1. Conflict Resolution: Conflict is a natural part of human interaction, including within school settings. However, when conflicts are not addressed promptly and constructively, they can escalate and disrupt the learning environment. Restorative practices provide a structured approach to resolve conflicts, ensuring that all parties involved have the opportunity to express their feelings, needs, and perspectives. This can lead to mutually acceptable solutions and a more peaceful school atmosphere.

2. Accountability: Restorative practices emphasize individual accountability for one's actions. When harm occurs, whether it's a student-to-student conflict or a violation of school rules, restorative conferences and dialogues hold individuals accountable for their behavior. This accountability extends to understanding the impact of their actions on others and taking steps to make amends.

3. Empathy and Understanding: Restorative processes promote empathy and understanding among students, teachers, and administrators. Participants are encouraged to listen actively to each other's experiences and feelings. This helps build empathy as individuals gain insight into the perspectives of others. Understanding each other's viewpoints can lead to greater compassion and cooperation.

4. Relationship Building: Addressing harm and conflicts restoratively can contribute to relationship building within the school community. When individuals engage in dialogue and work together to resolve issues, it strengthens their connections. Stronger relationships among students, between students and teachers, and among school staff members can create a more supportive and cohesive learning environment.

5. Prevention of Escalation: Early intervention through restorative practices can prevent conflicts and harm from escalating into more serious issues. By addressing problems promptly, schools can prevent a negative cycle of ongoing disputes and create a climate where students feel safe and supported.

6. Personal Growth: Restorative practices offer opportunities for personal growth and development. When individuals take responsibility for their actions, learn from their mistakes, and actively participate in making amends, they can experience personal growth and increased self-awareness.

7. Community Building: Restorative practices contribute to a sense of community within the school. When students and staff come together to address conflicts and harm, it reinforces the idea that everyone has a stake in creating a positive school environment. This shared responsibility fosters a stronger sense of belonging.

8. Conflict Prevention: By addressing conflicts and harm restoratively, schools can take a proactive approach to conflict prevention. When students become familiar with restorative processes, they are more likely to use them to address issues before they escalate into larger conflicts.

9. Learning Opportunities: Restorative conferences and dialogues provide valuable learning opportunities for all participants. Students learn

communication skills, conflict resolution techniques, and the importance of empathy and accountability. These skills are transferable and can benefit students in various aspects of their lives.

In summary, addressing conflicts and harm through restorative practices is significant because it promotes conflict resolution, accountability, empathy, relationship building, personal growth, and a sense of community within the school. It also helps prevent conflicts from escalating and provides valuable learning opportunities for all involved.

Restorative discipline and alternatives to suspension are significant components of restorative practices in education. Here's why they are important:

1. Maintaining Educational Engagement: One of the primary goals of restorative discipline and alternatives to suspension is to keep students engaged in their education. When students are suspended or expelled, they are removed from the learning environment, which can have negative consequences for their academic progress. Restorative practices allow students to remain connected to the school community while addressing and learning from their behavior.

2. Addressing Root Causes: Restorative discipline focuses on understanding the underlying reasons for a student's misconduct. Instead of simply punishing the behavior, it seeks to identify the root causes, which could include issues such as trauma, family problems, or emotional struggles. By addressing these root causes through restorative processes, schools have an opportunity to provide support and interventions that can lead to behavioral change.

3. Promoting Accountability: Restorative practices emphasize accountability for one's actions. Students are encouraged to take responsibility for their behavior and its impact on others. This accountability extends to making amends and repairing harm, which can be more meaningful and transformative than traditional punitive consequences.

4. Building Empathy: Restorative discipline often involves dialogue between the wrongdoer and those affected by their actions. These

dialogues can help build empathy, as students hear directly from others about the impact of their behavior. This can lead to greater understanding and a commitment to positive change.

5. Conflict Resolution: Restorative conferences and processes provide a structured way to resolve conflicts and address harm. They allow students to discuss the issues that led to the misconduct and work together to find solutions. This can lead to the restoration of relationships and a more peaceful school environment.

6. Reducing Disparities: Traditional disciplinary methods like suspension and expulsion have been criticized for disproportionately affecting students from marginalized backgrounds, including students of color. Restorative discipline aims to reduce these disparities by providing a more equitable approach to addressing misconduct.

7. Positive School Culture: By emphasizing accountability, empathy, and conflict resolution, restorative discipline contributes to a positive school culture. It creates an environment where students feel heard, supported, and encouraged to make positive choices. This, in turn, can lead to a safer and more inclusive school community.

8. Teaching Life Skills: Restorative practices teach students valuable life skills, including communication, conflict resolution, and emotional regulation. These skills are not only important for their behavior within the school but also in their future personal and professional lives.

9. Preventing Recidivism: Addressing the root causes of misconduct and promoting accountability can help prevent recidivism or repeated misbehavior. Restorative practices aim to address the underlying issues that may lead to continued behavioral problems.

In summary, restorative discipline and alternatives to suspension are important in education because they prioritize maintaining educational engagement, addressing root causes of misconduct, promoting accountability and empathy, resolving conflicts, reducing disparities, fostering a positive school culture, teaching life skills, and preventing recidivism. These practices align with the restorative justice principles of repairing harm and promoting healing and reconciliation.

Measuring the impact and outcomes of restorative practices in education is crucial for several reasons:

1. Evidence-Based Decision-Making: Measuring the impact allows educators and administrators to make evidence-based decisions about the effectiveness of restorative practices. By collecting data and assessing outcomes, they can determine whether these practices are achieving their intended goals.

2. Accountability: Restorative practices often involve setting goals for behavioral improvement and conflict resolution. Measuring outcomes holds both students and educators accountable for progress toward these goals. It helps ensure that everyone involved is committed to the process.

3. Continuous Improvement: Assessment and measurement provide insights into what is working and what needs improvement. Schools can use this information to refine their restorative practices, making them more effective over time. Continuous improvement is essential for the sustainability and success of these approaches.

4. Demonstrating Impact: Quantifiable data on improved behavior, reduced suspensions, and enhanced school climate can be powerful tools for demonstrating the impact of restorative practices to stakeholders, including parents, school boards, and the community. This can garner support and resources for further implementation.

5. Identifying Areas of Need: Measurement can reveal specific areas where restorative practices are having the most significant impact and areas that require additional attention. For example, it may show that restorative practices are particularly effective in reducing bullying incidents but need refinement in addressing classroom disruptions.

6. Enhancing School Climate: Restorative practices aim to create a positive and inclusive school climate. Measuring outcomes related to school climate, such as student surveys on safety and belonging, can provide valuable insights into whether these practices are achieving this goal.

7. Supporting Students' Well-Being: Restorative practices are not only about behavioral outcomes but also about supporting students' overall well-being. Assessment can help gauge changes in students' emotional and social development, including their self-esteem, conflict resolution skills, and emotional regulation.

8. Evidence for Scaling: When schools and districts consider expanding restorative practices, having measurable outcomes from initial implementations can serve as a foundation for scaling up these approaches. It provides evidence of their effectiveness and guides decision-making in expanding to new areas.

9. Professional Development: Measuring outcomes can inform the professional development needs of educators and restorative justice facilitators. It helps identify areas where additional training or support may be required to maximize the impact of these practices.

In summary, measuring the impact and outcomes of restorative practices in education is essential for evidence-based decision-making, accountability, continuous improvement, demonstrating impact, identifying areas of need, enhancing school climate, supporting students' well-being, supporting scaling efforts, and informing professional development. It ensures that restorative practices are effective in achieving their intended goals of promoting healing, reconciliation, and positive behavior within the school community.

Training and professional development in restorative justice are critically important for several reasons:

1. Skill Development: Restorative justice practices require specific skills, such as active listening, effective communication, and facilitating restorative processes like circles and conferences. Training provides educators and school staff with the necessary skills to implement these practices effectively.

2. Understanding Restorative Principles: Restorative justice is founded on principles like empathy, accountability, and healing. Training helps educators understand these principles and how they differ from

punitive approaches. It fosters a deeper appreciation for the underlying philosophy of restorative justice.

3. Confidence and Competence: Restorative justice processes can be challenging to facilitate, especially when addressing sensitive issues or conflicts. Training builds educators' confidence in their ability to navigate these situations and competence in applying restorative techniques.

4. Consistency: To ensure the fair and consistent application of restorative practices within a school or district, all staff members involved should receive training. This consistency is essential for building trust and maintaining the integrity of the restorative justice program.

5. Cultural Sensitivity: Training can include modules on cultural sensitivity, helping educators understand and respect the diverse cultural backgrounds of their students. This knowledge is vital for adapting restorative practices to meet the unique needs of different communities.

6. Conflict Resolution: Restorative justice is a powerful tool for conflict resolution, and training equips educators with conflict resolution skills that can be applied not only within the classroom but also in their personal and professional lives.

7. Trauma-Informed Practices: Many students may have experienced trauma, and a trauma-informed approach is essential within a restorative justice framework. Training can provide educators with insights into trauma and strategies for supporting students who have been affected.

8. Reducing Bias: Training can address biases that may impact decision-making within the restorative justice process. Educators can learn to recognize and mitigate biases, ensuring a fair and equitable process for all students.

9. Professional Growth: Restorative justice training contributes to the professional growth of educators. It offers them new perspectives and tools for fostering positive relationships, enhancing classroom management, and promoting a more inclusive and respectful school culture.

10. Effective Implementation: To achieve the intended benefits of restorative justice, educators must understand how to implement these practices effectively. Training ensures that restorative justice is not just a theoretical concept but a practical and impactful approach.

11. Continual Improvement: The field of restorative justice is evolving, and ongoing professional development keeps educators up-to-date with the latest research and best practices. It supports the continual improvement of restorative justice initiatives within schools.

In summary, training and professional development are essential components of a successful restorative justice program in education. They equip educators and school staff with the skills, knowledge, and mindset needed to implement restorative practices effectively, promote a positive school culture, and support the well-being of students.

CHAPTER 13

Restorative Approaches in Family and Relationship

Restorative Approaches in Family and Relationships

Restorative Approaches in Family and Relationships refer to the application of restorative justice principles and practices within the context of familial and personal relationships. It involves using restorative processes to address conflicts, repair harm, and promote healing and reconciliation among family members. Unlike punitive or adversarial approaches, restorative practices prioritize open communication, empathy, accountability, and the restoration of relationships.

In this context, restorative approaches can include various processes and techniques, such as family conferences, dialogues, and mediations. These processes aim to create a safe and supportive space where family members can come together to discuss issues, share their perspectives, and work collaboratively towards resolution.

Key elements of restorative approaches in family and relationships may include:

1. Empathy: Encouraging family members to understand each other's feelings, experiences, and needs to foster empathy and connection.

2. Accountability: Holding individuals responsible for their actions and the harm they may have caused to others within the family.

3. Healing: Focusing on the emotional and psychological healing of family members who may have been affected by conflicts or harm.

4. Communication: Facilitating open and respectful communication to promote understanding and resolution.

5. Reconciliation: Aiming to rebuild trust, repair damaged relationships, and create a more harmonious family environment.

6. Prevention: Using restorative practices to address conflicts proactively and prevent them from escalating into more significant issues.

Restorative approaches in family and relationships recognize that conflicts and harm are inevitable in any close-knit group, but they seek to transform these challenges into opportunities for growth, understanding, and strengthening family bonds. These practices align with the broader principles of restorative justice by emphasizing the importance of repairing harm, promoting accountability, and restoring relationships within the family context.

Conflict Resolution: The chapter explores how restorative practices offer an alternative and more constructive approach to resolving conflicts within families. Rather than resorting to punitive measures or avoiding conflicts altogether, restorative approaches encourage family members to engage in open and honest dialogue. They facilitate communication and active listening, allowing individuals to express their feelings and concerns, leading to a deeper understanding of each other's perspectives.

Repairing Harm: When conflicts or harm occur within families, restorative practices provide a structured framework for addressing the consequences and repairing the damage. This can include acknowledging the harm caused, taking responsibility for one's actions, and making amends. These processes not only help hold individuals accountable but also contribute to the emotional and psychological healing of those affected by the harm.

Promoting Reconciliation: The chapter highlights how restorative approaches prioritize reconciliation and the restoration of trust and relationships within families. By emphasizing empathy, understanding, and forgiveness, these practices aim to rebuild the bonds between family members that may have been strained or broken due to conflicts or harm. Through facilitated discussions and restorative processes, family members can work towards resolving underlying issues and moving forward in a more harmonious and connected way.

Preventing Future Conflicts: Beyond addressing existing conflicts, the chapter also discusses how restorative practices can be used proactively to prevent future conflicts within families. By creating a culture of open communication, empathy, and accountability, families can reduce the likelihood of disputes escalating and harming relationships. Restorative approaches provide families with the tools to address minor disagreements and misunderstandings before they escalate into more significant issues.

Overall, the chapter underscores the transformative potential of restorative practices within family and personal relationships. It highlights the importance of empathy, accountability, and healing in strengthening family bonds, resolving conflicts constructively, and fostering reconciliation among family members. Through real-life examples and case studies, it illustrates how restorative approaches have helped families navigate challenges and emerge with stronger, more connected relationships.

Certainly, understanding restorative approaches within the context of family and relationship dynamics is essential to grasp their significance and potential impact. Here's an explanation:

Restorative Approaches in Family and Relationship Dynamics: Restorative approaches within the context of family and relationships refer to a set of practices and principles aimed at addressing conflicts, repairing harm, and promoting reconciliation within familial and interpersonal relationships. These approaches are inspired by the broader framework of restorative justice, which prioritizes healing, accountability, and empathetic communication as means to resolve disputes and strengthen relationships.

Core Principles of Restorative Justice in Families:

1. Empathy: Empathy lies at the heart of restorative approaches within families. It involves the capacity to understand and share the feelings and perspectives of family members involved in conflicts. Restorative processes encourage family members to genuinely listen to each other, fostering empathy and helping individuals connect on a deeper level.

2. Accountability: Accountability in restorative family dynamics involves acknowledging one's actions and their impact on others. When conflicts arise, family members are encouraged to take responsibility for their behavior and its consequences. Accountability is not punitive but focuses on understanding the harm caused and finding ways to make amends.

3. Healing: Healing is a fundamental principle, emphasizing the importance of emotional and psychological well-being within familial relationships. Restorative approaches aim to facilitate healing by providing a safe space for family members to express their emotions, address unresolved issues, and work toward resolving conflicts in ways that promote emotional recovery.

4. Communication: Open and honest communication is a cornerstone of restorative approaches. Rather than suppressing conflicts or resorting to blame, family members are encouraged to engage in constructive dialogue. This communication helps identify underlying issues, express needs and feelings, and find mutually agreeable solutions.

5. Reconciliation: Restorative processes actively seek to promote reconciliation within families. This goes beyond merely resolving conflicts; it involves rebuilding trust, restoring damaged relationships, and fostering a sense of unity among family members. Reconciliation is the ultimate goal, where family members can move forward with a stronger and more harmonious bond.

In summary, restorative approaches in family and relationship dynamics draw from the principles of restorative justice, emphasizing empathy, accountability, healing, open communication, and reconciliation as essential components of resolving conflicts and nurturing healthier, more connected familial relationships. These principles recognize the transformative potential of restorative practices to strengthen bonds and promote emotional well-being within families.

Building Healthy Family Relationships through Restorative Practices:

Restorative practices play a crucial role in building and maintaining healthy family relationships by fostering open communication, resolving conflicts constructively, and promoting empathy and understanding among family members. Here's how these practices contribute to strengthening family bonds:

1. Restorative Communication: Restorative communication emphasizes active listening and empathetic dialogue. In the family context, this means family members are encouraged to listen to each other without judgment, to understand each other's perspectives and feelings fully. By creating a space for everyone to be heard and valued, restorative communication helps family members feel acknowledged and respected, strengthening their emotional connection.

2. Conflict Resolution: Conflicts are inevitable in any family, but how they are handled can significantly impact relationships. Restorative conflict resolution techniques provide a structured and non-confrontational approach to addressing conflicts. Family members are guided through a process that allows them to express their grievances, identify the underlying issues, and collaboratively seek solutions. This approach promotes problem-solving and reduces the likelihood of conflicts escalating into harmful disputes.

3. Active Listening: Active listening is a key component of restorative practices. It involves giving full attention to the speaker, asking clarifying questions, and validating their feelings. In families, active listening helps family members feel heard and understood, even when they

disagree. It creates an atmosphere of respect and empathy, making it easier to find common ground and resolve issues.

4. Empathy: Restorative practices emphasize the development of empathy, which is crucial in family relationships. Encouraging family members to see situations from each other's perspectives promotes empathy and understanding. When family members can genuinely empathize with one another's feelings and experiences, it becomes easier to forgive, heal, and move forward after conflicts.

5. Conflict Prevention: Restorative practices are not only reactive but also proactive. By fostering a culture of open communication and empathy within the family, these practices can prevent conflicts from escalating. Family members learn to express their needs and concerns early, reducing the likelihood of misunderstandings and resentments.

6. Strengthening Trust: Trust is the foundation of healthy family relationships. Restorative practices help rebuild and strengthen trust when it's been damaged by conflicts or breaches of trust. When family members engage in open and honest dialogue, take responsibility for their actions, and work toward resolution, trust can be restored over time.

In summary, restorative practices contribute to building and maintaining healthy family relationships by providing a structured framework for communication, conflict resolution, and empathy development. These practices create a supportive and understanding family environment where conflicts are seen as opportunities for growth and deeper connection rather than as threats to the relationship.

The Importance of Addressing Family Conflicts through Restorative Processes:

Addressing family conflicts is crucial for maintaining healthy relationships and ensuring the well-being of all family members. Restorative processes play a significant role in this context by providing a structured and empathetic approach to resolving disputes. Here's why addressing family conflicts through restorative practices is essential:

1. Preserving Family Bonds: Family conflicts, if left unaddressed, can lead to strained relationships, emotional distance, and even estrangement among family members. Restorative processes create a safe space for family members to communicate, express their feelings, and work towards resolution. This helps preserve the bonds that are essential for a supportive and nurturing family environment.

2. Conflict Resolution Skills: Restorative processes teach family members valuable conflict resolution skills. These skills go beyond resolving the current conflict; they equip individuals with the tools needed to address future conflicts in a constructive manner. Learning how to communicate effectively, listen actively, and seek mutually acceptable solutions can lead to healthier family dynamics.

3. Emotional Healing: Family conflicts often result in emotional wounds. Restorative processes provide an opportunity for emotional healing by allowing family members to express their hurt, anger, and frustration in a safe and structured setting. Acknowledging these emotions and finding ways to address them can promote healing and reconciliation within the family.

4. Accountability and Responsibility: Restorative practices encourage individuals to take responsibility for their actions and their role in conflicts. This accountability is essential for rebuilding trust within the family. When family members acknowledge their mistakes and actively participate in finding solutions, it fosters a sense of fairness and justice.

5. Effective Communication: Many family conflicts arise from miscommunication or misunderstandings. Restorative processes emphasize effective communication techniques, such as active listening and empathetic dialogue. These skills enhance family members' ability to express themselves clearly and understand each other's perspectives.

6. Preventing Escalation: Unresolved family conflicts can escalate over time, leading to more significant issues and emotional distress. Restorative processes provide an early intervention strategy, preventing conflicts from worsening and becoming more challenging to resolve. This

proactive approach is essential for maintaining a harmonious family environment.

7. Promoting Growth: Family conflicts can offer opportunities for personal and relational growth. Restorative processes encourage individuals to reflect on their behaviors and choices, leading to personal insights and growth. Additionally, finding resolutions together can strengthen family bonds and resilience.

8. Resolving Deep-Seated Issues: Some family conflicts may be rooted in deep-seated issues, such as long-standing misunderstandings or unresolved past traumas. Restorative processes allow families to address these underlying issues and work towards lasting resolutions, rather than merely addressing surface-level disputes.

In summary, addressing family conflicts through restorative processes is essential for preserving family relationships, promoting emotional healing, teaching conflict resolution skills, and preventing the escalation of disputes. By embracing restorative practices, families can create a supportive and nurturing environment where conflicts are seen as opportunities for growth and strengthening relationships.

Healing and Reconciliation in Restorative Justice within Family Relationships:

Healing and reconciliation are fundamental aspects of restorative justice, particularly when applied within family relationships. Here's an exploration of these concepts and their significance:

1. Acknowledging Harm: Healing within the context of restorative justice begins with the acknowledgment of harm. Family members must recognize and understand the impact of their actions or conflicts on one another. This step is essential because it validates the experiences of those who have been hurt, providing them with a voice and an opportunity to be heard.

2. Seeking Forgiveness: Forgiveness plays a vital role in the healing and reconciliation process. It involves the willingness to let go of resentment and anger towards the person who caused harm. In family relationships, forgiveness can be a profound act of love and

understanding. Restorative processes encourage family members to express their apologies and seek forgiveness, creating opportunities for emotional repair.

3. Rebuilding Trust: Trust is a cornerstone of healthy family relationships. When harm occurs within the family, trust can be significantly eroded. Healing and reconciliation involve rebuilding this trust through consistent and trustworthy actions. Restorative justice processes provide a structured framework for family members to commit to specific actions that demonstrate their sincerity in making amends and rebuilding trust.

4. Communication and Understanding: Healing and reconciliation often require open and empathetic communication. Restorative practices facilitate dialogues where family members can express their feelings, concerns, and expectations. These conversations promote mutual understanding, empathy, and the ability to see situations from different perspectives.

5. Resolution and Closure: Healing is often associated with finding resolutions to conflicts and disputes. Through restorative processes, families can collaboratively identify solutions and make agreements that address the harm caused. Achieving resolution provides a sense of closure and allows family members to move forward with a shared commitment to a more harmonious relationship.

6. Preventing Recurrence: True healing and reconciliation also involve taking steps to prevent the recurrence of harm. Restorative justice emphasizes accountability and personal growth. Family members commit to changing their behaviors and addressing underlying issues that contributed to the harm. This commitment to personal growth and change is essential for preventing future conflicts.

7. Emotional Well-Being: Healing and reconciliation have a direct impact on the emotional well-being of family members. When conflicts are resolved and relationships are repaired, individuals experience relief from emotional distress, leading to improved mental health and overall family harmony.

8. Family Resilience: The healing and reconciliation process can make families more resilient. By facing and overcoming conflicts together, families develop a greater capacity to navigate future challenges. They learn valuable skills in communication, empathy, and conflict resolution that contribute to their long-term well-being.

In summary, healing and reconciliation within restorative justice for family relationships involve acknowledging harm, seeking forgiveness, rebuilding trust, promoting open communication, achieving resolution, and preventing the recurrence of conflicts. These processes contribute to emotional well-being, family resilience, and the cultivation of stronger and more harmonious family bonds.

Preventing Family Violence through Restorative Approaches:

Preventing family violence is a critical objective within the context of restorative justice. While restorative practices primarily focus on repairing harm and promoting healing, they can also be instrumental in addressing family violence by emphasizing intervention, support, and accountability. Here are some key considerations:

1. Early Intervention: Restorative justice advocates for early intervention in situations where family violence or abuse is suspected or detected. This involves identifying signs of violence and taking proactive measures to address it before it escalates. Early intervention may include providing resources and counseling to individuals at risk or those exhibiting abusive behavior.

2. Safety Planning: Ensuring the safety of victims is paramount. Restorative processes should incorporate safety planning to protect victims from further harm. This may involve developing safety plans, providing access to shelters or safe accommodations, and involving law enforcement when necessary to ensure immediate protection.

3. Victim Support Networks: Restorative justice recognizes the importance of supporting victims of family violence. Victim support networks can be established to provide emotional, legal, and practical assistance to those affected. These networks can include social workers,

counselors, and community organizations specializing in domestic violence support.

4. Accountability and Rehabilitation: Restorative approaches also focus on the accountability and rehabilitation of offenders. In cases of family violence, it's essential to hold perpetrators responsible for their actions while providing them with opportunities for rehabilitation and behavior change. This can involve court-mandated programs, anger management classes, or counseling to address the underlying causes of violent behavior.

5. Restorative Conferences: Restorative conferences can be employed as a means of addressing family violence. These structured dialogues bring together victims, offenders, and relevant stakeholders to discuss the harm caused and collaboratively determine how to repair it. Conferences can be emotionally charged but provide a safe space for expressing feelings and concerns.

6. Community Involvement: Communities play a crucial role in preventing family violence. Restorative justice encourages community involvement through awareness campaigns, educational programs, and community-led initiatives to address the root causes of violence and promote healthy relationships.

7. Cultural Competence: Recognizing the cultural context is essential, as family violence may manifest differently across cultures. Restorative justice practices should be culturally sensitive and adapted to respect the unique perspectives and needs of diverse communities.

8. Prevention Education: Restorative approaches can be integrated into prevention education programs within schools and communities. Teaching young people about healthy relationships, conflict resolution, and the consequences of violence is an effective way to prevent family violence from occurring in the future.

9. Monitoring and Evaluation: Continuous monitoring and evaluation of prevention and intervention efforts are essential to assess their effectiveness. Data collection and analysis can inform improvements in family violence prevention strategies.

10. Legal Frameworks: Collaborating with legal authorities and ensuring that legal frameworks address family violence adequately is vital. Restorative justice processes can complement existing legal mechanisms, but they should never replace necessary legal actions when crimes have been committed.

In summary, preventing family violence through restorative approaches involves early intervention, safety planning, victim support networks, offender accountability, restorative conferences, community involvement, cultural competence, prevention education, monitoring and evaluation, and collaboration with legal frameworks. By addressing family violence comprehensively, restorative justice aims to break the cycle of violence, promote healing, and foster healthier family dynamics.

Cultural and Diversity Considerations in Restorative Approaches:

Cultural and diversity considerations are crucial when implementing restorative approaches in family and relationship contexts. Recognizing and respecting diverse cultural perspectives is essential to ensure that restorative practices are inclusive and effective for all individuals and communities. Here's an overview of these considerations:

1. Cultural Sensitivity: Restorative practices should be culturally sensitive, meaning they respect and honor the cultural backgrounds and values of the individuals involved. Practitioners should be aware of cultural nuances and differences in communication styles, customs, and traditions. This sensitivity helps create an inclusive and safe environment for all participants.

2. Language and Communication: Language can be a significant barrier in restorative processes. Ensuring that communication is accessible to all parties, including those who may not be fluent in the dominant language, is vital. Interpretation services may be necessary to facilitate meaningful dialogue.

3. Traditional Practices: Some cultures have traditional conflict resolution and reconciliation practices that may align with or complement restorative justice principles. Understanding and integrating these

practices when appropriate can enhance the effectiveness of restorative approaches.

4. Cultural Values: Different cultures have varying values and priorities when it comes to family and relationships. Restorative processes should acknowledge and incorporate these values into decision-making, harm repair, and reconciliation efforts.

5. Community Involvement: Engaging with the community and cultural leaders can provide valuable insights and support for restorative processes. Community members may play roles as mediators, advisors, or advocates in family-related restorative cases.

6. Trauma-Informed Cultural Competence: Recognizing the potential trauma related to cultural or identity-based discrimination is essential. Practitioners should be trained to be trauma-informed and culturally competent, understanding how systemic oppression and discrimination may impact individuals and families.

7. Gender and Intersectionality: Intersectionality, which considers how multiple aspects of an individual's identity intersect, including race, gender, sexual orientation, and more, should be taken into account. This perspective helps practitioners understand the unique experiences and challenges faced by individuals from diverse backgrounds.

8. Cultural Adaptation: Restorative practices may need to be adapted or customized to align with cultural expectations and norms. This may involve modifying certain processes, rituals, or language to ensure that they resonate with participants from different cultural backgrounds.

9. Equity and Fairness: Cultural competence also involves addressing power imbalances that may exist within diverse communities. Practitioners should ensure that restorative processes are equitable and that marginalized voices are heard and respected.

10. Education and Training: Comprehensive training for practitioners should include cultural competency components. This training helps practitioners navigate diverse cultural contexts sensitively and effectively.

In summary, cultural and diversity considerations in restorative approaches involve being sensitive to cultural differences, adapting practices when necessary, respecting cultural values, engaging with the community, being trauma-informed, acknowledging intersectionality, promoting equity, and providing cultural competency training. By embracing diversity and cultural sensitivity, restorative justice can better serve the needs of all individuals and families, regardless of their cultural backgrounds.

Challenges and Opportunities in Implementing Restorative Approaches in Families:

Implementing restorative approaches in family contexts presents both challenges and opportunities. Here's a closer look at these aspects:

Challenges:

1. Resistance to Change: Families, like any social system, can resist change. Some family members may be accustomed to traditional conflict resolution methods or may be skeptical of restorative practices, making it challenging to introduce these new approaches.

2. Power Dynamics: Family dynamics often involve power imbalances, such as those between parents and children or among siblings. Addressing these imbalances and ensuring that restorative processes are fair can be complex.

3. Complex Family Histories: Many families have complex histories of conflict and harm. These histories may involve unresolved issues, traumas, or deeply ingrained patterns of behavior, which can complicate the application of restorative approaches.

4. Emotional Barriers: Family conflicts can be emotionally charged, making it difficult for participants to engage in restorative dialogues objectively. Emotional barriers may hinder productive communication and reconciliation.

5. Privacy Concerns: Family matters are often considered private, and some family members may be uncomfortable with involving external mediators or facilitators. Maintaining privacy while still addressing harm can be a delicate balance.

Opportunities:

1. Healing and Reconciliation: Restorative approaches provide a unique opportunity for healing and reconciliation within families. They encourage open dialogue, empathy, and understanding, allowing family members to address past conflicts constructively.

2. Empowerment: Restorative processes empower family members to actively participate in conflict resolution and decision-making. This sense of agency can lead to more lasting and meaningful solutions.

3. Improved Communication: Restorative practices focus on effective communication, active listening, and empathy. These skills can significantly enhance family members' ability to express themselves and understand one another better.

4. Building Stronger Relationships: Through restorative approaches, families have the potential to build stronger, more resilient relationships. They can learn conflict resolution skills that serve them well in future challenges.

5. Preventing Escalation: Restorative practices can address conflicts at an early stage, preventing them from escalating into more significant problems. This proactive approach can lead to healthier family dynamics.

6. Teaching Conflict Resolution: When families engage in restorative processes, they model constructive conflict resolution for younger generations. This can have a positive ripple effect on how future conflicts are handled within the family.

7. Promoting Accountability: Restorative practices emphasize accountability for one's actions. Holding family members accountable for their behavior can contribute to a more responsible and respectful family environment.

8. Creating Safe Spaces: Restorative processes create safe spaces for family members to express their feelings and concerns without fear of judgment. This safety encourages honest and open communication.

In summary, implementing restorative approaches in families can be challenging due to resistance, power dynamics, complex histories, emotional barriers, and privacy concerns. However, it also offers opportunities for healing, empowerment, improved communication, stronger relationships, prevention of escalation, conflict resolution education, accountability promotion, and the creation of safe spaces for meaningful conversations. These opportunities can lead to healthier and more harmonious family dynamics over time.

In conclusion, the exploration of restorative approaches within the context of family and relationships reveals a promising path towards healthier and more harmonious dynamics. Key takeaways from this examination underscore the transformative potential of restorative practices in this intimate setting.

Restorative practices prioritize empathy, accountability, and healing as foundational elements. These principles can lead to improved communication, a deeper understanding among family members, and the resolution of conflicts in constructive ways. Instead of perpetuating cycles of harm and resentment, restorative practices promote healing and reconciliation.

By embracing restorative approaches, families can create safe spaces for open dialogue, address conflicts proactively, and empower each member to take an active role in conflict resolution and decision-making. This not only strengthens the family unit but also sets a positive example for future generations, teaching valuable conflict resolution skills.

In essence, restorative practices offer a pathway towards more compassionate, understanding, and accountable family interactions. They remind us that even in the face of conflicts and harm, healing and reconciliation are possible, fostering stronger bonds and a more harmonious family environment.

CHAPTER 14
Restorative Justice in the Community

Healing Trauma and Addressing Harm

Understanding the impact of trauma is foundational when considering restorative justice in the context of addressing harm and facilitating healing. Here's why it's crucial:

Empathy and Sensitivity: Recognizing the effects of trauma allows practitioners to approach survivors and offenders with empathy and sensitivity. Trauma survivors may experience a range of emotions and responses, including fear, anxiety, and distrust. Understanding these reactions helps practitioners create safe and non-retraumatizing environments.

Tailored Support: Different types of trauma can have varying effects on individuals. For instance, survivors of physical trauma may have distinct needs from survivors of emotional or psychological trauma. By understanding these differences, restorative justice processes can be tailored to meet the specific needs of survivors, enhancing their chances of healing and recovery.

Safety and Avoiding Retraumatization: Trauma survivors are often vulnerable and may have concerns about their safety. Understanding the impact of trauma ensures that restorative justice processes prioritize the emotional and physical safety of survivors, avoiding any actions or language that might trigger further trauma.

Communication and Engagement: Trauma can affect a survivor's ability to engage in restorative processes. Some survivors may struggle with communication or have difficulty expressing their feelings.

Understanding these challenges enables practitioners to adapt their approach, use trauma-informed techniques, and provide the necessary support for survivors to participate effectively.

Long-Term Healing: Trauma can have enduring effects that extend far beyond the immediate incident. Understanding this long-term impact helps practitioners appreciate that the healing process may take time. It underscores the importance of ongoing support and follow-up care for survivors as they navigate their journey toward recovery.

Preventing Revictimization: Restorative justice processes must not retraumatize survivors or expose them to further harm. Understanding the impact of trauma helps practitioners design processes that are non-retraumatizing and respectful of survivors' boundaries and needs.

In summary, understanding the impact of trauma is essential in ensuring that restorative justice processes are responsive, empathetic, and conducive to the healing and recovery of trauma survivors. It enables practitioners to create environments that prioritize survivors' well-being, dignity, and agency, ultimately enhancing the effectiveness of restorative practices in addressing harm and trauma.

Restorative Justice as a Tool for Healing:

Restorative justice as a tool for healing is a paradigm shift in how society addresses harm and trauma. Here's why it's important:

Trauma-Informed Approach: Restorative justice adopts a trauma-informed approach, recognizing that many individuals involved in the justice system, including survivors and offenders, may have experienced trauma. By understanding and addressing the impact of trauma, restorative justice processes aim to create environments that are safe, supportive, and conducive to healing.

Repairing Harm: Restorative justice places a central emphasis on repairing the harm caused by wrongdoing. This approach acknowledges that harm extends beyond the immediate victim and affects communities and relationships. By engaging all relevant parties in meaningful dialogue, restorative justice seeks to address the full scope of harm and promote healing for everyone involved.

Empowerment and Agency: Trauma can leave survivors feeling disempowered and voiceless. Restorative justice processes empower survivors by giving them a voice in the resolution of their cases. It allows survivors to express their needs, concerns, and expectations, which can be a crucial part of their healing journey.

Accountability and Responsibility: Restorative justice holds offenders accountable for their actions while also focusing on their responsibility to make amends and contribute to the healing process. This dual emphasis on accountability and responsibility fosters personal growth and transformation for offenders, which can be an essential component of community healing.

Community Support: Restorative justice often involves the broader community in the healing process. Community members play roles as facilitators, support persons, or observers. This community involvement can create a supportive network for survivors and contribute to the restoration of trust within the community.

Long-Term Healing: Healing from trauma is not a linear process, and it may take time. Restorative justice processes provide the flexibility needed for long-term healing. They offer opportunities for survivors to revisit the process, seek additional support, or engage in follow-up actions as needed.

Preventing Retraumatization: Traditional punitive approaches can retraumatize survivors by subjecting them to adversarial and dehumanizing processes. Restorative justice prioritizes creating a safe and respectful space for survivors, reducing the risk of further harm or retraumatization.

In summary, restorative justice as a tool for healing recognizes the profound impact of trauma on individuals and communities and seeks to address harm in a way that promotes genuine healing and recovery. It prioritizes the well-being and agency of survivors, acknowledges the needs of offenders, and engages the community in the restoration process. Ultimately, it offers a more compassionate and effective response to harm and trauma than punitive measures.

Trauma-Informed Restorative Practices:

Trauma-informed restorative practices are an essential aspect of applying restorative justice principles in situations involving trauma and harm. Here's a closer look at what they entail:

Sensitivity to Trauma: Trauma-informed practices acknowledge that trauma can significantly impact an individual's mental, emotional, and physical well-being. Practitioners are trained to recognize the signs and symptoms of trauma and to approach survivors with empathy and understanding.

Creating Safe Spaces: These practices prioritize creating safe and non-threatening environments for survivors to engage in restorative processes. Safety is crucial because survivors may have a heightened sense of vulnerability, and any perceived threat can trigger further distress.

Empowering Survivors: Trauma-informed approaches aim to empower survivors by giving them a voice and control in the process. Survivors are provided with choices and options, allowing them to participate on their terms and at their own pace.

Avoiding Re-Traumatization: One of the key goals of trauma-informed restorative practices is to prevent re-traumatization. This means avoiding any actions, language, or behaviors that could unintentionally trigger or exacerbate trauma symptoms in survivors.

Understanding Triggers: Practitioners are trained to understand potential trauma triggers and to take steps to mitigate them during restorative processes. This includes being aware of sensitive topics or situations that might be distressing for survivors.

Cultural Sensitivity: Cultural competence is essential within trauma-informed practices. Practitioners need to understand that cultural backgrounds and experiences can influence how trauma is experienced and expressed. Cultural sensitivity ensures that survivors' unique cultural perspectives are respected.

Collaboration and Support: These practices often involve collaboration with trauma specialists or mental health professionals who can provide additional support and resources to survivors when needed.

Self-Care for Practitioners: Recognizing that working with trauma survivors can be emotionally challenging, practitioners are encouraged to engage in self-care and seek support for themselves to prevent burnout.

Flexibility and Adaptability: Trauma-informed restorative practices are flexible and adaptable to meet the evolving needs of survivors. This flexibility allows for adjustments in the process as survivors progress in their healing journey.

In summary, trauma-informed restorative practices are designed to ensure that restorative justice processes are safe, supportive, and respectful of trauma survivors. They prioritize the well-being and agency of survivors, aim to prevent re-traumatization, and recognize the importance of cultural competence and collaboration in addressing trauma and promoting healing.

Healing and Recovery:

Healing and recovery, within the context of restorative justice, are vital aspects of addressing harm and trauma effectively. Here's a deeper understanding of these concepts:

Healing:

Healing refers to the process of restoring well-being, wholeness, and emotional health for individuals who have experienced harm or trauma. In restorative justice, healing is a fundamental goal. It involves several key components:

Acknowledgment of Harm: Healing often begins with the acknowledgment of the harm or trauma that has been experienced. This acknowledgment can be a powerful step toward validating survivors' experiences.

Validation and Empathy: Restorative justice processes prioritize creating spaces where survivors are heard, validated, and supported. Practitioners and participants offer empathy and understanding, helping survivors feel less isolated in their experiences.

Participation and Agency: Empowering survivors to actively participate in the process is crucial for healing. When survivors have agency and control over decisions related to the harm, it can contribute significantly to their sense of empowerment and healing.

Reconciliation and Closure: Healing may involve a process of reconciliation, where survivors and offenders, when appropriate, work toward understanding and finding common ground. Closure, in this context, refers to reaching a point where survivors feel they can move forward with their lives.

Recovery:

Recovery extends the concept of healing beyond individuals to encompass broader communities or systems affected by harm or trauma. In restorative justice, recovery implies addressing the harm's ripple effects and rebuilding trust within communities. Key aspects of recovery include:

Community Healing: Recovery recognizes that harm and trauma can affect entire communities. Restorative justice processes aim to restore the well-being of these communities, fostering a sense of unity and cohesion.

Rebuilding Relationships: Restorative practices promote the rebuilding of relationships among community members. These practices help communities come together to address shared challenges and conflicts.

Addressing Systemic Issues: Recovery may involve addressing systemic issues or inequalities that contributed to the harm or trauma. Restorative justice seeks to address root causes and work toward systemic change.

Preventing Future Harm: Recovery also involves strategies for preventing future harm. By addressing the underlying issues that led to harm, restorative justice can contribute to creating safer and more resilient communities.

In summary, healing and recovery are central to the restorative justice approach. Healing focuses on the well-being and empowerment of individuals who have experienced harm or trauma, while recovery extends these principles to encompass broader community and systemic well-being, ultimately working toward preventing future harm.

Application of Restorative Justice in Trauma Cases:

The application of restorative justice in trauma cases is of paramount importance. Here's why:

Addressing Trauma's Long-Term Effects: Trauma can have enduring effects on survivors, affecting their mental and emotional well-being for years. Restorative justice provides a framework for addressing these long-term effects by prioritizing survivors' needs for healing and closure.

Empowering Survivors: Restorative justice empowers survivors by giving them a voice and agency in the process. Survivors can share their experiences, express their feelings, and be heard and validated. This empowerment is essential for their emotional recovery.

Acknowledgment of Harm: Restorative justice processes begin with the acknowledgment of the harm caused. This acknowledgment can be a significant step in helping survivors feel that their experiences are recognized and taken seriously.

Promoting Emotional Healing: Through dialogue and communication, restorative justice practices create opportunities for emotional healing. Survivors can express their emotions, receive empathy and support, and potentially find a path to forgiveness or reconciliation if they choose.

Preventing Retraumatization: Traditional punitive approaches within the justice system can sometimes retraumatize survivors by subjecting them to adversarial processes. Restorative justice minimizes the potential for retraumatization by focusing on empathy, understanding, and the survivor's well-being.

Community Support: Restorative justice often involves the participation of community members who can provide emotional support to survivors. This sense of community can be a crucial element in the survivor's healing process.

Rebuilding Trust: For survivors, trust can be shattered due to the harm experienced. Restorative justice processes can help rebuild trust by facilitating communication, acknowledgment of responsibility, and a commitment to making amends.

Resolution and Closure: Restorative justice seeks to reach resolutions that satisfy the needs of survivors. Achieving a sense of closure and resolution can be instrumental in a survivor's journey toward healing.

Preventing Future Harm: By addressing the root causes of harm and focusing on accountability and understanding, restorative justice processes contribute to preventing future harm and trauma, benefiting both survivors and society as a whole.

In summary, applying restorative justice in trauma cases is crucial for supporting survivors' healing and well-being. It provides a compassionate and effective alternative to punitive approaches, allowing survivors to find closure, rebuild trust, and, in some cases, experience reconciliation and resolution.

Challenges and Considerations:

Working with trauma survivors within a restorative justice framework presents several challenges and considerations:

Ethical Considerations: Practitioners must navigate ethical dilemmas when working with trauma survivors. Respecting survivors' autonomy, choices, and boundaries while facilitating a healing process requires a delicate balance.

Power Dynamics: Power imbalances can exist between trauma survivors and those who caused harm. Ensuring that survivors have a voice and agency in the process, without feeling pressured or retraumatized, is essential.

Safety and Well-Being: Trauma survivors may have safety concerns, especially if they fear retaliation or harm from those responsible. Ensuring the safety and well-being of survivors is paramount, often requiring safety planning and protective measures.

Triggers and Emotional Responses: Trauma survivors may experience triggers and intense emotional responses during restorative processes. Practitioners must be prepared to provide emotional support and resources to help survivors cope with these reactions.

Privacy and Confidentiality: Respecting survivors' privacy and confidentiality is critical. Sharing sensitive information without consent can be retraumatizing and unethical.

Trauma-Informed Training: Practitioners need specialized training in trauma-informed care and restorative practices to effectively work with trauma survivors. Understanding the nuances of trauma and its impact is essential.

Secondary Trauma: Practitioners themselves may experience secondary trauma when working with survivors' stories. Self-care and emotional support for practitioners are essential to prevent burnout.

Cultural Sensitivity: Consideration of cultural diversity and sensitivity is crucial when working with survivors from diverse backgrounds. Cultural competency ensures that practices are respectful and inclusive.

Legal and Ethical Boundaries: Restorative justice processes must align with legal and ethical boundaries. Practitioners must be aware of legal obligations, such as mandatory reporting of certain types of harm.

Complex Cases: Some cases involving trauma may be highly complex, with multiple parties and intricate histories. These cases may require additional time and resources to address fully.

Balancing Accountability and Healing: Balancing the principles of accountability and healing can be challenging. The restorative justice process should support survivors' healing while still addressing the harm caused.

Long-Term Impact: Assessing the long-term impact of restorative justice processes on survivors' well-being and recovery is essential. Tracking outcomes and providing ongoing support may be necessary.

In summary, while restorative justice has the potential to facilitate healing for trauma survivors, it requires practitioners to navigate complex ethical, emotional, and practical challenges. Trauma-informed training, cultural sensitivity, and a commitment to survivors' well-being are essential considerations in this work.

Conclusion:

In conclusion, this chapter underscores the transformative potential of restorative justice, particularly when applied with a trauma-informed approach. It highlights several key takeaways:

Understanding Trauma: Recognizing the profound impact of trauma on individuals and communities is essential for practitioners and society as a whole.

Healing and Recovery: Restorative justice can play a crucial role in the healing and recovery of trauma survivors by providing safe spaces for sharing, validation, and empowerment.

Trauma-Informed Practices: Practitioners must adopt trauma-informed practices to create supportive and respectful environments that prioritize survivors' well-being, dignity, and agency.

Empathy and Accountability: Restorative justice processes should foster empathy, promote accountability, and prioritize healing, aligning with survivors' needs and choices.

Real-Life Examples: Real-life case studies illustrate the effectiveness of restorative practices in trauma cases, showcasing the potential for survivors to find closure, rebuild trust, and experience a sense of justice and resolution.

Challenges and Ethical Considerations: Addressing the challenges and ethical considerations when working with trauma survivors is crucial, emphasizing the importance of practitioner training and ongoing support.

In essence, applying restorative justice within trauma contexts is a powerful approach to addressing harm and facilitating healing. By embracing empathy, accountability, and a trauma-informed mindset, restorative practices can make a significant positive impact on the lives of those affected by trauma and harm.

CHAPTER 15

Restorative Justice in Conflict Resolution

Restorative justice in conflict resolution refers to an approach that prioritizes repairing harm, fostering accountability, and promoting healing in the aftermath of conflicts and disputes. Unlike traditional punitive methods that often focus on punishment and blame, restorative justice seeks to bring together those involved in the conflict, including victims, offenders, and sometimes community members, to engage in a facilitated dialogue.

The primary goals of restorative justice in conflict resolution include:

1. Repairing Harm: Restorative processes aim to address the tangible and intangible harm caused by the conflict, such as physical injuries, emotional distress, and damage to relationships.

2. Accountability: Restorative justice holds offenders accountable for their actions by encouraging them to take responsibility for their behavior, acknowledge the impact on victims, and make amends.

3. Communication: It facilitates open and honest communication between all parties involved, allowing victims to express their needs and

feelings, offenders to understand the consequences of their actions, and communities to support the resolution process.

4. Reconciliation: Ultimately, restorative justice seeks to promote reconciliation and healing, aiming for a resolution that restores a sense of dignity, safety, and peace for all parties involved.

This approach can be applied in various settings, from schools and communities to criminal justice systems, offering a more humane and effective way to address conflicts and repair the harm they cause.

The application of restorative justice principles and practices in resolving conflicts of various types and scales is broad and versatile. Here are some common scenarios in which restorative justice can be applied:

1. Personal Relationships: Restorative practices can address conflicts within families, between friends, or in romantic relationships. Through facilitated dialogues, parties can openly discuss their feelings, needs, and expectations, aiming for understanding and reconciliation.

2. Schools: Restorative justice is used in educational settings to address conflicts between students, between students and teachers, and even among school staff. It can help reduce bullying, improve school climate, and foster a sense of belonging among students.

3. Communities: Restorative processes can resolve conflicts within communities, whether they involve neighbors, community organizations, or different groups with competing interests. It can promote dialogue and collaboration, leading to more harmonious communities.

4. Workplaces: Restorative justice can address conflicts in the workplace, including disputes between coworkers or between employees and management. It can help rebuild trust, enhance communication, and maintain a productive work environment.

5. Criminal Justice: In the criminal justice system, restorative justice programs offer an alternative to traditional sentencing. Offenders meet with victims to discuss the impact of the crime, make amends, and address the root causes of criminal behavior.

6. Societal Conflicts: On a broader scale, restorative justice principles can be applied to address societal conflicts and injustices. It can be used in peacebuilding efforts, reconciliation processes following civil conflicts, and addressing systemic issues like racial inequality.

7. Organizations: Restorative practices can be implemented in organizations to address internal conflicts, disputes, and workplace ethics violations. This can lead to improved employee relationships and organizational culture.

8. Cyberbullying and Online Disputes: With the rise of online conflicts and cyberbullying, restorative justice can provide a way for parties to address harm, find resolution, and learn about responsible digital behavior.

In all these contexts, restorative justice seeks to empower those affected by conflicts, encourage accountability, and promote healing and reconciliation. Its adaptability and focus on dialogue make it a valuable tool for addressing conflicts of various types and scales.

The emphasis on understanding and adopting restorative practices for conflict resolution is rooted in their transformative potential. Here's a breakdown of why this is important:

1. Constructive Conflict Resolution: Traditional conflict resolution methods often focus on assigning blame and punishment, which can escalate conflicts and perpetuate resentment. Restorative practices, on the other hand, prioritize healing and reconciliation. By understanding and adopting these practices, individuals and communities can address conflicts in a way that seeks to repair harm and rebuild relationships rather than exacerbating them.

2. Promoting Understanding: Restorative practices encourage open and honest communication. Participants in a restorative process have the opportunity to share their perspectives, feelings, and needs. This promotes a deeper understanding of one another's experiences and motivations, fostering empathy and reducing misunderstandings.

3. Facilitating Reconciliation: Through restorative processes like dialogues or conferences, conflicting parties can work towards

reconciliation. This means not only resolving immediate issues but also addressing the underlying causes of conflicts. Reconciliation can lead to stronger, more harmonious relationships in personal, community, or organizational settings.

4. Preventing Future Harm: Restorative justice aims not only to address the current conflict but also to prevent its recurrence. By engaging in meaningful dialogue, participants can identify ways to avoid similar conflicts in the future. This proactive approach contributes to long-term conflict prevention.

5. Empowerment: Restorative practices empower individuals by involving them in the resolution process. Victims have a voice in expressing their needs and the harm they've experienced, while offenders have an opportunity to take responsibility for their actions and make amends. This empowerment can lead to a sense of agency and closure for those involved.

6. Lasting Resolution: By focusing on addressing the root causes of conflicts and promoting understanding, restorative practices can lead to more lasting resolutions. Parties are more likely to adhere to agreements reached through restorative processes because they have a personal investment in the outcomes.

In summary, understanding and adopting restorative practices in conflict resolution not only address immediate disputes but also contribute to a more compassionate, empathetic, and harmonious society. By prioritizing understanding, reconciliation, and prevention, restorative justice offers a path to resolving conflicts in ways that can lead to long-lasting positive outcomes.

PART III
Challenges and Critiques

Part III of this book delves into the challenges and critiques surrounding restorative justice. While restorative justice offers a human-centered and transformative approach to addressing harm and conflicts, it is not without its complexities and criticisms.

The first section explores the challenges practitioners and communities may face when implementing restorative justice processes. These challenges can range from resistance to change in established punitive systems to concerns about consistency and due process. It's essential to acknowledge these hurdles as they impact the successful adoption of restorative practices.

The second section delves into the ethical considerations and dilemmas associated with restorative justice. While restorative processes emphasize empathy, healing, and reconciliation, ethical questions can arise concerning issues like power imbalances, the involvement of marginalized communities, and the potential for secondary victimization. It's crucial to address these ethical concerns to ensure that restorative justice remains a just and equitable approach.

The third section of this part explores the critiques leveled against restorative justice. Some argue that restorative processes might not be appropriate or effective in all situations, especially for cases involving severe violence or offenders with little motivation for accountability. Critics also point out potential pitfalls in the application of restorative justice, such as retraumatization of victims or offenders exploiting the process.

Lastly, this part examines the ongoing debates within the field of restorative justice. These debates include discussions about the scope of restorative justice, its relationship with the traditional criminal justice system, and the need for further research and evaluation to better understand its impact. By addressing these challenges and critiques, restorative justice advocates can refine and strengthen its practices while promoting a more just and compassionate approach to conflict resolution and harm repair.

CHAPTER 16

Obstacles to Restorative Justice

The resistance within punitive systems is a formidable obstacle to the widespread adoption of restorative practices. In the context of Chapter 16, "Obstacles to Restorative Justice," this resistance is likely explored in greater detail. Here are some key points that might be discussed regarding the resistance within punitive systems:

1. Historical Precedence: Punitive justice systems have a long history and established traditions that prioritize punishment as a means of addressing wrongdoing. This historical precedence can make it challenging to introduce restorative practices, which represent a departure from the punitive approach.

2. Cultural Norms: Society often perceives punishment as a form of justice. The idea that wrongdoers should suffer consequences for their actions is deeply ingrained in cultural norms. This cultural acceptance of punitive measures can create resistance to alternatives like restorative justice.

3. Institutional Inertia: Criminal justice institutions, including courts, law enforcement agencies, and corrections facilities, may resist change due to institutional inertia. There can be bureaucratic and structural obstacles to implementing restorative practices within these systems.

4. Concerns About Accountability: Critics within punitive systems may express concerns about whether restorative justice truly holds offenders accountable for their actions. They may argue that punitive measures, such as incarceration, are more effective in ensuring accountability.

5. Lack of Understanding: Some individuals working within punitive systems may have limited knowledge or understanding of restorative justice principles and practices. This lack of familiarity can lead to skepticism and resistance.

6. Fear of Leniency: There might be fears that restorative justice could be perceived as lenient, especially when dealing with serious offenses. Critics may worry that it could send a message that offenders can escape significant consequences for their actions.

7. Resource Allocation: Implementing restorative practices may require a reallocation of resources within the justice system. This can be met with resistance from those who are concerned about the financial and logistical implications of such a shift.

Addressing the resistance within punitive systems often requires comprehensive education, training, and a shift in institutional culture. It involves demonstrating the benefits of restorative practices, such as reduced recidivism, improved victim satisfaction, and the potential for transformative change in offenders. Overcoming this resistance is crucial for the broader acceptance and integration of restorative justice into the criminal justice landscape.

In the context of Chapter 16, "Obstacles to Restorative Justice," an examination of power dynamics within restorative justice processes is vital. Here's a more detailed exploration of this aspect:

Power Dynamics in Restorative Justice:

Restorative justice processes can involve various parties, including victims, offenders, facilitators, community members, and even institutional representatives. Each of these individuals or groups may bring different levels of power and privilege to the table, which can influence the dynamics of the process. Here are some key considerations:

1. Authority and Facilitators: Restorative justice facilitators play a crucial role in guiding the process. However, the authority they wield can affect the balance of power. It's essential for facilitators to maintain a neutral and impartial stance to ensure fairness.

2. Victim-Offender Dynamics: In cases involving a victim and an offender, there can be a significant power imbalance. The victim may feel vulnerable or intimidated, while the offender may have a history of exerting power over them. Restorative processes aim to address and mitigate this imbalance.

3. Community Involvement: In some cases, community members may participate in restorative processes. Their roles can vary, but it's essential to consider their influence and power within the community context.

4. Privilege and Marginalization: Issues related to race, class, gender, and other forms of identity can intersect with power dynamics. Those with privilege may have more influence, while marginalized individuals or groups may face additional challenges in these processes.

Addressing Power Imbalances:

Addressing power imbalances within restorative justice processes is fundamental to ensuring fairness and justice. Strategies to achieve this include:

1. Facilitator Training: Restorative justice facilitators should receive comprehensive training on identifying and addressing power dynamics. This training should emphasize the importance of neutrality and fairness.

2. Ensuring Participant Voice: It's critical to create an environment where all participants, especially victims and marginalized

individuals, feel safe and empowered to express their perspectives and needs.

3. Community Involvement: Engaging the broader community can help balance power dynamics. However, careful consideration should be given to who participates and how their influence is managed.

4. Structural Changes: In some cases, structural changes within restorative justice programs or processes may be necessary to reduce power imbalances. This could include modifying the role of facilitators or involving mediators with specialized training.

5. Cultural Competency: Recognizing and respecting cultural differences and identities is essential. Cultural competency training can help facilitators and participants navigate power dynamics in culturally sensitive ways.

By addressing power dynamics within restorative justice processes, practitioners can work toward more equitable and just outcomes. This ensures that the principles of empathy, accountability, and healing are applied consistently and fairly to all participants, regardless of their relative power or privilege.

Training and education in restorative justice principles and practices are essential components of ensuring the effectiveness and ethical application of this approach. In Chapter 16, "Obstacles to Restorative Justice," the challenges and importance of such training are discussed in more detail:

The Importance of Training and Education:

1. Skill Development: Restorative justice processes require specific skills, including active listening, effective communication, conflict resolution, and facilitation. Training equips individuals with these skills, allowing them to navigate complex emotional situations and ensure the process remains productive.

2. Understanding Restorative Principles: Training helps participants understand the underlying principles of restorative justice, such as empathy, accountability, and healing. This understanding is crucial for aligning restorative practices with these principles.

3. Ethical Considerations: Restorative justice operates within an ethical framework that prioritizes fairness, respect, and the well-being of all participants. Training helps individuals navigate ethical dilemmas that may arise during the process.

4. Cultural Competency: Training also addresses cultural competency, emphasizing the importance of understanding and respecting diverse cultural perspectives. This ensures that restorative justice processes are culturally sensitive and inclusive.

5. Process Implementation: Restorative justice involves various steps and procedures, such as convening circles, facilitating dialogues, and reaching agreements. Training ensures that individuals can effectively implement these processes.

Challenges in Providing Training:

1. Resource Constraints: Comprehensive training programs require resources, including funding, qualified trainers, and time commitment. Limited resources can hinder the availability of training opportunities.

2. Access to Training: Ensuring that training is accessible to a wide range of individuals, including those in underserved communities or marginalized groups, can be challenging. Addressing issues of access and equity is essential.

3. Quality of Training: The quality of training programs can vary. Ensuring that training meets established standards and is delivered by experienced trainers is crucial for effective skill development.

4. Ongoing Training: Restorative justice is a dynamic field that evolves over time. Providing ongoing training to practitioners is essential to keep them updated on the latest developments and best practices.

5. Certification and Accreditation: Establishing certification or accreditation mechanisms for restorative justice practitioners can help ensure that individuals have met specific training standards and maintain their competence.

In summary, training and education are vital to the successful implementation of restorative justice. They equip practitioners with the necessary skills, ethical understanding, and cultural competency to conduct fair and effective restorative processes. Overcoming challenges related to resources, access, and quality is essential to ensure that training reaches a broad and diverse audience, ultimately promoting the principles of empathy, accountability, and healing within restorative justice practices.

Secondary victimization, within the context of restorative justice, refers to the unintentional harm or distress that can be experienced by a victim or survivor when participating in the restorative process. While restorative justice aims to provide healing and resolution, it is essential to be aware of the potential for secondary victimization and take steps to minimize its occurrence. Here are some key points related to secondary victimization in restorative justice:

1. Trauma Sensitivity: Many individuals who have experienced harm or victimization may have already gone through significant trauma. Participating in a restorative justice process can sometimes trigger or exacerbate trauma-related reactions. Restorative practitioners must be sensitive to this possibility and approach survivors with care and understanding.

2. Respect and Empathy: To prevent secondary victimization, it is crucial for facilitators and participants to show respect, empathy, and active listening to survivors. Their experiences should be validated, and they should be given space to express their feelings and needs.

3. Informed Consent: Informed consent is essential in restorative justice processes. Victims and survivors should be fully informed about what to expect during the process and should voluntarily choose to participate. This allows them to make an informed decision about whether the process is right for them and helps reduce the risk of secondary victimization.

4. Support Networks: Restorative justice programs should offer access to support networks, such as victim advocates or mental health professionals, who can provide assistance and guidance to survivors before, during, and after the process.

5. Clear Boundaries: Setting clear boundaries within the restorative process is important. Facilitators should ensure that discussions remain focused on repairing harm and achieving resolution rather than becoming confrontational or retraumatizing.

6. Monitoring and Feedback: Restorative justice programs should have mechanisms in place for monitoring and collecting feedback from participants, including survivors. This feedback can help identify areas where the process may need improvement to minimize secondary victimization.

7. Flexibility: Restorative justice processes should be flexible and adaptable to the unique needs and comfort levels of survivors. If a survivor feels uncomfortable or distressed during the process, facilitators should be prepared to make adjustments or provide additional support.

Overall, while restorative justice can be a powerful tool for healing and reconciliation, it is essential to approach it with sensitivity to the experiences of victims and survivors. Preventing secondary victimization requires a trauma-informed approach, clear communication, and a commitment to prioritizing the well-being and dignity of all participants.

Ethical considerations in the context of restorative justice are essential to ensure that the process remains fair, just, and respectful of the rights and needs of all participants. Here are some key aspects of ethical considerations in restorative justice:

1. Balancing the Needs and Rights: Restorative justice often involves bringing together victims and offenders to address harm and seek resolution. Ethical dilemmas may arise when balancing the needs and rights of both parties. Facilitators must ensure that neither party feels coerced or disadvantaged during the process.

2. Impartial Facilitation: Ethical facilitation is crucial to maintain the integrity of the restorative process. Facilitators should remain impartial and not take sides or show favoritism. Their role is to guide the process neutrally, ensuring that all voices are heard and respected.

3. Accountability and Healing: Restorative justice seeks to hold offenders accountable for their actions while promoting healing for

victims and communities. Ethical considerations include ensuring that accountability is achieved without causing additional harm to either party and that the healing process is genuine and meaningful.

4. Informed Consent: Ethical practices in restorative justice require obtaining informed consent from all participants. This means that participants should fully understand the process, their rights, and what to expect. Informed consent ensures that individuals willingly choose to participate.

5. Confidentiality and Privacy: Respecting the privacy and confidentiality of participants is an ethical imperative. Information shared during the restorative process should be kept confidential unless there are legal or safety concerns that require disclosure.

6. Cultural Competency: Ethical considerations include cultural sensitivity and competency. Restorative practitioners must be aware of and respect diverse cultural perspectives, norms, and values when facilitating processes involving participants from different cultural backgrounds.

7. Transparency and Honesty: Restorative justice processes should be transparent and honest. Ethical facilitators provide clear information about the process and its goals, ensuring that participants have realistic expectations.

8. Ongoing Evaluation: Ethical practices involve ongoing evaluation and feedback mechanisms. This helps identify any ethical concerns or shortcomings in the process and allows for continuous improvement.

9. Survivor-Centered Approach: An ethical approach in restorative justice prioritizes the well-being and choices of survivors. Survivors should never be pressured into participating or made to feel retraumatized by the process.

10. Avoiding Harm: Ethical considerations in restorative justice also involve actively working to avoid causing further harm to anyone involved. Facilitators should be prepared to address situations where harm might occur and take steps to prevent it.

Ethical considerations are integral to maintaining the credibility and effectiveness of restorative justice practices. Practitioners and facilitators should receive training and guidance on ethical principles and dilemmas to ensure that the restorative process remains a safe, respectful, and transformative experience for all participants.

Cultural sensitivity, within the context of restorative justice, refers to the awareness, understanding, and respect for diverse cultural perspectives, values, and norms when implementing restorative processes. It recognizes that individuals and communities from different cultural backgrounds may have unique ways of perceiving and addressing conflict, harm, and justice. Here's why cultural sensitivity is crucial in restorative justice:

1. Respect for Diversity: Cultural sensitivity acknowledges and respects the diversity of cultural backgrounds, traditions, and worldviews. It recognizes that there is no one-size-fits-all approach to addressing harm and resolving conflicts.

2. Effective Communication: Different cultures may have distinct communication styles and expectations. Cultural sensitivity ensures that facilitators and participants are aware of these differences to facilitate effective and respectful dialogue during restorative processes.

3. Cultural Competency: Restorative justice practitioners should strive to be culturally competent, which means having the knowledge and skills to work effectively with individuals from various cultural backgrounds. This includes understanding cultural norms, values, and customs related to conflict resolution.

4. Avoiding Cultural Insensitivity: Without cultural sensitivity, restorative processes can inadvertently be culturally insensitive or even offensive. This can hinder the success of the process and potentially harm relationships between participants.

5. Inclusivity: Cultural sensitivity promotes inclusivity within restorative justice. It ensures that everyone, regardless of their cultural background, feels welcomed and heard during the process. This inclusivity is essential for building trust and achieving meaningful outcomes.

6. Conflict Resolution that Resonates: Different cultures may have unique ways of conceptualizing harm and justice. Cultural sensitivity allows restorative justice practitioners to tailor the process so that it resonates with the cultural values and expectations of the participants.

7. Conflict Prevention: Understanding cultural nuances can help prevent conflicts from arising in the first place. Cultural sensitivity allows communities to address underlying issues that may lead to conflicts and harm.

8. Community Buy-In: Restorative justice processes are more likely to be embraced by a community when they are culturally sensitive. When communities see that their cultural values and traditions are respected, they are more likely to participate and support these practices.

Cultural sensitivity is not just about avoiding cultural stereotypes; it's about actively engaging with and respecting the unique cultural contexts in which restorative justice processes are applied. Practitioners and facilitators should be trained to be culturally sensitive, and they should collaborate with communities to ensure that restorative justice is relevant, respectful, and effective for all participants, regardless of their cultural background.

Evaluating the effectiveness and outcomes of restorative justice practices is a critical aspect of understanding their impact. Here are some key points related to this topic:

1. Empirical Evidence: Restorative justice programs have been subject to extensive research and evaluation. Studies have examined their effectiveness in various settings, such as criminal justice, schools, and communities. The empirical evidence generally suggests that restorative practices can lead to positive outcomes, including reduced recidivism, improved victim satisfaction, and better social and emotional development among participants.

2. Variability: The effectiveness of restorative justice can vary depending on several factors, including the specific program or model used, the quality of implementation, and the characteristics of the

participants. Not all restorative programs yield the same results, and some may be more effective than others.

3. Measuring Success: Success in restorative justice is often measured by multiple factors, including the extent to which harm is repaired, the degree of victim satisfaction, and the level of offender accountability. Restorative processes aim to address the underlying causes of harm and conflict, leading to more meaningful and long-lasting outcomes.

4. Long-Term Impact: One of the strengths of restorative justice is its potential for long-term impact. By addressing the root causes of harm and promoting understanding and empathy, restorative practices can contribute to lasting behavioral change and reduced rates of reoffending.

5. Challenges and Critiques: While there is empirical support for restorative justice, it is not without its challenges and critiques. Some studies have questioned its effectiveness in certain contexts or with specific populations. Critics have raised concerns about potential retraumatization of victims and the need for rigorous evaluation of restorative programs.

6. Qualitative Data: In addition to quantitative research, qualitative data is often used to assess the outcomes of restorative justice. Personal narratives, testimonials, and case studies can provide insights into the transformative potential of restorative processes from the perspectives of participants.

7. Community-Level Impact: Restorative justice is not solely focused on individual outcomes. It also aims to strengthen communities by addressing underlying social issues and promoting social cohesion. Community-level impact may include reduced crime rates, improved community relationships, and greater trust in the justice system.

8. Ongoing Evaluation: Effective restorative justice programs engage in ongoing evaluation and quality improvement efforts. This allows for adjustments and refinements to be made based on feedback and emerging research.

In conclusion, the effectiveness and outcomes of restorative justice are complex and multifaceted. While empirical evidence generally supports its positive impact, there is no one-size-fits-all answer, as outcomes can vary depending on numerous factors. Ongoing research and evaluation are essential to continually refine and improve restorative practices, ensuring that they meet the needs of participants and contribute to more just and compassionate societies.

Overcoming challenges is crucial in the context of restorative justice for several reasons:

1. Enhancing Effectiveness: Addressing challenges head-on can lead to more effective restorative justice practices. By identifying and mitigating obstacles, restorative processes are more likely to achieve their intended goals, such as repairing harm, promoting accountability, and fostering healing.

2. Ensuring Fairness: Many challenges in restorative justice relate to issues of fairness, equity, and access. Overcoming these challenges is essential to ensure that restorative practices are applied fairly to all participants, regardless of their background or circumstances.

3. Building Trust: Trust is a cornerstone of restorative justice. Overcoming challenges, particularly those related to power dynamics and cultural sensitivity, can help build trust among participants. When people believe that the process is fair and respectful, they are more likely to engage fully.

4. Promoting Inclusivity: Restorative justice aims to be an inclusive and adaptable approach. Overcoming challenges related to cultural diversity and secondary victimization ensures that restorative processes are accessible and relevant to a wide range of individuals and communities.

5. Ethical Considerations: Ethical challenges, such as balancing the needs of victims and offenders or addressing power imbalances, require careful consideration. Overcoming these challenges involves ethical decision-making that upholds the principles of restorative justice.

6. Continuous Improvement: Restorative justice is an evolving field. Overcoming challenges leads to continuous improvement. Strategies

for addressing challenges can lead to more refined practices, better training for facilitators, and improved outcomes for participants.

7. Preventing Harm: Some challenges, such as the potential for secondary victimization, are directly related to preventing further harm. Overcoming these challenges is essential to ensure that restorative processes do not inadvertently retraumatize individuals.

8. Wider Acceptance: For restorative justice to become more widely accepted and integrated into various justice systems, educational settings, and communities, addressing challenges is vital. Policymakers and stakeholders may be more likely to embrace restorative practices when they see that challenges are acknowledged and addressed effectively.

In summary, overcoming challenges in restorative justice is fundamental to its success and continued growth. By actively addressing these challenges through research, training, policy development, and ongoing evaluation, the field can evolve and better serve the needs of individuals, communities, and society as a whole.

Public perception plays a significant role in the adoption and success of restorative justice. Here are some key points to consider regarding public perception:

1. Misconceptions: Public perception can be shaped by misconceptions or misunderstandings about what restorative justice is and how it works. These misconceptions may include beliefs that restorative justice is solely about forgiveness, that it lets offenders off the hook, or that it's not effective.

2. Education and Awareness: Overcoming misconceptions and fostering a more positive public perception requires education and awareness campaigns. These initiatives can help inform the public about the principles, processes, and outcomes of restorative justice, dispelling myths and providing accurate information.

3. Community Buy-In: Public perception can influence whether communities and individuals are willing to participate in restorative processes. Positive perceptions of restorative justice can lead to greater

community buy-in, which is essential for the success of restorative programs.

4. Support for Policy Change: Policymakers often take public opinion into account when considering changes to justice systems. A favorable public perception of restorative justice can lead to increased support for policy changes that integrate restorative practices into existing systems.

5. Media Influence: The media plays a significant role in shaping public perception. Positive media coverage and accurate reporting on successful restorative justice cases can contribute to a more favorable image of these practices.

6. Testimonials and Stories: Personal stories and testimonials from individuals who have benefited from restorative justice can be powerful tools for changing public perception. These stories humanize the process and demonstrate its positive impact.

7. Research and Data: Providing empirical evidence of the effectiveness of restorative justice can sway public opinion. Research studies that show positive outcomes, such as reduced recidivism and increased victim satisfaction, can help build support.

8. Community Engagement: Engaging with communities and involving them in the development and implementation of restorative programs can foster a sense of ownership and investment. This, in turn, can lead to more positive perceptions.

9. Addressing Concerns: It's important to address concerns and criticisms openly. Acknowledging that restorative justice is not a panacea and that challenges exist can build credibility and trust with the public.

10. Continuous Dialogue: Maintaining a continuous dialogue with the public, stakeholders, and those directly affected by restorative justice processes is key. This ongoing conversation can help address questions and concerns as they arise.

In conclusion, public perception plays a pivotal role in the success and expansion of restorative justice. Efforts to educate, inform, and engage the public can help dispel misconceptions, build support, and create a more favorable environment for the adoption of restorative practices in various contexts.

CHAPTER 17
Restorative Justice and Social Injustice

Restorative justice and Social justice:

The relationship between restorative justice and social justice is multifaceted and interconnected. Restorative justice is a framework and set of practices that aim to address harm, promote accountability, and foster healing through dialogue and community involvement. When examining their relationship, several key points become evident:

Addressing Systemic Injustices: Restorative justice can be a powerful tool for addressing harm stemming from systemic injustices, such as racism, sexism, economic disparities, and discrimination. It provides a space for dialogue and accountability, allowing marginalized communities to voice their experiences and seek reparation for systemic wrongs.

Promoting Equity and Inclusivity: Restorative justice principles emphasize inclusivity, empathy, and cultural sensitivity. These principles are aligned with the goals of social justice, as they seek to create equitable processes that respect the dignity and rights of all participants, regardless of their background.

Access and Equity: However, challenges related to access and equity may arise within restorative justice processes. Some communities may have less access due to systemic barriers or lack of resources. Ensuring that restorative practices are accessible and equitable for all is an ongoing concern in the pursuit of social justice.

Potential for Co-optation: There is a risk that restorative justice can be co-opted or misused by systems of power. Instead of challenging existing inequalities, it might be used to maintain the status quo. This highlights the importance of critically examining how restorative practices are implemented and whether they genuinely address social injustices.

Cultural Competency: Recognizing the diversity of experiences and perspectives within society is essential for effective restorative justice. Cultural competency and an understanding of different worldviews are vital for addressing social injustices while respecting the needs and experiences of various communities.

In summary, the relationship between restorative justice and social justice is one of potential and complexity. Restorative justice has the capacity to contribute to social justice by addressing harm, promoting accountability, and fostering healing. However, it also faces challenges related to access, co-optation, and the need for cultural competency. Understanding and navigating this relationship is crucial for advancing both restorative and social justice goals.

What is the capacity of restorative justice to redress social injustices?

Restorative justice has the capacity to redress social injustices by providing a framework and practices that address harm resulting from systemic discrimination, racism, economic disparities, and other forms of social injustice. Here's how restorative practices can be utilized for this purpose:

Community Dialogue: Restorative justice often involves facilitated dialogues that bring together affected parties, including marginalized communities and those in positions of power or privilege.

These dialogues create a safe space for open and honest conversations about the impacts of social injustices.

Voice and Empowerment: Restorative processes emphasize giving voice to those who have been marginalized or oppressed. Participants are encouraged to express their experiences, concerns, and needs, which can lead to greater empowerment and agency for marginalized individuals and communities.

Accountability for Systemic Wrongs: Restorative justice promotes a broader understanding of accountability. It recognizes that accountability extends beyond individual actions to include institutions and systems. Through restorative processes, systemic wrongs can be acknowledged, and steps can be taken to address and rectify these injustices.

Community Healing: Healing is a central component of restorative justice. Addressing social injustices often requires collective healing for affected communities. Restorative practices can facilitate this healing by acknowledging past harms, validating the experiences of survivors, and promoting a sense of unity and support.

Action Plans and Reparations: Restorative processes can lead to the development of action plans aimed at rectifying social injustices. These plans may include policy changes, resource allocation, or initiatives designed to reduce disparities and promote equity. Reparations, in various forms, can also be part of restorative justice outcomes.

Building Solidarity: Restorative justice processes can foster a sense of solidarity among participants. This solidarity can extend beyond individual cases and lead to broader movements for social change and justice.

However, it's essential to recognize that while restorative justice has the capacity to address social injustices, it may not be a sole or immediate solution. Systemic injustices often require multifaceted approaches, including legal reforms, policy changes, and broader societal shifts. Restorative justice can be a valuable complement to these efforts, offering a space for healing, dialogue, and accountability within the context of social justice initiatives.

What are challenges restorative justice faces in the context of social injustices?

Restorative justice faces several challenges when addressing social injustices:

Access and Equity: Restorative justice processes may not be equally accessible to all communities, particularly marginalized or disadvantaged groups. Barriers such as financial constraints, lack of awareness, or distrust of the justice system can limit access to restorative practices. Addressing these disparities is essential to ensuring that restorative justice is genuinely inclusive.

Power Imbalances: Social injustices often result from power imbalances within society. Restorative processes must grapple with these power dynamics, especially when involving parties with differing levels of privilege and influence. Facilitators need to be skilled in managing these imbalances to ensure fair and just proceedings.

Co-Optation: There's a risk that restorative justice practices can be co-opted or instrumentalized by systems of power to maintain the status quo. For example, restorative processes might be used to placate communities affected by social injustices without addressing underlying structural issues. Vigilance is necessary to prevent restorative justice from being misused for cosmetic or tokenistic purposes.

Legal and Policy Frameworks: Legal and policy frameworks may not always align with restorative justice principles. This misalignment can hinder the effective integration of restorative practices into existing justice systems. Advocacy and policy reform efforts are needed to ensure that restorative justice is recognized and supported within legal systems.

Resource Allocation: Adequate resources, including funding and training, are essential for the successful implementation of restorative justice initiatives. Resource disparities can limit the expansion and sustainability of restorative programs, particularly in marginalized communities.

Cultural Sensitivity: Restorative justice must be culturally sensitive and adaptable to diverse communities. Failing to account for cultural differences and practices can lead to cultural insensitivity and potential harm during restorative processes.

Public Perception: Changing public perceptions and attitudes toward restorative justice, especially in the context of addressing social injustices, can be challenging. Public education and awareness campaigns are needed to combat misconceptions and promote the benefits of restorative approaches.

Measuring Impact: Measuring the impact of restorative justice on addressing social injustices can be complex. Traditional metrics and evaluation methods may not capture the nuanced outcomes of restorative processes, making it challenging to demonstrate their effectiveness.

Overcoming these challenges requires collaboration among policymakers, practitioners, advocates, and affected communities. It also involves ongoing dialogue and critical reflection on how restorative justice can best contribute to addressing social injustices while remaining true to its principles of empathy, accountability, and healing.

Cultural competency:

Cultural competency within restorative justice is of paramount importance for several reasons:

Respect for Diverse Perspectives: Cultural competency ensures that restorative justice practitioners and processes respect and value the diverse cultural backgrounds and perspectives of participants. It recognizes that individuals from different cultures may have unique ways of understanding harm, conflict, and justice.

Effective Communication: Understanding cultural nuances and communication styles is essential for effective dialogue and conflict resolution. Cultural competency equips facilitators with the skills to navigate cross-cultural interactions, promoting meaningful and respectful communication.

Avoiding Harm: Insensitivity to cultural differences can inadvertently cause harm during restorative processes. Being culturally competent helps prevent misunderstandings, offense, or retraumatization, ensuring that the restorative experience is safe and healing for all participants.

Inclusivity: Restorative justice seeks to be inclusive and accessible to all, regardless of cultural background. Cultural competency promotes inclusivity by removing barriers that might discourage or alienate individuals from participating in restorative processes.

Addressing Systemic Injustices: Many social injustices are rooted in systemic biases and discrimination. Cultural competency allows restorative justice to address these deeper issues effectively, acknowledging how cultural factors intersect with systemic inequalities.

Community Engagement: Involving culturally competent practitioners within communities affected by social injustices builds trust and credibility. It ensures that restorative justice efforts are seen as respectful and genuinely concerned with the well-being of those involved.

Tailored Approaches: Cultural competency allows restorative justice practices to be adapted to suit the specific needs and preferences of different cultural groups. This flexibility ensures that restorative processes remain relevant and effective across diverse contexts.

In essence, cultural competency in restorative justice aligns with the overarching principles of fairness, equity, and inclusivity. It recognizes that social injustices affect people from various cultural backgrounds and that addressing these issues effectively requires an approach that values and integrates cultural diversity.

CHAPTER 18

Restorative Justice in a Global Context

Cultural Sensitivity:

Cultural sensitivity is a fundamental aspect of restorative justice that underscores the need to be aware of and respectful toward the diverse cultural backgrounds and perspectives of individuals and communities involved in restorative processes. It recognizes that different cultures have their own distinct values, traditions, norms, and ways of addressing harm and conflict.

Within the context of restorative justice, cultural sensitivity involves:

Respecting Diversity: Acknowledging and respecting the diversity of cultural backgrounds and identities among participants in restorative processes. This includes understanding that individuals may come from various ethnic, religious, linguistic, and social backgrounds.

Adaptability: Recognizing that restorative practices should be adaptable and flexible to meet the specific needs and preferences of different cultural groups. What works effectively in one cultural context may need adjustments in another.

Inclusivity: Ensuring that restorative processes are inclusive and welcoming to all, regardless of their cultural background. Participants should feel that their cultural identity is respected and valued throughout the process.

Cultural Competency: Developing cultural competency among practitioners and facilitators involved in restorative justice. This involves being knowledgeable about the cultural norms and practices of the communities they serve and being sensitive to cultural nuances during the process.

Avoiding Cultural Stereotypes: Being mindful not to rely on cultural stereotypes or assumptions when interacting with participants. Every individual is unique, and it's essential to approach each case with an open mind.

Community Engagement: Engaging with the local community and involving community leaders or cultural experts when appropriate. This helps ensure that restorative practices align with the cultural values and expectations of the community.

Cultural sensitivity is vital to the success of restorative justice processes because it promotes inclusivity, trust, and effective communication. When participants feel that their cultural identities are respected and considered, they are more likely to engage meaningfully in the process, leading to more positive outcomes and strengthened community relationships. It also aligns with the principle of equity in restorative justice, ensuring that all individuals, regardless of their cultural background, have equal access to fair and just processes.

Legal Frameworks:

Legal frameworks are essential when considering the implementation of restorative justice, and here's why they are important:

Legitimacy and Recognition: Legal frameworks provide legitimacy and recognition to restorative justice practices. When restorative justice is incorporated into the legal system, it gains official status and support. This can help ensure that restorative processes are taken seriously and have the backing of the legal authorities.

Guidance and Standards: Legal frameworks establish guidelines and standards for how restorative justice processes should be conducted.

They outline the roles and responsibilities of various parties involved, such as facilitators, victims, and offenders. This clarity helps maintain consistency and fairness in restorative practices.

Protection of Rights: Legal frameworks help protect the rights of all participants. They ensure that individuals engaging in restorative processes have access to due process, legal representation, and safeguards against coercion or manipulation.

Enforcement: Legal frameworks can enforce the outcomes of restorative processes. When agreements or restitution orders are reached through restorative justice, the legal system can enforce compliance if necessary. This provides a level of accountability and ensures that agreements are not merely voluntary.

Integration with the Legal System: Legal frameworks allow restorative justice to be integrated with the existing legal system. This means that restorative justice can be used as an alternative or complementary approach to traditional criminal justice processes. Offenders may have the option to participate in restorative processes as part of their sentencing or rehabilitation.

Consistency: Legal frameworks help maintain consistency in the application of restorative justice. They prevent arbitrary or ad-hoc use of restorative practices and ensure that they are applied in a systematic manner.

Public Confidence: Having restorative justice incorporated into legal frameworks can boost public confidence in the justice system. It demonstrates a commitment to innovative and effective approaches to addressing harm and conflict.

Accountability: Legal frameworks hold the legal system itself accountable for the proper implementation of restorative justice. This means that there are mechanisms for oversight and evaluation to ensure that restorative practices are meeting their intended goals.

In summary, legal frameworks provide a structured and regulated environment for the practice of restorative justice. They help balance the principles of restorative justice with the need for accountability, fairness, and protection of participants' rights within the broader legal system. This integration allows restorative justice to function effectively while upholding the rule of law.

Implementing restorative justice on a global scale presents both challenges and opportunities:

Challenges:

Resource Constraints: In many parts of the world, there may be limited resources, including trained facilitators, to support restorative justice initiatives. This can hinder widespread adoption.

Cultural Sensitivity: Restorative justice practices must be adapted to fit diverse cultural contexts. What works in one culture may not work in another, and there is a risk of imposing Western models on non-Western societies.

Power Dynamics: Power imbalances, whether due to gender, race, or socioeconomic factors, can affect the equitable application of restorative justice. Addressing these dynamics is crucial.

Legal and Institutional Barriers: Some legal systems may not easily accommodate restorative justice principles. Changing existing laws and institutions to align with restorative practices can be a lengthy and challenging process.

Resistance to Change: There may be resistance to adopting restorative justice from those within the traditional punitive justice system who fear a loss of control or job security.

Opportunities:

Conflict Resolution: Restorative justice can play a significant role in resolving conflicts and promoting reconciliation in post-conflict or conflict-affected regions. It offers a nonviolent means of addressing grievances and building peace.

Community Empowerment: Restorative justice empowers communities to take an active role in resolving conflicts and addressing harm. This can strengthen social bonds and foster community resilience.

Victim-Centered Approaches: Restorative justice's emphasis on meeting the needs of victims aligns with broader efforts to enhance victim rights and support worldwide.

Human Rights: Restorative justice principles often align with human rights values, emphasizing dignity, respect, and participation. This can help promote human rights and access to justice globally.

Innovation and Adaptation: Restorative justice's flexibility allows it to adapt to different cultural and legal contexts. This adaptability is an opportunity to create innovative approaches tailored to local needs.

Research and Knowledge Sharing: As restorative justice gains traction globally, there is more opportunity for international research and knowledge sharing. This can help refine practices and address challenges collaboratively.

Community Building: Restorative justice contributes to community building and social cohesion, which can be especially important in regions recovering from conflict or facing social divisions.

In summary, implementing restorative justice on a global scale is a complex endeavor with various challenges, but it also offers significant opportunities for conflict resolution, community empowerment, and the promotion of human rights. Success often depends on adaptability, collaboration, and a commitment to addressing social injustices through transformative practices.

What are the International Restorative Justice Initiatives?

International restorative justice initiatives involve various organizations and efforts dedicated to advancing restorative practices globally:

United Nations: The United Nations has recognized the value of restorative justice in conflict resolution, reconciliation, and post-conflict peacebuilding. Various UN bodies and agencies have promoted restorative justice principles and practices in conflict-affected regions.

European Forum for Restorative Justice: This organization brings together practitioners, policymakers, and researchers from Europe and beyond to exchange knowledge and promote restorative justice in criminal matters, juvenile justice, and other areas.

Restorative Justice International: RJI is a global network that connects individuals and organizations working in the field of restorative justice. It serves as a platform for sharing resources, research, and best practices.

International Institute for Restorative Practices: IIRP offers training and resources in restorative practices, with a focus on education, criminal justice, and organizational settings. It collaborates with institutions worldwide to implement restorative principles.

European Institute for Restorative Approaches: EFRJ works to develop restorative justice practices in Europe and beyond. It supports research, training, and policy development related to restorative justice.

International Center for Transitional Justice: ICTJ explores the use of restorative justice in transitional contexts, where societies are recovering from conflict or dictatorship. It seeks to integrate restorative principles into transitional justice processes.

International Juvenile Justice Observatory: IJJO promotes restorative justice approaches in juvenile justice systems worldwide, with an emphasis on the rights and needs of young offenders.

These initiatives collaborate with governments, NGOs, and local communities to raise awareness about restorative justice, build capacity, and advocate for the adoption of restorative principles in legal systems, conflict resolution, and social programs. They play a vital role in fostering a global network of practitioners and researchers dedicated to the advancement of restorative justice.

CHAPTER 19

Ethical Considerations and Cultural Sensitivity

Ethical Foundations of Restorative Justice:

The ethical foundations of restorative justice are the fundamental principles and values that underpin its practice. These principles serve as guiding lights, shaping the way restorative justice processes are designed and implemented. Some of the key ethical foundations of restorative justice include:

Respect for Human Dignity: At the core of restorative justice is a deep respect for the inherent dignity of every individual. It recognizes that all participants, whether victims, offenders, or community members, deserve to be treated with respect and fairness throughout the process.

Fairness and Equity: Restorative justice strives to ensure fairness and equity in its procedures and outcomes. It aims to balance the needs and rights of all parties involved, seeking to rectify power imbalances and promote a sense of justice.

Accountability: Restorative justice promotes accountability for one's actions. Offenders are encouraged to take responsibility for the harm they've caused, and this accountability is seen as a key step toward repairing the harm and preventing future wrongdoing.

Empathy and Compassion: Empathy and compassion are integral to restorative justice. Practitioners are encouraged to listen with empathy, victims are given a platform to express their feelings, and offenders are supported in understanding the impact of their actions on others.

Inclusivity and Participation: Restorative justice values inclusivity and encourages the active participation of all stakeholders, including victims, offenders, and the community. It seeks to involve everyone affected by the harm in the decision-making and resolution processes.

Community and Relationship Building: Restorative justice recognizes the importance of building and maintaining healthy relationships within communities. It fosters a sense of belonging and interconnectedness among community members.

Healing and Restoration: A central ethical principle of restorative justice is the focus on healing and restoration. It aims to repair the harm caused by the offense and support the well-being of victims, offenders, and the community as a whole.

Non-Violence: Restorative justice advocates for non-violent responses to harm and conflict. It seeks to break the cycle of violence and retribution often associated with punitive justice systems.

These ethical foundations are not only theoretical principles but are put into practice in restorative justice processes. They guide practitioners in creating safe and respectful spaces for dialogue and reconciliation, ultimately aiming to transform the way society responds to harm and conflict.

Ethical Dilemmas and Decision-Making:

Ethical dilemmas within restorative justice processes can be complex and challenging. They often involve finding a balance between the needs and rights of victims, offenders, and other stakeholders while upholding the core principles of restorative justice. Some common ethical dilemmas and considerations include:

Balancing Accountability and Healing: One ethical dilemma centers on the balance between holding offenders accountable for their actions and prioritizing the healing and well-being of victims. Restorative justice seeks to achieve both, but determining the appropriate emphasis in each case can be challenging.

Impartial Facilitation: Restorative justice processes rely on impartial facilitation to ensure fairness. Ethical dilemmas may arise if facilitators have personal biases or connections to those involved in the process, potentially affecting their neutrality.

Informed Consent: Obtaining informed consent from all participants is crucial in restorative justice. Ethical concerns can emerge if participants feel pressured to participate or if they are not fully informed about the process and its implications.

Privacy and Confidentiality: Respecting the privacy and confidentiality of participants is essential. Balancing the need for transparency and accountability with the privacy rights of individuals can present ethical challenges.

Power Dynamics: Addressing power imbalances between participants, such as between victims and offenders, is fundamental in restorative justice. Ethical dilemmas can arise when power dynamics are not adequately recognized or when some participants feel marginalized.

Community Involvement: Ethical considerations may arise regarding the extent of community involvement in the process. Decisions about who should participate and to what degree can raise questions about inclusivity and fairness.

Safety and Re-Traumatization: Ensuring the emotional and physical safety of participants, particularly victims, is paramount. Ethical dilemmas can occur when there are concerns about re-traumatization during the process.

To address these ethical dilemmas, restorative justice practitioners often use decision-making models that guide their actions. These models may involve ethical reflection, consultation with colleagues or supervisors, and a commitment to upholding the principles of restorative justice.

Training and ongoing professional development also play a vital role in helping practitioners navigate ethical challenges effectively while promoting the integrity of the process.

Cultural Sensitivity and Diversity:

Cultural sensitivity and diversity within the context of restorative justice are crucial considerations, as they reflect the need to recognize and respect the cultural backgrounds, beliefs, and values of all participants.

Here are key points regarding cultural sensitivity and diversity:

Respecting Cultural Diversity: Restorative justice processes should honor the diversity of participants' cultural backgrounds. This includes acknowledging differences in customs, traditions, communication styles, and worldviews.

Cultural Competency: Practitioners and facilitators involved in restorative justice must strive to develop cultural competency. This means understanding the cultural norms and expectations of participants to create an inclusive and respectful environment.

Effective Communication: Cultural sensitivity extends to communication. Restorative justice practitioners should be aware of how language, tone, and non-verbal cues can vary across cultures. Effective communication promotes understanding and trust.

Interpretation of Harm: Cultural diversity can influence how individuals perceive harm and justice. Some cultures may prioritize collective well-being, while others focus on individual rights. Acknowledging these differences is essential for fair and meaningful restorative processes.

Inclusivity: Cultural sensitivity ensures that restorative justice processes are inclusive, allowing all participants to have their voices heard and their perspectives valued. This inclusivity promotes a sense of belonging and equity.

Cultural Adaptation: Restorative justice practices may need to be adapted to align with the cultural norms and preferences of specific communities or individuals. This flexibility demonstrates respect for cultural diversity.

Avoiding Cultural Stereotypes: Practitioners should avoid making assumptions or relying on stereotypes related to culture. Each participant is an individual with unique experiences and perspectives.

Cultural Safety: Cultural safety means ensuring that participants feel safe and respected within the restorative justice process, regardless of their cultural background. It involves addressing any potential bias or discrimination.

Community Involvement: Cultural sensitivity extends to the involvement of communities in restorative justice. Communities may have their own restorative practices and traditions that should be respected and integrated where appropriate.

In summary, cultural sensitivity and diversity in restorative justice underscore the need for an inclusive and respectful approach that recognizes and values the cultural identities and backgrounds of participants. By embracing cultural competency and adapting practices as needed, restorative justice can effectively address harm and promote healing within diverse communities and contexts.

Why is important to Address Cultural Differences?

Addressing cultural differences is essential within restorative justice for several reasons:

Respect for Individual Identities: Cultural differences are a fundamental aspect of an individual's identity. Ignoring or dismissing these differences can lead to feelings of exclusion and disrespect. Restorative justice aims to honor and respect each person's unique identity, including their cultural background.

Effective Communication: Cultural differences can significantly impact communication styles and norms. To ensure that participants in restorative processes understand one another and feel heard, it's crucial to navigate these differences skillfully. This can involve adapting communication approaches and employing interpreters when necessary.

Avoiding Cultural Stereotypes: Making assumptions or relying on cultural stereotypes can be harmful and counterproductive. By addressing cultural differences, restorative justice processes can steer clear of these stereotypes and instead focus on the individual experiences and perspectives of participants.

Cultural Interpretation of Harm: Cultural backgrounds can influence how individuals perceive harm and justice. Some cultures may emphasize collective well-being, while others prioritize individual rights. Understanding these differences allows for more nuanced discussions and resolutions in restorative justice.

Inclusivity and Equity: Restorative justice is founded on principles of inclusivity and equity. To achieve these goals, cultural sensitivity is vital. It ensures that individuals from all cultural backgrounds have equal access to and participation in restorative processes.

Cultural Competency: Practitioners and facilitators involved in restorative justice should possess cultural competency. This means having the knowledge and skills to navigate diverse cultural contexts sensitively. It's important for creating a safe and respectful environment.

Community Engagement: Communities often have their own restorative practices and traditions. Understanding and respecting these cultural practices is key to effective community engagement within restorative justice. It fosters collaboration and trust.

Conflict Resolution Across Borders: In a globalized world, restorative justice can extend across borders. Cultural differences become even more critical when addressing conflicts involving participants from various countries and backgrounds.

In summary, addressing cultural differences in restorative justice ensures that the process is respectful, effective, and equitable for all participants. It requires cultural sensitivity, adaptability, and a commitment to valuing the diverse backgrounds and perspectives of those involved.

What is The Intersection of Ethics and Cultural Sensitivity?

The intersection of ethics and cultural sensitivity within restorative justice is a critical area of consideration. Here's a closer look at how these two aspects intersect:

Respect for Cultural Diversity: Ethical principles in restorative justice, like respect for human dignity and fairness, are inherently tied to cultural sensitivity. Respecting diverse cultural backgrounds and perspectives is essential to upholding these ethical principles. It means recognizing that each individual's cultural identity is a part of their human dignity.

Fairness Across Cultures: Ethical fairness requires equitable treatment of all participants, regardless of their cultural background. Cultural sensitivity ensures that restorative justice processes do not favor one culture over another, leading to fair and just outcomes for everyone involved.

Avoiding Ethical Pitfalls: Lack of cultural sensitivity can lead to ethical pitfalls, such as unintentional discrimination or perpetuating stereotypes. Recognizing and addressing cultural differences helps practitioners navigate these pitfalls and maintain ethical integrity.

Inclusive Decision-Making: Ethical decision-making within restorative justice should include input from all participants. Cultural sensitivity ensures that individuals from diverse backgrounds have an equal voice in the decision-making process, aligning with the ethical principle of inclusivity.

Accountability and Healing: Ethical principles emphasize accountability and healing as central goals of restorative justice. Cultural sensitivity ensures that accountability and healing processes are culturally relevant and sensitive to the needs of all participants.

Ethical Cultural Competency: Practitioners within restorative justice must possess ethical cultural competency. This means not only having knowledge about cultural diversity but also applying ethical principles to navigate cultural differences with sensitivity and fairness.

Community Engagement: Ethical practice extends to engaging communities effectively. Cultural sensitivity helps build trust and collaboration within communities, fostering a sense of ownership over the restorative justice process.

In summary, the intersection of ethics and cultural sensitivity in restorative justice reinforces the importance of aligning ethical principles with an understanding of cultural diversity. It ensures that ethical practice is culturally competent, fair, inclusive, and respectful of the diverse backgrounds and perspectives of participants.

CHAPTER 20

The Future Restorative Justice

The Future of Restorative Justice: A Call to Action

"The Future of Restorative Justice: A Call to Action" is likely the concluding chapter of the book, where the authors draw together the key themes, ideas, and discussions presented throughout the book to provide a forward-looking perspective. Here's an expanded explanation of what this chapter could encompass:

Reflection on the Journey: The chapter may begin by reflecting on the journey covered in the preceding chapters. It might recap the historical development of restorative justice, its philosophical underpinnings, and the various applications and case studies that have been explored.

Challenges Acknowledged: It could acknowledge the challenges and obstacles that have been discussed in earlier chapters, emphasizing that these challenges are not insurmountable but require collective action and commitment to overcome.

The Vision of Restorative Justice: This chapter might articulate a vision for the future of restorative justice. This vision could encompass a world where restorative principles are integrated into legal systems, educational institutions, workplaces, and communities as a means of addressing conflicts, promoting healing, and fostering accountability.

Call to Action: As the subtitle suggests, this chapter is likely to issue a "Call to Action." It may call upon readers, policymakers, practitioners, and communities to actively engage with restorative justice. This could involve advocating for policy changes, participating in restorative justice training, supporting community-led initiatives, and fostering a restorative mindset in everyday life.

Expanding Restorative Justice: The chapter may discuss strategies for expanding the reach of restorative justice beyond its current applications. This could involve exploring new contexts where restorative practices can be employed and adapting them to meet the unique needs of various communities and cultures.

Community Engagement: Recognizing the importance of communities, this chapter might emphasize the role of community engagement and mobilization. It may showcase successful examples of communities that have embraced restorative justice and highlight the positive impacts on social cohesion and conflict resolution.

Global Perspective: Considering the global context, the chapter could delve into the international spread of restorative justice principles and practices. It may discuss how restorative justice contributes to addressing global issues like peacebuilding, reconciliation, and human rights.

The Transformative Power: Ultimately, the chapter is likely to underscore the transformative power of restorative justice in addressing social injustices, healing trauma, and fostering a culture of empathy and accountability. It may convey the idea that restorative justice has the potential to bring about profound positive changes in society.

Closing Thoughts: The chapter will likely conclude with a final call to action, urging readers to become advocates and ambassadors for restorative justice. It may offer resources and guidance on how individuals and organizations can actively support and promote restorative practices.

In essence, "The Future of Restorative Justice: A Call to Action" is expected to provide a compelling and inspirational conclusion to the book, motivating readers to take concrete steps toward making restorative justice a more central and transformative force in society.

Reflection on Key Takeaways:

The "Reflection on Key Takeaways" section of the chapter is likely to serve as a summarization of the most significant lessons and insights presented throughout the book. Here's what it might entail:

Core Principles of Restorative Justice: This section would revisit and emphasize the fundamental principles of restorative justice, such as repairing harm, fostering empathy, and promoting accountability. It could underscore how these principles distinguish restorative justice from punitive approaches.

Impact on Individuals and Communities: The reflection may highlight the transformative impact of restorative justice on individuals who have experienced harm and offenders who have taken responsibility for their actions. It may also discuss the broader community benefits, such as reduced recidivism, improved relationships, and enhanced social cohesion.

Challenges and Barriers: Acknowledging the challenges and barriers discussed in previous chapters, this section might emphasize that understanding and addressing these obstacles are essential for the successful implementation of restorative practices.

Ethical Considerations: The reflection could touch on the ethical considerations and cultural sensitivity discussed earlier in the book. It might stress the importance of ensuring that restorative justice processes are ethically sound and culturally relevant.

Global Perspective: Given the global context explored in the book, this section may underscore the universal appeal of restorative justice principles while recognizing the need for cultural adaptations to make them effective in diverse contexts.

Empowerment and Healing: Reflecting on the chapters related to trauma, family dynamics, and conflict resolution, the chapter might highlight how restorative justice empowers individuals to heal and rebuild their lives.

The Vision of Restorative Justice: This section could introduce the vision of the future of restorative justice, emphasizing its potential to create a more just, empathetic, and accountable society.

Call to Action: Building on the reflections, this section may issue a call to action, urging readers to engage with restorative justice in their personal and professional lives. It could provide practical steps for individuals to support the restorative justice movement.

Overall, the "Reflection on Key Takeaways" section aims to reiterate and reinforce the core messages of the book, offering readers a concise yet comprehensive summary of the journey through the world of restorative justice and its transformative potential.

The Evolving Landscape:

The "Evolving Landscape" section is likely to provide an overview of how the field of restorative justice has evolved over time. Here's what it might cover:

Historical Evolution: The chapter could start by briefly summarizing the historical development of restorative justice, from its indigenous roots to its modern resurgence in the justice system.

Shift in Public Perception: It may discuss how public perception of restorative justice has changed over the years. This could include a shift away from punitive approaches toward more empathetic and restorative methods of addressing harm.

Legislative Advancements: The section might highlight legislative advancements that have recognized and integrated restorative practices into the formal justice system. This could include the adoption of restorative justice programs in various jurisdictions and their impact on reducing recidivism.

Integration in Various Contexts: It could discuss how restorative justice principles have expanded beyond the criminal justice system. This might include their integration into education, family dynamics, workplace conflict resolution, and even international conflict resolution.

Research and Evidence-Based Practices: The chapter may touch upon the growing body of research supporting the effectiveness of restorative justice. This could include studies on reduced reoffending rates, increased victim satisfaction, and improved community outcomes.

Global Adoption: It might explore how restorative justice has been adopted and adapted in different countries and regions around the world, showcasing its global relevance.

Challenges and Controversies: Acknowledging that the evolving landscape isn't without its challenges, this section could briefly discuss controversies or criticisms that have emerged as restorative justice has gained prominence.

Overall, the "Evolving Landscape" section is likely to illustrate how restorative justice has progressed from a relatively niche approach to a more recognized and accepted method for addressing harm and promoting accountability in various contexts.

Challenges and Opportunities:

"Remaining Challenges and Opportunities" section of Chapter 20 is likely to explore the ongoing issues and prospects for restorative justice. Here's what it might cover:

Cultural Sensitivity: The chapter may discuss the need for continued improvement in cultural sensitivity within restorative justice practices. This includes acknowledging and addressing cultural differences and ensuring that restorative processes are inclusive and relevant to diverse communities.

Access and Equity: It might highlight the importance of expanding access to restorative justice programs and services. This could involve addressing barriers such as financial constraints, geographic limitations, and disparities in access among different demographic groups.

Power Imbalances: The section may delve into the persistent issue of power imbalances within restorative processes. It could explore strategies for mitigating these imbalances to ensure that all participants have an equal voice and are treated fairly.

Intersectionality: The chapter might touch upon the concept of intersectionality, emphasizing the need to consider the unique experiences and challenges faced by individuals with intersecting identities, such as race, gender, and socioeconomic status.

Community Engagement: It could discuss opportunities for enhancing community engagement in restorative justice initiatives. This might involve strengthening partnerships between community organizations, government agencies, and restorative justice practitioners.

Youth Engagement: The section might focus on the role of young people in shaping the future of restorative justice. It could explore how involving youth in restorative practices can contribute to more inclusive and effective approaches.

Research and Evaluation: The chapter could stress the importance of ongoing research and evaluation to refine restorative justice practices. This includes studying the long-term outcomes of restorative processes and identifying areas for improvement.

Advocacy and Education: It may encourage advocacy efforts and educational campaigns aimed at raising awareness about restorative justice and its potential benefits. This could involve engaging policymakers, community leaders, and the public in discussions about restorative practices.

Overall, the "Remaining Challenges and Opportunities" section is likely to underscore that while significant progress has been made in the field of restorative justice, there are still areas in need of attention and improvement to realize its full potential for promoting healing, accountability, and justice.

A Vision for the Future:

The "Vision for the Future" section in Chapter 20 is expected to provide a forward-looking perspective on restorative justice. Here's what it might entail:

Expanding Adoption: The chapter may advocate for the widespread adoption of restorative justice principles and practices, not only within the criminal justice system but also in various other contexts such as education, family, and community settings.

Policy Changes: It might call for policy reforms and legislative changes to integrate restorative justice more comprehensively into existing legal and justice systems. This could involve advocating for restorative justice programs to be established as a standard option alongside traditional punitive approaches.

Community Empowerment: The section may emphasize the role of communities in driving the restorative justice movement. It could encourage communities to take ownership of restorative initiatives and advocate for their implementation.

Education and Training: It could highlight the importance of ongoing education and training for practitioners, educators, and community leaders in restorative justice practices. This would ensure that individuals are equipped with the skills needed to facilitate restorative processes effectively.

Research and Innovation: The chapter might underscore the need for continued research and innovation in restorative justice. This includes exploring new approaches, evaluating existing programs, and documenting best practices to refine the field.

Youth Engagement: It may emphasize the role of young people in shaping the future of restorative justice. Encouraging youth involvement in restorative practices and decision-making processes could be a key element of the vision.

Global Collaboration: The section could advocate for increased collaboration and knowledge-sharing among countries and regions to promote restorative justice on a global scale. This might involve supporting international initiatives and partnerships.

Cultural Sensitivity: It might stress the importance of cultural sensitivity and diversity within the restorative justice movement, recognizing that the principles and practices must be adaptable and respectful of various cultural perspectives.

Victim-Centered Approaches: The chapter may highlight the importance of maintaining a victim-centered focus within restorative justice processes, ensuring that survivors' needs and voices are consistently prioritized.

Healing and Reconciliation: It could underline the potential for restorative justice to contribute to healing and reconciliation at individual, community, and societal levels.

Overall, the "Vision for the Future" section is likely to inspire individuals and communities to actively engage with restorative justice and work towards a future where it plays a central role in addressing harm, fostering accountability, and promoting social justice. It may serve as a call to action to collectively shape a more just and compassionate society.

Expanding Restorative Justice:

Expanding restorative justice is crucial for several reasons:

Broader Impact: By extending restorative justice beyond its traditional criminal justice context, it can have a more significant impact on society. Its principles of accountability, empathy, and healing can benefit various facets of life, including education, workplaces, and community interactions.

Prevention: Restorative practices in schools, workplaces, and communities can help prevent conflicts and harm from occurring in the first place. By fostering better communication, empathy, and conflict resolution skills, it contributes to a more peaceful environment.

Personal Growth: Restorative justice principles can promote personal growth and development. In educational settings, they encourage students to reflect on their actions and take responsibility, leading to improved behavior and decision-making.

Accountability: Expanding restorative justice emphasizes the importance of accountability in everyday life. It encourages individuals to take responsibility for their actions, make amends when necessary, and contribute positively to their communities.

Community Building: Restorative practices in community settings strengthen bonds among residents and promote a sense of belonging. It empowers communities to address conflicts and challenges collaboratively, enhancing overall well-being.

Conflict Resolution: In workplaces, restorative approaches can improve workplace relationships and resolve conflicts more constructively. This can lead to higher job satisfaction and productivity.

Equity and Social Justice: Expanding restorative justice can contribute to addressing systemic issues of inequality and social injustice. It provides a framework for discussing and addressing these issues at both individual and community levels.

Holistic Approach: By expanding restorative justice, it becomes a holistic approach to societal issues, not limited to responding to wrongdoing but also proactively promoting positive interactions, empathy, and healing.

Cultural Sensitivity: Tailoring restorative practices to different settings and communities ensures cultural sensitivity and relevance, making it more accessible and effective for a diverse range of people.

Transformative Potential: Expanding restorative justice recognizes its transformative potential beyond the individual. It acknowledges that embracing these principles can lead to more compassionate and just communities.

In essence, expanding restorative justice aligns with the vision of creating more compassionate, accountable, and equitable societies. It recognizes that these principles are not limited to one specific context but can be applied wherever conflicts arise and relationships need to be repaired and strengthened.

Role of Advocacy Restorative Justice:

Advocacy plays a vital role in advancing restorative justice for several reasons:

Policy Change: Advocacy efforts can influence policymakers to adopt and implement restorative justice policies and practices within the criminal justice system, education, workplaces, and communities.

Awareness: Advocacy helps raise awareness about the benefits of restorative justice among the public, professionals, and decision-makers. It educates people about the principles and potential of restorative practices.

Community Engagement: Advocacy encourages community members to get involved in restorative justice initiatives. It fosters a sense of ownership and responsibility for creating more just and compassionate communities.

Victim Support: Advocacy can focus on improving support services for victims of crime. By advocating for victim-centered restorative processes, survivors can have a more significant role in the justice process and access the support they need.

Offender Rehabilitation: Restorative justice advocacy can emphasize the potential for offender rehabilitation and reintegration into society. It highlights the role of restorative processes in addressing the root causes of offending behavior.

Conflict Prevention: Advocacy efforts can promote the use of restorative practices as a means of preventing conflicts and harm in various settings, reducing the need for punitive responses.

Equity and Social Justice: Advocacy can address issues of systemic inequality and advocate for restorative approaches to contribute to social justice and equity.

Legislation: Advocacy can lead to changes in laws and regulations that support the use of restorative justice. It can influence the development of policies that prioritize accountability, empathy, and healing.

Research and Evaluation: Advocacy can support research initiatives that assess the effectiveness of restorative practices. Gathering evidence of positive outcomes can bolster advocacy efforts.

International Collaboration: Advocacy can facilitate international collaboration and knowledge-sharing on restorative justice best practices, fostering a global community of restorative practitioners and advocates.

Restorative Culture: Advocacy can work toward creating a culture that values restorative principles, emphasizing empathy, accountability, and healing in everyday interactions.

In summary, advocacy is a powerful tool for expanding the use of restorative justice and integrating its principles into various aspects of society. It helps shape policies, raise awareness, engage communities, and ultimately contributes to creating more empathetic, accountable, and just environments.

How important is Community Engagement in restorative justice?

Community engagement is of paramount importance in restorative justice for several compelling reasons:

Ownership and Empowerment: Engaging communities in restorative justice processes gives them a sense of ownership over the outcomes. It empowers individuals to actively participate in resolving conflicts and repairing harm, fostering a more just and accountable society.

Conflict Prevention: Communities can use restorative practices to prevent conflicts and tensions from escalating into harm or violence. By addressing issues at an early stage, they contribute to a safer and more harmonious environment.

Building Social Capital: Restorative justice fosters trust, understanding, and positive relationships within communities. These connections create social capital, strengthening bonds and cooperation among community members.

Resolving Local Issues: Restorative processes can address issues that are specific to a community's context and culture. Communities can tailor restorative approaches to meet their unique needs and priorities.

Support for Victims: Restorative justice allows communities to provide meaningful support to victims of harm. This can include emotional, practical, and financial assistance, helping survivors in their journey toward healing and recovery.

Accountability: Communities can hold individuals accountable for their actions and ensure they take responsibility for harm caused within the community. This accountability reinforces community norms and values.

Restorative Culture: Engaging in restorative practices cultivates a culture of empathy, respect, and accountability within communities. It promotes a way of resolving conflicts that aligns with community values.

Conflict Transformation: Communities can transform conflicts into opportunities for growth and learning. Restorative processes encourage individuals to understand the impact of their actions and work together to find constructive solutions.

Education and Awareness: Community engagement in restorative justice can educate members about the principles and benefits of restorative practices, contributing to increased awareness and acceptance.

Preventing Recidivism: Communities can support the rehabilitation and reintegration of individuals who have caused harm. This reduces the likelihood of reoffending and contributes to community safety.

Restorative Justice Initiatives: Communities can initiate and sustain restorative justice programs, circles, and dialogues tailored to their unique needs. These initiatives empower communities to address conflicts on their terms.

In summary, community engagement is vital in promoting restorative justice because it empowers communities to take an active role in conflict resolution, accountability, and the promotion of empathy and healing. When communities embrace restorative principles, they contribute to creating more compassionate and equitable societies.

Global Perspective:

A global perspective on restorative justice reveals its expanding presence and relevance in addressing pressing global challenges:

Conflict Resolution: Restorative justice principles are increasingly recognized as valuable tools in resolving conflicts at various levels, from interpersonal disputes to international conflicts. The focus on dialogue, understanding, and reconciliation aligns with the goals of peace and conflict resolution.

Peacebuilding: Restorative justice contributes to peacebuilding efforts by promoting reconciliation, healing, and the rebuilding of trust in post-conflict societies. It helps communities and nations address the legacies of violence and division.

Human Rights: Restorative justice aligns with human rights principles, emphasizing the dignity and agency of all individuals. It offers a human-centered approach to justice that prioritizes the well-being and rights of victims and offenders alike.

Transitional Justice: In contexts of transitional justice, where societies grapple with past atrocities and human rights abuses, restorative justice mechanisms like truth and reconciliation commissions play a vital role in uncovering the truth, acknowledging harm, and facilitating healing.

Community and Social Healing: Restorative justice can address systemic injustices and inequalities that contribute to conflict and harm. It offers a means of addressing structural issues and promoting social healing within and between communities.

Cross-Cultural Exchange: Restorative justice practices are adapted and applied in diverse cultural and societal contexts. This cross-cultural exchange fosters mutual understanding and learning, contributing to the global dissemination of restorative principles.

Rehabilitation and Reintegration: Restorative justice approaches can support the rehabilitation and reintegration of individuals involved in conflicts or violence, reducing recidivism rates and contributing to the rehabilitation of societies.

Victims' Rights: Restorative justice emphasizes the rights and needs of victims, aligning with international human rights instruments that seek to protect and empower survivors of harm.

Advocacy and Collaboration: Global networks and organizations advocate for the adoption of restorative justice practices. Collaborative efforts facilitate knowledge-sharing, capacity-building, and the promotion of restorative principles on a global scale.

Sustainable Development: Restorative justice contributes to sustainable development by fostering inclusive and peaceful societies. It aligns with Sustainable Development Goal 16, which aims to promote peace, justice, and strong institutions.

In a global context, restorative justice serves as a means of addressing complex and interconnected challenges. Its emphasis on empathy, accountability, and healing aligns with the values and aspirations of societies worldwide seeking more just and peaceful coexistence. The global dissemination of restorative principles reflects the growing recognition of its potential to contribute to a more equitable and compassionate world.

The Transformative Potential:

The transformative potential of restorative justice is a powerful force for change in addressing social injustices, healing trauma, and fostering a more just and compassionate society. Here's how this potential can be highlighted:

Social Injustices: Restorative justice offers a pathway to address systemic social injustices by acknowledging historical wrongs, promoting accountability for structural discrimination, and facilitating meaningful dialogue between affected communities and institutions.

Healing Trauma: Restorative justice provides a space for individuals and communities to heal from trauma by recognizing and validating their experiences, fostering empathy, and supporting their journey toward recovery and well-being.

Accountability: Restorative justice promotes a sense of accountability that goes beyond punitive measures. It encourages offenders to take responsibility for their actions and make amends, contributing to their personal growth and rehabilitation.

Reconciliation: The emphasis on dialogue and understanding in restorative processes fosters reconciliation between victims, offenders, and communities. It helps rebuild trust and relationships that may have been strained or broken.

Community Building: Restorative justice strengthens communities by involving them in the resolution of conflicts and harm. It empowers communities to play an active role in promoting healing and social cohesion.

Prevention: Restorative justice has the potential to prevent future harm by addressing the root causes of conflicts and addressing them at their source. It encourages individuals to reflect on their actions and make positive changes.

Empowerment: Restorative practices empower individuals and communities by giving them a voice in the justice process. This empowerment can lead to increased civic engagement and advocacy for social change.

Diversity and Inclusion: Restorative justice adapts to diverse cultural and societal contexts, respecting different perspectives and values. It promotes inclusivity and equity by recognizing the unique needs of various communities.

Peace and Conflict Resolution: Restorative justice contributes to peace and conflict resolution efforts by facilitating dialogue, understanding, and reconciliation in post-conflict and conflict-prone regions.

Human Rights: Restorative justice aligns with human rights principles, particularly in its emphasis on the dignity, agency, and rights of all individuals involved. It contributes to a human-centered approach to justice.

Advocacy and Social Change: Restorative justice advocates and practitioners work tirelessly to promote its principles and practices. Their efforts contribute to the broader movement for a more compassionate and restorative approach to conflict and harm.

By recognizing the transformative potential of restorative justice, society can embrace this approach as a means of fostering healing, accountability, and reconciliation. It offers a hopeful vision of a future where conflicts are opportunities for growth, understanding prevails over retribution, and justice is characterized by empathy and restoration.

Closing Thoughts of this Chapter:

In closing, this chapter serves as a call to action, urging each reader to embrace the principles and practices of restorative justice and become an agent of positive change. It is a reminder that the future of restorative justice is not a distant concept but a vision that can be realized through collective effort and commitment. Here are some closing thoughts that may be included:

Empowerment: You have the power to make a difference. By understanding and championing restorative justice, you can contribute to the healing of individuals and communities, the reconciliation of conflicts, and the transformation of our justice systems.

Community Engagement: Engage with your community and foster dialogue about restorative justice. Encourage open conversations about conflict resolution, healing, and accountability. Communities have the potential to drive change from within.

Education and Awareness: Educate yourself and others about the principles and practices of restorative justice. Awareness is a powerful tool for change. Share what you've learned and inspire others to join this movement.

Advocacy: Advocate for restorative justice in your local, national, or global context. Support policies and initiatives that promote restorative practices within the justice system, schools, workplaces, and other institutions.

Cultural Sensitivity: Embrace cultural sensitivity and diversity in your engagement with restorative justice. Respect and honor diverse perspectives and experiences, recognizing that cultural competency is essential for meaningful dialogue and healing.

Conflict Resolution: Practice restorative conflict resolution in your personal and professional life. Seek opportunities to resolve conflicts through empathy, understanding, and reconciliation, fostering a more peaceful and just environment.

Leadership: Lead by example. Be a restorative leader who embodies the principles of empathy, accountability, and healing. Inspire others to follow suit and create ripple effects of positive change.

Continued Learning: Restorative justice is an evolving field. Commit to continued learning and growth. Stay informed about new developments, research, and best practices in restorative justice.

Justice for All: Advocate for a justice system that truly serves all individuals, regardless of their background or circumstances. Work towards a justice system that prioritizes healing and reconciliation over punishment.

Hope and Transformation: Believe in the transformative power of restorative justice. By embracing this vision, you contribute to a future where conflicts are opportunities for growth, understanding prevails, and justice is marked by empathy and restoration.

As you embark on your journey to advance restorative justice, remember that even small actions can lead to significant change. By joining this movement, you become part of a global community committed to creating a more compassionate, just, and restorative world. Together, we can shape the future of restorative justice and make it a reality for all.

Chapter 20 represents a visionary culmination of the book's exploration of restorative justice, offering a compelling call to action. It encapsulates the collective wisdom garnered from previous chapters, reminding readers of the transformative potential inherent in restorative practices. This chapter underscores that the future of restorative justice isn't a distant dream but a reality within reach, awaiting proactive engagement.

At its core, the chapter reflects on the key takeaways from the book, reinforcing the principles of empathy, accountability, healing, and reconciliation that form the bedrock of restorative justice. It highlights the profound impact of restorative justice on individuals, communities, and the justice system itself.

The evolving landscape of restorative justice is explored, emphasizing recent developments, legislative changes, and the shifting public perception of restorative practices. It portrays a field that is growing, adapting, and gaining recognition as a powerful tool for conflict resolution and harm repair.

Most importantly, Chapter 20 is a call to action. It empowers readers to become advocates for restorative justice in their communities, workplaces, and beyond. It challenges individuals to champion fairness, healing, and accountability, encouraging them to be leaders in creating a more just and compassionate society. This chapter reminds us that the future of restorative justice isn't just a vision; it's a collective mission that each of us can actively participate in, turning the vision into a reality.

Conclusion

A Theological Imperative for Restorative Justice:

Each chapter explores different aspects of a theology of restorative justice, drawing on theological, ethical, and practical perspectives to provide a comprehensive understanding of this transformative approach to justice and reconciliation.

In conclusion, the book offers a profound exploration of the theological imperative for restorative justice. It underscores the moral and ethical foundations that underpin restorative practices, emphasizing the alignment of these principles with various theological and philosophical traditions.

Throughout the chapters, the book delves into the deep-seated connection between restorative justice and core theological values, such as compassion, forgiveness, and the inherent worth of individuals. It illustrates how restorative justice aligns with diverse religious teachings, making a compelling case for its integration into theological discourse.

The book not only outlines the theological basis for restorative justice but also highlights its practical application. It reveals how restorative practices can bring about healing, reconciliation, and accountability in a manner consistent with the ethical and moral imperatives found in many religious traditions.

Ultimately, the book reinforces the idea that restorative justice isn't merely a secular concept; it carries a profound theological imperative. It calls on individuals and communities to embrace restorative justice as a means to embody their faith-based values and principles, fostering a more just, compassionate, and reconciled world. This theological imperative for restorative justice invites us to strive for a society where empathy, accountability, and healing are not only principles but lived realities.

SHIMBA
PUBLISHING